America

Who Stole the Dream?

America

Who Stole the Dream?

Donald L. Barlett
and James B. Steele
of the *Philadelphia Inquirer*

ANDREWS AND MCMEEL
A Universal Press Syndicate Company
Kansas City

Library of Congress Cataloging-in-Publication Data

Barlett, Donald L.
    America: who stole the dream ? / Donald L. Barlett and James
B. Steele.
      p.   cm.
      Includes bibliographical references and index.
      ISBN 0-8362-1314-9 (ppb)
      1. Income distribution – United States. 2. Middle class –
United States. 3. United States – Economic policy – 1981-1993.
4. United States – Economic conditions – 1981 – I. Steele, James
B. II. Title. HC110.I5B367   1996
     330.973'092–dc20   96-41610
                                                      CIP

ISBN: 0-8362-1314-9

Contents

Contents

Acknowledgments

In a book that is a sweeping indictment of the people who run the federal government—or more accurately, the people at the very top— it seems only fitting to note that further down in the ranks are truly dedicated and sincere civil servants.

They have answered our many questions with good humor over the years, and furnished us with reams of statistical material, much of it in response to arcane questions. Their numbers are many, but we would like to thank in particular the employees of the public records rooms of the Office of Training Adjustment and Assistance of the Department of Labor, the United States Trade Representative, the United States Trade Commission and the Foreign Agents Registration unit of the Department of Justice, who probably saw more of us than they would care to admit, but never let on. We would especially like to thank Maureen Greene of the Bureau of Labor Statistics in Philadelphia, who was most patient and helpful in answering our questions and directing us to data that proved so crucial in telling this story.

As always, we are indebted to librarians at public, private and university libraries across the country, including those at Lippincott Library of the University of Pennsylvania, the government publications room of the Free Library of Philadelphia, and at numerous other libraries around the country, among them the Smyth-Bland Regional Library in Marion, Va.

We especially want to thank the gifted and hard-working library staff of the *Inquirer*. In particular, Denise Boal, Frank Donahue, Joe Daley, Alletta Bowers, Sandra Simmons and Ed Voves spent untold hours researching our queries and unearthing hard-to-find information from electronic databases and other sources. Other *Inquirer* librarians also made important contributions to the project—Jennifer Ewing Elliott, Steve Elliott, Virginia Graham, Gene Lolelo, Marla Otto, Michael Panzer, Michael Porter and Connie Pickett. To former staff members Teresa Banik and M. J. Crowley, we will also always be grateful.

Acknowledgments

We owe a special debt to a group of talented and energetic editorial assistants from the *Inquirer* staff who worked with us at varying times—John Brumfield, Bing Mark, Harold L. Brubaker and Tirdad Derakhshani—each of whom made invaluable contributions. We will be forever indebted to Bill Allison, an *Inquirer* editorial assistant who also happens to be one of the great researchers we have ever encountered. To our benefit, he worked with us almost from the start, and it is safe to say the book before you could not have existed without Bill, who was as caught up in this project as we were and whose grasp of this exceedingly complex topic made it possible to push the research to new plateaus.

In addition to those who helped in the research, we are most appreciative of the time and energy devoted to this project by the group of editors with whom we worked: assistant managing editor Lois Wark, assistant to the executive editor Peter Kaufman and assistant managing editor Marietta Dunn.

A special word of thanks to Maxwell E. P. King, the editor of the *Philadelphia Inquirer,* who proposed this project and who has been its committed and enthusiastic supporter from day one, contributing both ideas and challenges to take the work to the next level. Max is probably the only newspaper editor in America willing to commit the time and resources to a project of this magnitude.

At Andrews and McMeel, we are, as usual, in the debt of more persons than we could possibly name here, but a special word of thanks goes to Donna Martin for her patience and thoughtfulness as an editor in helping us bring this complex and demanding venture to a close.

And finally, a word about Andrews and McMeel's production people. They are an extraordinary lot who managed to produce this book in a most timely fashion, while laboring under an enormous handicap: authors who delayed delivery of the manuscript for week after week.

Introduction

Seven years ago, in 1989, we first set out across the country to interview the working man and woman. The results were published by the *Philadelphia Inquirer* in October 1991 in a nine-part series of articles entitled *America: What Went Wrong?* The series was expanded into a book by the same title that was published in 1992.

That work chronicled the lives of middle-class Americans under siege from corporate raiders and Wall Street, the people doing the raiding and the people in government who made it all possible.

The response to *America: What Went Wrong?* was extraordinary—an outpouring of thousands of letters from individuals from all walks of life from every part of the nation. Many urged us to continue to write about the plight of the middle class—not only what is happening to them, but why.

America: Who Stole the Dream? is the result, published as a series by the *Philadelphia Inquirer* in September 1996, and in this book at the same time.

As with *America: What Went Wrong?*, we began by listening to people. If one had to choose a single word to describe the hundreds of people we have interviewed over these years, it would be *gracious*. They patiently answered the endless questions of intruders, who often descended on their homes, or telephoned them, in times of great stress—when they had lost their jobs, were about to lose their unemployment benefits, had lost their health insurance or pensions.

Many were interviewed at length in person. On occasion we returned for second and third interviews. Some we know only after prolonged and frequent telephone interviews. They are white, black, Hispanic and Asian. They are blue collar, white collar and professional. They are married with children, single, divorced and alone, divorced with children, married without children, married with grown children on their own.

Introduction

Out of all these conversations we have been left with a series of vivid impressions. But perhaps foremost is a remarkable strain of common sense that seems to be so prevalent in working Americans—and so lacking among the people in Washington.

To a person, they expressed as much concern or more for fellow citizens as they did for themselves. There were others, they said, in more desperate straits. And to a person, they expressed uniform displeasure with the federal government's failure to deal forthrightly with so many critical issues—from health care to taxes, from global trade to the growing concentration of corporate power.

In addition to all the interviews, we have received thousands of letters since 1991, written in response to *America: What Went Wrong?* and a second book, *America: Who Really Pays the Taxes?* In all, more than 30,000 letters.

They came from nearly all the 50 states. They were written by men and women. Rich and poor. Teenagers and seniors citizens. Employed and unemployed. Blue collar and professional. Affected by corporate layoffs and unaffected. White and black. Big-city residents and rural dwellers.

Some were brief notes of a personal nature. Some offered detailed proposals for solutions. As was the case with the people we interviewed, the letters reflected a remarkable degree of common sense.

Typical of those letters was one that arrived in August 1996 from a Philadelphia resident who, after reading *America: Who Really Pays the Taxes?* drew up a set of principles and a plan for a more equitable tax system. One of those principles could stand for American economic life overall. It was this: "A company should never be rewarded for doing harm."

The letter-writer was talking in particular about corporations that enjoy tax reductions after laying off workers. But his principle has many other applications, both for business and individuals.

On the pages that follow, you will read one story after another about people who were rewarded for doing just that—harming other people. In most cases, the harmful actions grew out of government policies.

Two brief notes to keep in mind while reading this book.

The subject of "global trade" will be found on many of the pages that follow. All that is written—and all the supporting statistics—deal with merchandise trade, the goods and commodities that are manufactured in this country and exported abroad, or are made elsewhere and imported here. No mention is made of trade in services, another statistic compiled by the U.S. government and widely reported by the news media. This omission was deliberate.

The United States did not win World War II because it excelled in attracting foreign tourists, or because it collected royalties for the overseas distribution of movies like *The Hunchback of Notre Dame* and licensing fees for the sale of Mickey Mouse products in foreign lands, all of which are counted in the service trade. Rather, it won the war because it had a superior military machine that was backed up by an equally superior—and overpowering—manufacturing base. That manufacturing base produced massive quantities of aircraft, ships, tanks, rifles, ammunition and other war materiel not just for the United States, but for our allies as well.

It would not be much of an exaggeration to say that if World War II broke out in the 1990s instead of the 1940s, the United States would lose because it no longer possesses a preeminent manufacturing capability. In short, trade in services is irrelevant to a country pretending to be a world power.

While what follows documents the ongoing decline of America's middle class, it must also be noted that not everyone has fallen on hard times. Some middle-class people are doing quite nicely. Across the country, there are indeed pockets of middle-class prosperity.

For purposes of this book, we have defined the middle class as working individuals and families who filed tax returns reporting adjusted gross incomes between $20,000 and $75,000. That range takes into account differences in living costs around the country. Needless to say, a family of four with an income of $20,000 in New York City would live in poverty. But a single person in a small Southern town, say Enterprise, Ala., could maintain a middle-class lifestyle. At the upper end, families with an income of $75,000 could afford to buy a home most anywhere.

Forty-six million tax returns with incomes between $20,000 and $75,000 were filed by individuals and families in 1993, the latest year for which complete tax statistics are available. They represented 47 percent of the total 98 million returns filed that year showing wage or salary income. Taxpayers with incomes over $75,000 accounted for 8 percent of the total. There were 8 million returns filed by taxpayers in this income group. Those who reported incomes under $20,000, who may be termed the working poor, made up 45 percent of all returns showing wage or salary income. There were 44 million tax returns in this income group.

Mark that $75,000 income figure as kind of rough divide in Washington's new economic order—the line between the have-mores and the have-lesses. Again, keep in mind these are fluid divisions. A family with no children and an income of $40,000 may well be in better financial condition than a family with an income of $125,000, paying full tuition for two children at an Ivy League school.

With that understanding, the have-mores, the people above $75,000, fall into three groups:

- Those at the very top who are accumulating more wealth than ever.
- Those just below, who are living a comfortable existence.
- And those at the bottom end, many of whom are striving to maintain their existing lifestyle.

The have-lesses, the people below $75,000, tend to fall into four groups:

- Those who are doing well enough to meet their obligations and have a little left over.
- Those whose incomes are declining as a result of lay-offs and forced job changes.
- Those who would have moved up the economic ladder in the past but are effectively barred under the existing economic rules.
- And an expanding underclass for whom there is little movement or hope.

This shifting profile of a few people who have more and more and ever-increasing numbers of people who have less and less poses one of the single greatest social and economic threats to American life. While the cure may be hotly debated, there is one point on which most would agree: This is not the American dream. Only by moving forcefully can it be prevented from becoming the American reality.

America

Who Stole
the Dream?

CHAPTER • ONE

Have-Mores and Have-Lesses

Who Revoked the Dream?

Let's suppose, for a moment, there was a country where the people in charge charted a course that eliminated millions of good-paying jobs. Suppose they gave away several million more jobs to other nations. Finally, imagine that the people running this country implemented economic policies that enabled those at the very top to grow ever richer while most others grew poorer.

You wouldn't want to live in such a place, would you?

Too bad.

You already do.

These are some of the consequences of failed U.S. government policies that have been building over the last three decades—the same policies that people in Washington today are intent on keeping or expanding. Under them, 100 million Americans, mostly working families and individuals—blue-collar, white-collar and professional—are being treated as though they were expendable.

Most significant of all, the American dream of the last half-century has been revoked for millions of people—a dream rooted in a secure job, a home in the suburbs, the option for families to live on one income rather than two, a better life than your parents had and a still-better life for your children.

U.S. government policies consistently have failed to preserve that dream in the face of growing international competition. Instead they've favored the very forces that shift jobs, money and influence abroad. As a result, the United States is about to enter the 21st century much the same way it left the 19th century: with a two-class society.

Both government and big business are encouraging the shift—dividing America into have-mores and have-lesses. While the

1

nation's richest 1 percent is accumulating wealth not seen since the robber-baron era of the last century, the middle class is shrinking.

There are, to be sure, some notable differences from a century ago. In the 1890s, most Americans were struggling to reach a middle-class lifestyle. By the 1990s, an overwhelming majority, having achieved it, were either losing it or struggling to hold on to it. In the 1890s, government responded to the prodding of reform-minded citizens and began to slowly create a framework of rules to guide the economy, control the excesses of giant business trusts and their allies, and generally to protect the interests of the average citizen. By the 1990s, that framework was being dismantled.

Who is responsible?

In a word: Washington.

Or, more specifically, members of Congress and presidents of the last three decades, Democrats and Republicans alike. Of course, they've had a lot of help—from lobbyists, special-interest groups, executives of multinational corporations, bankers, economists, think-tank strategists and the wheelers and dealers of Wall Street. These are some of the emerging winners in this changing America.

The losers? Working Americans who have been forced to live in fear—fear of losing their jobs and benefits, fear of the inability to pay for their children's education, fear of what will happen to their aging parents, fear of losing everything they've struggled to achieve.

The winners say if you're not a part of this new America, you have no one to blame but yourself. They say the country is undergoing a massive structural change comparable to the Industrial Revolution of the 1800s, when Americans moved off the farms and into factories. They say you have failed to retrain yourselves for the new emerging economy. That you don't have enough education. That you're not working smarter. That you failed to grasp the fact that companies aren't in the business of providing lifetime employment. And, they say, it's all inevitable anyway.

It is inevitable that factories and offices will close, that jobs will move overseas or be taken by newly arriving immigrants, that people's living standards will fall, that you may have to work two or three part-time jobs instead of one full-time job. These things are inevitable, they say, because they are the product of a market economy, and thus beyond the control of ordinary human beings and, most especially, beyond the control of government.

Don't believe it.

They are, in fact, the product of the interaction between market forces and government policies—laws and regulations enacted or not enacted, of people finding ways to turn government to their advantage. The policies that are driving these changes range across the breadth of government—from international trade to immigration, from antitrust enforcement to deregulation, from lobbying laws to tax laws.

Because of these changes, American society is being recast, as the bottom-line mentality of the global business world is transferred to the country at large. Along the way, workers, entire communities and a way of life once the envy of people around the world have become dispensable.

Michael Rothbaum and Darlene Speer are at opposite ends of this new two-class society.

Rothbaum, a corporate executive, lives in an exclusive gated community called St. Andrews Country Club in Boca Raton, Fla. Set amid 718 acres of lakes, fairways and landscaped grounds, St. Andrews is typical of the luxury communities that many wealthy Americans now inhabit—self-contained enclaves sealed off from everyone else.

St. Andrews has its own 24-hour security patrol, shopping complex, sports pavilion, restaurants and two championship 18-hole golf courses where residents can play after paying a $75,000 membership fee. Rothbaum lives in a 5,000-square-foot home, with pool and spa, built in 1991. According to the Palm Beach county assessor's office, the property is valued at $636,000.

Darlene Speer, on the other hand, works two jobs. She is a full-time office worker for a furniture manufacturer and a part-time clerk at a video store in Marion, Va. She lives in a one-bedroom unit in an apartment complex in Marion, a community of 8,500 in the mountains of southwestern Virginia.

Until 1992, Speer worked in the sewing department of Harwood Industries, a clothing manufacturer that was one of Marion's largest private employers. But in August 1992, Harwood Industries, whose principal owner was Michael Rothbaum, announced it would close the department. After that, all apparel production was in Honduras and Costa Rica, where labor costs are much cheaper. The company said it was under pressure from retailers to cut costs.

Not that Darlene Speer and her coworkers drove Harwood Industries to Central America with their bloated salaries. After 13

1% of the town has **30%** of the wealth.

The Very Rich: 3 Families

Houses worth $5.6 million each.

ENTERING
Inequityville
A TOWN DIVIDED

Inequityville is the U.S. class structure in miniature. Reduced to 300 families and in proportion to the nation's distribution of wealth, this graphic shows what each house in the town would be worth.

Inequityville's total wealth amounts to $55 million. Here's how the real numbers translate: America's 96 million households are worth a total of $17.6 trillion, an average of $183,500 each. That amount multiplied by Inequityville's 300 houses comes to $55 million.

SOURCE: Internal Revenue Service, Federal Reserve Board and the Federal Home Loan Mortgage Corp.

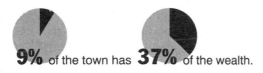

9% of the town has **37%** of the wealth.

The Well-Off: 27 Families

Houses worth $750,000 each.

Houses worth
$67,000 each.

The Middle Class and Working Poor:
270 Families

90% of the town has **33%** of the wealth.

years, Speer was earning less than nine dollars an hour. But women in Honduras work for a lot less—about 48 cents an hour.

Before leaving town, Rothbaum's company agreed to pay severance of about $1,200 to each employee. The total for 120 women, who had collectively worked more than 1,500 years in the sewing department, amounted to less than one-quarter of the value of Rothbaum's home.

The Widening Divide

Take a glimpse into the new America of Michael Rothbaum and Darlene Speer.

The Top 1 Percenters—Growing Richer. These are the families and individuals with incomes that begin at about $182,000 and go all the way up into the tens of millions of dollars—the top 1 percent of all tax filers. There are 1.1 million of them. Most are doing quite well. Some spectacularly well. The average income in this top group, according to IRS tax return statistics, ballooned from $147,700 in 1980 to $464,800 in 1992—a jump of 215 percent.

That was three times the growth recorded by the bottom 90 percent of tax filers, the 101.4 million families and individuals whose incomes begin at the minimum wage and go up to about $65,000. Their average income rose just 67 percent, from $13,200 in 1980 to $22,100 in 1992.

While the increase in incomes of the majority of Americans lagged behind the 70 percent increase in the cost of living, the income of the top 1 percenters went up three times as fast as the inflation rate.

The Bottom 90 Percenters—Growing Poorer. In 1980, the bottom 90 percenters accounted for 68 percent of all income reported on tax returns. By 1992, their share had fallen to 61 percent. In dollars, that meant they lost one-tenth of their income. Meanwhile, the top 1 percent of tax filers saw their share of all income rise from 8 percent in 1980 to 14 percent in 1992.

Looked at another way, the 90 percent of the people at the bottom transferred 9 percent of their income to the people at the very top. They transferred another 1 percent to those tax filers in the 90 to 99 percent range, the 10.1 million families and individuals with incomes between about $65,000 and $182,000. That group's share of all income edged up from 24 percent in 1980 to 25 percent in 1992.

Concentration of Wealth. The United States has the widest gap between rich and poor of any industrialized nation. The in-

Income Shifts to the Wealthy

The bottom 90% of U.S. taxpayers — those making less than $65,000 — saw their share of the nation's income, as reported on tax returns, drop dramatically in just 12 years. In effect, a portion of their income shifted upward.

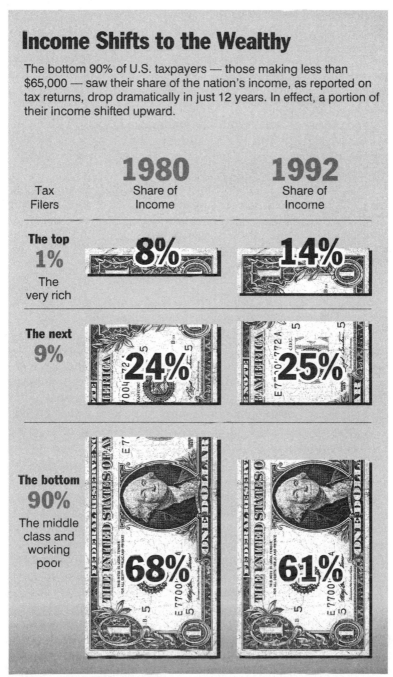

Tax Filers	1980 Share of Income	1992 Share of Income
The top **1%** The very rich	8%	14%
The next **9%**	24%	25%
The bottom **90%** The middle class and working poor	68%	61%

SOURCE: Internal Revenue Service

equality is reversing the gains that carried millions to middle-class prosperity following World War II.

How bad is it? Picture a town called Inequityville that is a perfect miniature version of the United States, a true microcosm of the nation's population and wealth. And suppose that all the wealth in this town amounted to $55 million and consisted of the houses of the 300 families living there. Here's how it would divide up: Three families would live in mansions worth $5.6 million each, and 27 families would live in very nice $750,000 houses. The remaining 270 families would live in row houses averaging $67,000 each.

In the real U.S.A., the top 1 percent of households controls almost one-third (30.4 percent) of the nation's net worth—that's total wealth, not income. The next 9 percent hold another third (36.8 percent) of the nation's wealth. Put the two together, and the top 10 percent of households own two-thirds (67.2 percent) of the wealth. The remaining 90 percent account for 32.8 percent of the wealth.

Exploding Disparity in Income. Over 20 years on the job, how would you like to see your salary go up by, say, 950 percent?

If you had a job in the retail trade, as a sales clerk in a department store making $5,660 a year two decades ago, today you'd be earning $59,400. Or if you were in manufacturing, perhaps turning out switch gears and earning $9,921 then, you'd be making $104,200 now. And if you were in a minimum-wage job 20 years ago, making $2.10 an hour, your hourly pay today would be $22.

Where can you find such lucrative work? You can't.

But that's what those jobs would pay if they'd gone up at the same rate as the salary and bonuses paid by General Electric Co. to its top executive between 1975 and 1995. When it comes to pay increases, executives of America's largest companies have left their workers far, far behind.

A *Philadelphia Inquirer* survey of 20 *Fortune* 500 corporations—in industries ranging from tractors to computers, from soft drinks to soap—shows that the salaries and bonuses of the highest-paid executives ballooned an average of 951 percent between 1975 and 1995, or five times the inflation rate.

By comparison, the average earnings of more than 73 million blue-collar and white-collar workers across all private industry—from shipping clerks to nurses, from truck drivers to musicians—went up just 142 percent, not even keeping up with the

8

inflation rate of 183 percent. Their average annual salary in 1995 was $20,559— down $3,529 from their inflation-adjusted earnings of $24,088 in 1975. Because of growing tax burdens, these workers were even worse off than that decline suggests.

Contrast that with GE's top bosses. In 1975, Reginald H. Jones earned $500,000 in salary and bonuses. By 1995, GE's chief executive officer, John F. Welch Jr., received $5.25 million. While the top executive's pay rose 950 percent, the number of GE employees plunged 41 percent, dropping from 375,000 to 222,000. Actually, that jobs reduction was even greater than it seems. For in 1985, GE bought RCA, which had 119,000 employees. When those workers are added in, over the 20 years GE eliminated 272,000 jobs—the equivalent of the entire RCA workforce, plus another 153,000 GE employees. The layoffs helped Welch earn the less-than-reverent nickname "Neutron Jack."

Oh, a footnote: In addition to a salary and bonus of $5.25 million, Welch also had GE stock options worth $35 million at the end of 1995.

More Executive Excess. America's corporations paid their top officers $221 billion in compensation in 1992, the latest year for which complete corporate statistics are available from the Internal Revenue Service. That exceeded the combined incomes of every working individual and family earning less than $50,000 a year in Arkansas, Kansas, Missouri, Oregon, Pennsylvania and Wisconsin—more than 12 million individuals and families.

To better understand those numbers, consider this: In 1975, Alden W. Clausen, then the Bank of America's top executive, earned $348,018. That was the equivalent of the pay of 53 bank employees, from janitors to tellers. In 1995, Richard M. Rosenberg, chairman and chief executive officer of Bank of America, earned $4,541,666 in salary and bonuses. That was the equivalent of the salaries of 116 *more* bank employees than for Clausen—or a total of 169.

Or compare salaries of people who provide services to corporate executives—like service station attendants. In 1995, Louis V. Gerstner Jr., chairman and CEO of IBM, earned $4.8 million in salary and bonuses. That was the equivalent of 407 gas station attendants' pay. Gerstner's salary was worth 320 *more* gas station attendants than his predecessor's pay was worth.

The Great Tax Burden: Federal. At the same time that middle-class family incomes have stagnated or fallen behind, local, state

Growing Gap Between Top Executives and the Average Family

In 1975, the CEO of General Electric made $500,000.

His pay equaled the income of

36 families

earning the U.S. median income of $13,719.

In 1995, the CEO of General Electric made $5,250,000.

His pay equaled the income of

133 families

earning the U.S. median income of $39,500.

SOURCE:
U.S. Securities
and Exchange
Commission

and federal tax burdens have soared, leaving families with less after-tax money to spend on food, housing and clothing.

Take a look at what Washington has done for you on the federal level. In 1955, the personal exemption was $600. For a family of four, that added up to $2,400. Median family income that year amounted to $4,418. So the personal exemption shielded 54 percent of family income from tax. By 1995, when median family income reached an estimated $39,500, the personal exemption was $2,500, or $10,000 for a family of four. Now the personal exemption shielded only 25 percent of family income from tax.

And there is the matter of rates. In 1955, the top tax rate was 91 percent. It applied to all taxable income over $400,000. By 1995, the top rate had been slashed to 39.6 percent, which applied to taxable income over $256,500.

The change in income-tax brackets means that Washington has pushed lower- and middle-income people closer to the top tax rate, and pushed those at the top closer to the middle rates. Thus, 71 percentage points separated the bottom from the top tax rates in 1955. In 1996, it was just 24.6 points.

Finally, consider Social Security and Medicare taxes. Those taxes paid by a median-income family spiraled 3,498 percent between 1955 and 1995. The amount deducted from paychecks rose from $84 in 1955, when only Social Security was withheld, to $3,022 in 1995, when both Social Security and Medicare taxes were deducted.

The Social Security tax is the most regressive levy of all. Because the amount of income subject to tax is capped at a specific figure—$62,700 in 1996—the more money you make, the lower your effective tax rate.

Taking all these taxes into account, the people in Washington have effectively canceled the progressive tax system. That system, built on the principle that tax rates go up as income rises, was in place during the great growth years of the middle class.

The Still-Greater Tax Burden: State and Local. While the people in Washington have been easing the tax burden on the wealthiest citizens, they have been shifting more responsibilities —and therefore taxes—to state and local governments. These taxes fall hardest on middle-income taxpayers. That's true whether it's state income and sales taxes or local real estate and excise taxes.

Overall, the local and state tax burdens have doubled in the last 40 years. In 1955, they consumed 12 percent of wage and salary income. By 1995, it was 23 percent. Put another way, if mo dian family income had gone up at the same pace as state and local taxes, 50 percent of all families today would earn more than $95,000 a year. In reality, only 4 percent do.

Some of the Rich Are Different from You. In 1980, a total of 198 individuals and families with incomes above $200,000 filed U.S. tax returns reporting that they owed not one cent in federal income tax. By 1992, the number had swelled to 1,896. The tax-free returns were perfectly legal, since filers took advantage of a variety of write-offs and tax shelters that one Congress after another inserted or preserved in the tax code.

Those provisions also allowed tens of thousands of affluent people who did pay income taxes to enjoy an effective rate below that of many middle-income families and individuals. For example, if your adjusted gross income was between $25,000 and $30,000 in 1992, you paid federal income tax at around double the rate paid by 5,598 families and individuals with incomes over $200,000. Their effective rate: less than 5 percent.

America's Not-So-Global Wages. The image of the highly paid American production worker exists more in talk-show rhetoric than in reality. Twenty years ago, the average hourly compensation—wages and benefits combined—of workers employed in U.S. manufacturing plants was higher than that of workers across most of the industrialized world. No more.

In 1975, the compensation of U.S. production workers averaged $6.36 an hour, compared with $6.35 for Germany, $6.09 for Switzerland, $4.51 for Austria, and $3 for Japan, according to a study by the Bureau of Labor Statistics.

By 1993, the last year for which figures are available, the U.S. average compensation of $16.79 an hour had been eclipsed by Germany, where wages and benefits reached $25.56; Switzerland, $22.66; Austria, $20.20; and Japan $19.20. For the European Union as a whole, hourly compensation in 1993 averaged $18.48—or $1.69 above the U.S. rate.

The New American Dream—Fortress Homes. The decline of America's middle class has been accompanied by the rise of a new generation of wealth. And many owners of that new wealth live in a way that is quite different from everyone else. They live in private preserves, so-called gated communities, where estate homes—the size of two or three typical suburban houses—are ringed by walls and protected by security guards 24 hours a day; where admittance to the neighborhood is by invitation only.

A brochure for The Reserve at Tampa Palms in Tampa, Fla., an exclusive enclave with its own championship golf course and lakes, says it offers "a sense of unequalled privacy and security [that] is enhanced by a tall, elegantly landscaped brick wall, creating a distinctive approach leading to the gatehouse entrance, which is staffed around the clock for your peace of mind."

A few lots remain. They range in price from $137,500 for a standard 21,875-square-foot lot, with no special amenities, to $249,000 for a 43,349-square-foot lot on the golf course. That's for the land. The house is extra. Many are in the million-dollar-plus range.

Even at the peak of the robber-baron era, the very richest industrialists lived in their communities. John D. Rockefeller, on many winter mornings, could be found skating on the outdoor rink he built next to his town house on West 54th Street in New York City. In the 1990s, even senior-level corporate managers have sealed themselves and their families off from the communities where they earn their living.

The Fading American Dream: A Nice Home. Beginning after World War II and continuing through the 1950s, '60s and '70s, successive generations achieved the American dream of owning their own home.

During the decade of the 1980s, home ownership among those 34 and younger, when people traditionally buy their first house, declined. It fell from 43.8 percent in 1980 to 39.6 percent in 1990.

In the 1950s, the largest home builder in the Philadelphia area —indeed, in the country—was Levitt & Sons Inc., which created Levittown, a planned community of 17,000 homes in Bucks County. Built for an emerging middle class, the homes were priced so that half the families in the area could afford to buy one.

In the 1990s, the largest home builder in the region is Toll Brothers Inc., which builds houses that sell for $210,000 to $400,000, a price range that excludes most families earning less than $65,000 a year. Based on the latest state income tax data, about 10 percent of working families in Philadelphia and the four surrounding Pennsylvania counties can afford to buy a Toll Brothers house; 90 percent are priced out of the market.

Nowhere to Turn. Over the years, American families have achieved or maintained their standard of living by exercising, one after another, a series of options. Women joined the workforce in larger numbers, often to bolster family income. Families had fewer children. College-age children and young adults returned home to live with their parents, saving on costs and sometimes even contributing to household income. And families began to live on credit cards.

Back in the 1950s, Americans, prudently, kept their overall debt loads below the amount of their weekly paychecks. In 1950, total consumer debt—mortgage and installment loans—amounted to $96 billion. That represented 65 percent of total wage and salary income of $147 billion. In 1960, consumer debt rose to 98 percent of wage and salary income. By 1995, that figure had climbed to 166 percent. Americans now are nearly two dollars in debt for every one dollar they receive in their paychecks.

As might be expected from such rising debt loads, another set of numbers also has shot up smartly—personal bankruptcies. They climbed from an annual average of 183,700 in the 1970s to 373,300 in the 1980s, and then soared to 811,100 so far in the 1990s.

Now, families are running out of options.

Down, Out and Angry

For this new America of lagging earnings, a widening gap in incomes and wealth, a falling standard of living and a bleak future for children and grandchildren, you can thank Washington and special interests, who have set the nation's economic agenda for years to come.

On a more personal level, the grim statistics merely reinforce the feelings shared by many working people, but seldom voiced beyond family, friends and coworkers. In interviews the authors conducted over the last two years with scores of white-collar, blue-collar and professional workers, the picture of the new America is decidedly downbeat. From Washington to Los Angeles, Chicago to Biloxi, the moods ranged from mild pessimism to hopelessness.

One after another, they talked about how their standard of living is dropping, how there is little job security, how loyalty to a corporation counts for nothing, how it is impossible to set aside money for their children's education and how the strain of both parents working—sometimes at multiple jobs—is putting stress on families. These were hard-working people, steeped in traditional American optimism and values, who once believed everything would turn out all right but now have doubts.

People like Jody Meyer of Eden Prairie, Minn. Married and the mother of three children, Meyer helped produce brochures, videos and other promotional items for 17 years for Prudential

Insurance Co. in Minneapolis, until 1994, when she and 1,500 coworkers were dismissed in a cost-cutting move.

Like anyone who loses a job, Meyer at first experienced what she described as a "sense of loss" and a feeling that the company, which is America's largest insurance firm, just "didn't care." But she soon rebounded and went into business for herself, arranging and catering weddings, parties and other social events. "I do a little bit of everything," she says.

It was difficult getting started, but her husband's salary from a courier service carried the family through. Meyer's new business gives her more flexibility to be with her children, a daughter and twin boys. But, in a theme that the authors heard over and over, she said she earns less than she made at Prudential.

What worries Jody Meyer most is what's happening to the middle class. "I have a feeling that we're going to start seeing some real critical movements throughout the country," Meyer said. "To individuals, the family is most important. But when you have to have people working two and three jobs, 24 hours a day, the stress levels in the family are so great that I am very concerned.

"I don't know how much more the middle class—supposedly we're middle class—are going to be able to withstand before you start seeing drastic problems. It is harder and harder to maintain decent physical and mental health, general wellness."

Harder yet for her to deal with is the feeling that the situation isn't getting any better. "I don't see that we are making great strides in any direction that would ease some of this," she said. "I just see everybody scrambling. . . . Literally everyone is tapped out. I have a lot of neighbors who are middle management, who have gotten laid off. It's over. And it's over not a month from now. It's over now. It's really scary. It's not even the American dream anymore. We're just striving to make it. . . .

"I don't foresee anything with the letter *W*, for wealth, in our future. I question Social Security—if it's even going to be there. I question whether my [pension] plan will even be there. All those things you thought were there, you're just not so sure they're going to be there."

Others interviewed were more bitter. The steady erosion of good-paying jobs, forcing down living standards, is building resentment and anger at the companies and Washington policy makers who are blamed for the changes.

James R. Rude of Chatham, N. J., who lost his job as a computer programmer when foreign workers were brought in to replace his department, says corporate America is killing its own market by eliminating the jobs of potential consumers. Like many interviewed by the authors, Rude is skeptical of the stories he reads about the robust American economy. He says most people he knows see another side of the economic picture.

"I can tell you what's happening," he said. "You got low mortgage rates, yet houses aren't selling. The middle class is scared. They are afraid they're going to lose their jobs and they won't be able to keep their house and keep their cars.

"So basically big business, by making [big] profits, is good to their stockholders, but they are taking the greatest market and destroying it. They sell their products and services basically to Americans, and they are cutting their own throats. Those quarterly profits look great now. But what will they be like five years from now?"

Most of all, workers are angry about the loss of control over their lives. At work, they appear outwardly docile. Inside, they seethe.

These are not members of any right-wing militia. They are not members of any hate group. They are ordinary people from a cross section of society. They are factory workers and college graduates with advanced degrees. They are Democrats and Republicans, although increasingly they are distancing themselves from both parties. Consider the observations of three workers, who reflect a largely silent but growing sentiment.

A factory worker in Kansas: "Are we just going to keep lowering our standard of living? When that happens, nobody is going to have money to put food on the table. Then you are going to see a revolution because people are not going to be able to feed their families."

A former teacher in Illinois: "The level of hostility and anger and frustration is astonishing."

A factory worker in Pennsylvania: "There's going to be bloodshed before we get out of this."

Washington Stacks the Deck

How did the most emulated society of the 20th century reach a point where average citizens talk quietly and matter-of-factly of revolution and bloodshed? It has come about gradually, the result of policies and decisions that, taken together, have stacked the economic deck against middle America.

Have-Mores and Have-Lesses

Pick a government policy, or a corporate business practice encouraged or abetted by a government policy, and it's likely to be working against the average American. Foreign trade and imports. Immigration. Taxes. Deregulation. Antitrust enforcement. Mergers and layoffs. Self-employment. Retraining.

In years gone by, the federal government crafted and implemented policies that encouraged the growth of a healthy, broad-based middle class.

No more.

Trading Away Jobs. The government's trade policies are ostensibly intended to create jobs for Americans making products to be exported. Instead, they have had the opposite effect. They have wiped out jobs and driven down wages.

That's because Washington policy makers have given foreign producers essentially unrestricted access to the world's richest consumer market—the United States—without insisting upon the same access in return. Indeed, the government has actually subsidized foreign access to the American consumer. This, at the same time that our trading partners, such as Japan, have maintained tight controls over their own markets.

Not surprisingly, imports have soared, far outstripping exports. In 1996, the United States will record its 21st consecutive merchandise trade deficit—a record unmatched by any other developed country. By year's end 1996, the nation's cumulative trade deficits since 1976 will add up to $1.9 trillion.

More significantly, because of all those imported products that make up the trade deficits, more than 3 million manufacturing jobs in the United States have been eliminated.

Immigrants and a Labor Glut. At the same time that trade policies were creating a surplus of laid-off manufacturing workers and managers, Washington rewrote the immigration laws, leading to a record flow of immigrants into a domestic job market that already was unable to create enough good-paying jobs.

Legal immigration in the 1990s will dwarf every previous decade in American history. No other industrial country has allowed in so many workers in so short a time, depressing wages and living standards. So far in the 1990s, the number of immigrants has been the equivalent of adding 13 new cities to the U.S. map—another Philadelphia; Boston; New Orleans; Fort Worth; Kansas City, Mo.; Portland, Ore; Tucson; Atlanta; Cincinnati; Buffalo; Louisville; Newark, N.J.; and Des Moines.

On top of those numbers, Congress made it possible for employers to bring in foreign workers, often at salaries below those paid their American employees. Add 2 million more people to the labor force, competing for a declining number of good jobs.

Antitrust: Busting the Trustbusters. Over the last decade, the government has retreated from its role as trustbuster, backing away from the authority built up painstakingly over nearly 100 years to prevent business combinations that reduce, or threaten to reduce, competition. That, too, has cost jobs.

Where once the government would block the merger of two major competitors, today it routinely rubber-stamps the formation of megacorporations. Federal regulators in 1995 and 1996 let stand such combinations as Wells Fargo & Co.'s $11.6 billion acquisition of First Interstate Bancorp., Kimberly-Clark's $9.4 billion takeover of Scott Paper Co., Chemical Bank's $10 billion merger with Chase Manhattan, Pharmacia A.B.'s $7 billion marriage with Upjohn Co., and Hoechst A.G.'s $7.1 billion takeover of Dow Chemical Co., to name only a few.

The mergers, as you might expect, were accompanied by job losses. The Wells Fargo and First Interstate union put 7,200 people on the street. Scott Paper shed 11,000 employees before its merger with Kimberly-Clark, then Kimberly-Clark cut 6,000 more. The Chemical Bank and Chase Manhattan marriage ended the jobs of 12,000 people. Pharmacia A.B.'s $7 billion merger with Upjohn Co. eliminated 3,000 jobs. Hoechst A.G.'s $7.1 billion takeover of Dow Chemical Co. resulted in 8,000 layoffs.

According to Mergerstat Review, a firm that tracks corporate acquisitions, the merger wave in 1995 set a record at $266.5 billion, far outstripping the previous high of $177 billion in 1988, at the height of the corporate takeover craze.

So far in the 1990s, the Justice Department has filed an average of 16 civil antitrust cases a year in U.S. district courts. That's down 63 percent from the 43 cases filed annually during the 1970s. Similarly, the number of restraint-of-trade investigations conducted by the Justice Department plunged 64 percent, falling from an annual average of 267 cases in the 1970s to 96 cases in the 1990s.

The Fall of Labor. As corporations have gained more power, influence and size, trade unions—which once served as a buffer to corporate power—have declined, both in members and political influence. Whatever your attitude toward unions, three trends overlap in this century:

The rise of labor in the 1930s and '40s coincided with enactment of federal safety-net programs—from Social Security to unemployment compensation to the minimum wage. Labor's continuing rise in the 1950s and '60s paralleled the growth of the country's broad-based middle class, which for the first time expanded to include blue-collar workers.

Conversely, the decline of labor in the 1970s,'80s and '90s—union membership fell from 35 percent of the workforce in 1955 to 14 percent in 1995—mirrors the decline of the middle class.

So, too, do strike statistics. With mergers and corporate downsizing, unions have had to concentrate on trying to save jobs, not striking for higher wages. During the 1950s, unions averaged 352 work stoppages a year. That dropped to 283 in the 1960s, then held steady at 289 in the 1970s. It plummeted to 83 in the 1980s, and to 38 thus far in the 1990s. The number of workers involved in strikes has fallen from an average of 1.6 million a year in the 1950s to 273,000 in the 1990s.

Caught in the Tax Trap. Tax policy over the last three decades has worked steadily against the middle class. Layered over the transition to a more regressive tax system has been another form of wealth-shifting: transfer of much of the corporate tax burden to individuals.

America's largest and most powerful businesses now pay federal income tax at a fraction of the rate they once paid. To understand the magnitude of the tax shift, consider this: If corporations paid federal income tax in 1996 at the effective rate paid in the 1950s, the U.S. Treasury would collect an extra $250 billion a year—wiping out the federal deficit overnight. The top corporate rate in the 1950s was 52 percent. In the 1990s, it's 36 percent.

Rise of the Influence Peddlers. To intercede with policy makers and members of Congress, U.S. multinational corporations and foreign companies—as well as foreign governments—hire high-priced Washington lobbyists. Usually, the lobbyists are former U.S. government officials who know the intricacies of U.S. economic policies and have personal relationships with those still in power.

A revolving door of Washington insiders who go from government jobs to lobbyist-consultants, and back again, has given insiders—and the people who hire them—enormous influence over government decision making. Working Americans have no comparable representation.

How effective is the Washington lobbying corps? In 1970, Japan, Mexico and South Korea fielded 47 registered agents to lobby the

U.S. government on their behalf. By 1995, their ranks had swelled to 118—an increase of 151 percent. During that same period, imports from the three countries increased by 2,900 percent, rising from $7 billion to $210 billion. If supporters of the minimum wage had enjoyed the same lobbying success with Congress and the White House as the foreign agents of Mexico, Japan and South Korea, the lowest-paid worker in America today would earn $48 an hour.

Terminated Workers: The Retraining Game. So far in the 1990s, several million workers have lost their jobs through corporate mergers or imports, or when U.S. multinational corporations moved production to low-wage countries.

The abruptly terminated employees received mixed treatment from the U.S. government—at a cost of many billions of taxpayer dollars. The government retrained some displaced workers for new occupations, but not others. It provided job counseling for some workers, but not others. It provided job-search assistance for some workers, but not others. It provided extended benefits to tide some workers over during lengthy retraining, but not others. Under this latter government program, many workers said they attended training courses not because they wanted to learn a new trade, but so they could collect an additional one year of unemployment benefits.

Even those workers serious about retraining fared poorly. In a study of one government program, only two of every five workers who completed retraining found jobs in their new fields. What's more, many workers receive training for jobs that don't exist, or for dead-end jobs.

Not all U.S. job losses, obviously, have been caused by imports, immigration or corporations seeking bigger profits. Technology, too, has eliminated jobs. Hardly an industry has escaped the revolution in computers. Tasks that once required dozens of workers can now be performed by one person sitting at a terminal.

The process of machines replacing human labor is hardly new. Yet in the past, when a new technology made an older one obsolete, it often created more jobs than it eliminated—when airplanes replaced passenger trains, for example. That is not happening today.

What is also different: Many of the jobs being eliminated are not casualties of changing technology or obsolete industries. We still use telephones, hammers, screwdrivers, air conditioners, paper clips, ceiling fans, notepaper, toys and windshield wipers. We still wear shoes, dresses, pants, shirts, sweaters, skirts and coats. We still watch television, listen to radios and play stereos. These and other products we buy, though, increasingly are made outside the United States. None has become obsolete, like the buggy whips and steam locomotives of old.

What's obsolete in the new American economy is the people who make them.

But isn't high technology the answer? Haven't entire new industries sprung up to provide jobs, so we no longer need the older manufacturing industries that are being shipped offshore?

The computer industry itself is an obvious example. The writing and production of software programs and the manufacture of computer hardware have created thousands of new jobs. Twenty-five years ago, there was no Microsoft Corp., the software developer whose operating system controls the workings of most personal computers in the world, a company that employs around 16,000 people. But already, the United States is facing challenges in high-tech jobs from developing nations, whose governments are targeting technology as a growth industry and whose computer technicians work more cheaply.

To be sure, the demand for computer systems analysts and scientists has grown steadily, from 359,000 in 1985 to 933,000 in 1995. But in a workforce of 116.6 million people, those jobs represented just eight-tenths of 1 percent of the total.

Meanwhile, other computer-industry jobs already are in decline. The number of workers in computer production and related jobs has fallen from a high of 298,000 in 1988 to 189,000 in 1995, as 109,000 jobs disappeared. And in yet another computer field, the U.S. Labor Department forecasts that "employment of computer and peripheral equipment operators is expected to decline sharply through the year 2005. Many experienced operators are expected to compete for the small number of openings that will arise each year. . . ."

Jobs That Might Have Been

All these and other changes are adding up to a great power shift—away from employees and communities, and toward corporations and shareholders. Under the new economic rules, corporations lay off employees in good times as well as bad; close plants at will; subcontract work out to shops where wages and benefits are less; export many jobs abroad to low-wage countries; bring in foreign workers, who will work longer hours for lower pay; and influence policy in Washington along lines that serve their interests exclusively.

It is not just employees who have been hurt; small companies and industries also have borne the brunt of these policies. Take a look at one segment of one small industry—flower growers. In 1971, there were 1,525 commercial growers of standard carnations in 36 states. They dominated the U.S. market. As cheaper imports flooded the country, the number of domestic growers dwindled to 95 in 1995—a falloff of 94 percent. Today, foreign growers of standard carnations control the American market, accounting for 88 percent of all such flowers sold. The result: loss of thousands of American jobs.

Or consider the disappearing autoworker. Over the last two decades, 40 percent of the hourly production and skilled workers at the Big Three auto plants have vanished. From 1978 to 1995, the GM, Ford and Chrysler workforces shrank from 667,000 to 398,000 hourly employees.

Not to worry. As Washington and Wall Street are quick to point out, new jobs were created throughout the country to replace the old. Why, employment by Wal-Mart alone has increased by 2,890 percent in less than two decades.

In 1978, Wal-Mart had 21,000 employees. In April 1996, the company issued a news release from its Bentonville, Ark., headquarters, announcing: "Wal-Mart's U.S. employment has climbed to 628,000—roughly the population of North Dakota—or one of every 200 civilian jobs." In short, Wal-Mart has roared ahead of GM, Ford and Chrysler as a major American employer.

There are, to be sure, several significant differences. First, 30 percent of Wal-Mart's workers are part-time; the Big Three autoworkers are full-time. As for pay, a GM assembler earns $18.81 an hour; a tool and die maker, $21.99 an hour. Most Wal-Mart employees earn a dollar or two above the minimum wage, $4.75 an hour in 1996.

Then there's the matter of benefits. The autoworkers have a guaranteed annual pension. The Wal-Mart employees do not. The autoworkers receive fully paid health care. Wal-Mart part-time workers receive no company-paid benefits and full-time workers must pay part of the cost of their health insurance.

Beyond the jobs eliminated, there is an equally serious problem: jobs that should have been created—but weren't.

It used to be that a new invention or a new technology introduced into the U.S. market would guarantee employment for thousands, often tens of thousands, of American workers for decades.

More than a century ago, in 1882, Western Electric Co. became the sole manufacturer and supplier of telephones for the American Bell Telephone Co., later AT&T. In 1905, Western Electric moved its main manufacturing facility from downtown Chicago to Hawthorne, Ill., on the outskirts of the city. Over the next seven decades, the Hawthorne works—which included more than 100 buildings—turned out telephones and telephone equipment. It provided jobs for as many as 43,000 workers, since all telephones used in the United States were manufactured in this country.

Then came cellular phones. Within a few years after their introduction in the mid-1980s, most cellular telephones were manufactured in other countries, including those that carried the AT&T and Bell company labels. The drain of phone-manufacturing and related-equipment jobs overseas had its impact at Hawthorne, and, in 1986, the plant closed.

A chief reason for cellular phones going offshore: U.S. government policies that lowered tariffs on imported products and encouraged corporations to manufacture their products in lower-wage countries and ship them back to the United States.

In 1990, sales of cellular telephones in the United States reached nearly 1.9 million units. Imports that year totaled 1.3 million units—or 68 percent of those sold. By 1994, most cellular phones sold in the United States were made abroad. The manufacturing jobs that once provided a middle-class lifestyle for American workers now provided employment for foreign workers. Between 1990 and 1994, imports of cellular phones from South Korea rose 446 percent, from 247,038 to 1,349,691. Imports from Mexico spiraled 1,836 percent, from 27,259 to 527,708. And imports from China shot up a whopping 11,428 percent, from 6,245 to 719,905.

All that job loss is from a single industry—cellular telephones. When viewed across all manufacturing, the loss of jobs that should have been but aren't is staggering. If the percentage of the workforce employed in manufacturing today was the same as in 1956, there would be an extra 20 million good-paying jobs for people who make things with their hands.

It was not supposed to turn out this way. Global trade was supposed to benefit American workers. The justification for various free-trade initiatives has been that they would stimulate the export of American products and create more jobs at home. This hasn't happened.

Just look at the scorecard on the cross-border trade between the United States and Mexico following implementation of the North American Free Trade Agreement (NAFTA), which tied together the markets of the United States, Mexico and Canada. When NAFTA was proposed in 1990, supporters insisted it would open the door to vast numbers of American products for sale in Mexico.

Said George Bush in 1991: "I don't have to tell anyone about Mexico's market potential: 85 million consumers who want to buy our goods. Nor do I have to tell you that as Mexico grows and prospers, it will need even more of the goods we're best at producing: computers, manufacturing equipment, high-tech and high-value products."

Said Frank D.Kittredge, president of the National Foreign Trade Council, in 1993: "The last point I think we cannot miss. . . . is the competitive advantage in the Mexican market that NAFTA gives to United States manufacturers. Talking about tilting the playing field, it really tilts the playing field in favor of U.S. manufacturers."

Said the *New York Times*, in a 1993 editorial: "NAFTA would lower Mexican tariffs by a lot and U.S. tariffs, because they are already low, only a little. That means the price of U.S. goods in Mexico will fall enough to make U.S. exports more affordable to Mexicans. . . . NAFTA will raise U.S. exports."

Proponents pointed to a United States trade surplus of $4.9 billion with Mexico in 1992 as evidence of the benefits of expanded trade with Mexico through NAFTA. "Already, we sell far more to Mexico than they do to us," the *Philadelphia Inquirer* editorialized on September 15, 1993.

President Clinton also cited the trade surplus in a September 14, 1993, speech urging congressional approval: "I believe that NAFTA will create a million jobs in the first five years of its impact. . . . NAFTA will generate these jobs by fostering an export boom to Mexico. . . . In 1987, Mexico exported $5.7 billion more of products to the United States than they purchased from us. We had a trade deficit. Because of the free-market, tariff-lowering policies of the Salinas government in Mexico, and because our people are becoming more export-oriented, that $5.7 billion trade deficit has been turned into a $5.4 billion trade surplus for the United States. It has created hundreds of thousands of jobs."

Well, how goes the export boom with Mexico?

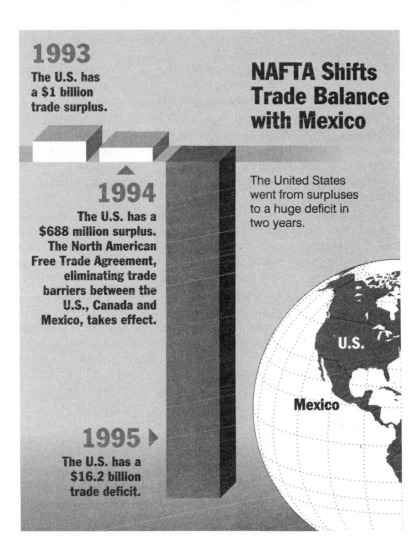

1993
The U.S. has a $1 billion trade surplus.

NAFTA Shifts Trade Balance with Mexico

1994
The U.S. has a $688 million surplus. The North American Free Trade Agreement, eliminating trade barriers between the U.S., Canada and Mexico, takes effect.

The United States went from surpluses to a huge deficit in two years.

U.S.

Mexico

1995 ▶
The U.S. has a $16.2 billion trade deficit.

SOURCE: U.S. Department of Commerce

The widely touted trade "surplus" with Mexico evaporated after NAFTA was approved. In 1995, the United States recorded a $16.2 billion merchandise trade deficit with Mexico, an all-time record. Indeed, the U.S. trade deficit with Mexico was greater than with all of Western Europe ($15.2 billion).

Exports of American goods to Mexico have gone up, from $41.5 billion in 1992 to $46.2 billion in 1995, an increase of 11.3 percent. But, in a story that has been repeated over and over in U.S. trade policy, imports from Mexico rose five times faster, going from $40.5 billion in 1992 to $62.4 billion in 1995, an increase of 54 percent.

Not everyone in Washington, of course, subscribed to the policies that are costing American jobs. And many who supported them acted out of good intentions, in actions that have had unforeseen consequences. But, taken together, these decisions are causing a relentless erosion of the middle class.

How have the people in Washington sold these policies?

In the case of foreign trade, they were promoted as providing the lowest possible prices and broadest choice for consumers—never mind who'd make money off the imports or whose jobs would be lost. Rep. David Dreier, a California Republican, put it this way in October 1993 during congressional debate over NAFTA: "Now, what is the goal of implementing a free-trade agreement like this? It is to help the consumer gain the ability to purchase the best-quality product at the lowest possible price."

Thus, if offshore workers earning 50 cents an hour can produce a shirt that sells for much less than one produced by Americans earning $4.25 an hour, the United States must import the cheaper shirt and workers in this country must forfeit their jobs.

Left unsaid is this: A society built on the economic principle that the lowest price is all that matters will be quite different from a society built on the principle that everyone who wants to work should receive a living wage. The former society—label it the bottom-line society—will be filled with retail clerks, warehouse helpers and shippers earning little more than minimum wage. The latter with skilled tradesmen, craftsmen and professional workers earning $20 an hour or more.

A New Kind of Job Sharing

Jim Rude learned about the bottom-line society the hard way. Married and the father of two children, one in college, Rude is a computer programmer. A native of northern New Jersey, he earned his bachelor's degree in computer science at Montclair State College.

After 18 years at Blue Cross of New Jersey, Rude went to work in 1989 at American International Group Inc. (AIG), one of the world's largest, richest and most influential insurance companies.

Working out of AIG's Livingston, N.J., offices, Rude was one of several hundred programmers. With worldwide operations, the data-processing unit was a booming enterprise for computer programmers, a case where global business generated jobs for Americans.

The pay and benefits were good, and Rude, at the encouragement of his superiors, enrolled in a program under which the company would pay part of his tuition toward a master's degree in computer science. "Everybody says you need more education, and I decided to make the effort and go for an advanced degree," Rude said. He did it for "the self-satisfaction" and to expand his opportunities at the company.

By the fall of 1994, Rude was only a few credits away from earning his degree when his continuing education—and his job—suddenly came to an end. To the astonishment of Rude and the 325 others in AIG's computer operations, the company announced it was dismissing them in two months. AIG had hired a subcontractor who would employ programmers from India, then streaming into the United States by the thousands to fill high-tech jobs.

Suddenly, professional workers were losing their jobs just like blue-collar workers before them—but with one notable difference. The blue-collar jobs disappeared when production work was moved offshore. Now, white-collar workers were being replaced by foreign nationals brought here to do the work. It was all part of a U.S. government immigration policy engineered in 1990 by the Republican Bush administration, a Democratic-controlled Congress and businesses with ties to both parties. The companies had used the threat of global competition to extract government approval to bring in foreign workers for high-tech occupations.

Next to losing his $64,000 salary, the worst part for Rude and the others was having to train the people who were taking their jobs. "We were told two months before our last day that we were leaving as of a certain day because we were going to be terminated," Rude said. "And for that two months, we had all those people coming over from India and we had to train them. And we were told, 'If you don't train these people, you will be terminated on the spot and you won't get your severance package.'"

In December 1994, Rude and his fellow programmers were out of a job. As incomes fell, so did their standard of living. Rude was unemployed nearly two months. When he landed a job, it was at roughly half his AIG salary. He became a recruiter placing programmers with companies. Since starting the new job, he has increased his income to $37,000 a year—or $27,000 less than he made before. Rude says AIG did what all large corporations are doing. "Big business today, if it can find a way to save a few bucks, they'll do it," he said. "The bean counters are running these companies anymore. Anything they can do to make their quarterly projections, they do."

Not everyone at AIG has fared badly under the new economic rules. Some have profited handsomely from such bottom-line decisions: Maurice R. (Hank) Greenberg, for one. At age 71, he represents both the present and the future.

Greenberg is chairman and chief executive officer of AIG. From an office near Wall Street, he presides over a business empire of 34,500 employees in more than 100 countries, with revenue of $25.9 billion in 1995—more than the gross domestic product of entire countries such as Bolivia, Ecuador, Guatemala, Panama or Uruguay. Greenberg is one of the 100 richest men in America, with a net worth estimated by *Forbes* magazine at $1 billion. He has an apartment bordering Central Park in New York City and an ocean-front condominium on Buccaneer Lane on Key Largo in Florida.

Greenberg has headed AIG since 1969, during which time he has earned a reputation as one of America's most abrasive, cocky and aggressive corporate executives. Once asked to sum up his business philosophy, Greenberg answered: "All I want in life is an unfair advantage."

Among his advantages has been instant access in Washington. In contrast to Jim Rude, who lost his job thanks to an immigration policy made by Congress, AIG has profited from its close ties to Washington policy makers. In 1986, for example, the company lobbied for a special provision in the tax reform act of that year exempting certain of its operations from a crackdown on foreign tax shelters.

If you pick up a copy of the Internal Revenue Code, you can read the custom-tailored tax law written for AIG. It states, in part, that this section of the new tax law will apply to everyone except "any controlled foreign corporation which on August 16, 1986, was a member of an affiliated group (as defined in section 1504(a) of the Internal Revenue Code of 1986 without regard to subsection (b)(3) thereof) which had as its common parent a corporation incorporated in Delaware on July 9, 1967, with executive offices in New York, New York. . . ." AIG was incorporated in Delaware on July 9, 1967, and has its executive offices in New York.

That little provision and a similarly arcane clause written for another big insurer—Cigna—were worth an estimated $20 million to the two companies. They would have been obliged to pay that much in taxes had not a friendly, but anonymous, member of Congress's tax-writing committees inserted the exemption into law.

You, of course, can't obtain such a tax break, since they go only to the politically well connected. But if you could secure your own tax law, it might read like this: "This section of the Internal Revenue Code does not apply to a resident of West Virginia born on January 31, 1949, who incorporated a business in Delaware on February 23, 1968."

Not possible, you think? Think again.

If you believe that's preposterous, ponder this tax amendment written by friendly members of Congress for favored constituents: "(E) Application of old rules to certain acquisitions.—In the case of a Texas resident whose birthdate is May 16, 1931, and a Michigan resident whose birthdate is November 16, 1941, in connection with a corporation incorporated in Texas on February 4, 1971, and a corporation incorporated in Florida on August 24, 1979. . . ."

Convinced?

In any event, 1986 was not the first time that AIG helped to write the tax laws. In 1976, the company was the prime beneficiary of a section in the tax reform act of that year entitled "Exclusion from Subpart F of Certain Earnings of Insurance Companies." That section exempted AIG and other large insurers from taxes on some of their offshore operations, saving the companies millions of dollars.

In addition to securing preferential tax breaks, AIG's tax lawyers, recruited from the ranks of former staff members of the congressional tax-writing committees, have succeeded in fending off other potentially harmful tax measures. One of the company's principal tax lawyers has been Robert E. Lighthizer, who was chief counsel and staff director of the Senate Finance Com-

29

mittee from 1981 to 1983, and is a partner in the Washington office of Skadden, Arps, Slate, Meagher & Flom.

Greenberg also has packed AIG's board of directors with political powerbrokers. Among them:

- Lloyd M. Bentsen, secretary of the treasury under President Clinton from 1993 to 1994 and former chairman of the Senate Finance Committee, which oversees tax legislation.
- Barber B. Conable Jr., former ranking Republican on the tax-writing House Ways and Means Committee and former president of the World Bank.
- Martin S. Feldstein, chairman of President Reagan's Council of Economic Advisers from 1982 to 1984.
- Carla A. Hills, former U.S. trade representative in the Bush administration, now one of Washington's premier consultants on international trade matters.

Those who know Greenberg say his strongest characteristic is his single-minded devotion to improving AIG's bottom line. It has propelled him into the ranks of the richest Americans.

In the wake of AIG's replacing its U.S. computer programmers, 1995 proved an especially good year for Greenberg. His salary and bonus totaled $4.15 million. That worked out to $80,000 a week, or more than the average AIG programmer earned in a year. Greenberg also held unexercised stock options valued at $23.6 million and owned 10.7 million shares of AIG stock worth $1 billion or so.

Let's summarize: In 1995 Jim Rude, a certified member of America's solid middle class, saw his earnings fall 42 percent. Maurice Greenberg saw the value of his AIG stock more than double, as he solidified his membership in America's Top 1 Percent Club.

No Middle Ground

What has complicated the debate about the nation's economic course is that most policy issues are cast in either/or terms. Either you're for free trade, or you're a raving protectionist. Either you want to throw open the doors to immigrants, or you'd erect walls to keep out foreigners. Either you want government off business's back, or you favor shackling American companies with onerous regulations. Either you're for lowering taxes, or you believe in soaking the rich.

Absent from the debate is serious talk about the need for a

middle ground—of a balance between the interests of corporations and of employees, between unrestricted trade and controlled trade, between preserving the nation's historic tolerance
of immigrants and protecting American workers from a glut in
the labor force.

And there is a middle ground—just as there is a middle ground
for all human behavior. For example, children may eat an occasional ice cream cone for a treat. But eating ice cream for dinner
every night would be harmful. Families may enjoy several hours
of television each week. But staying glued to the television set 12
hours a day, 7 days a week, would be disastrous for the family
and all its members.

And so it is with trade, immigration, taxes, protectionism and
government regulatory policies. Yet for a variety of reasons, special interests, Washington, Wall Street and the news media have
cast these and other issues as either/or propositions: Either it's
ice cream for the main meal every night and 12 hours of daily
television. Or it's no ice cream, no television. If that sounds sim-
plistic, it is—and so are government policies set at the edge, rather
than in the middle. Yet for their own reasons, partisans in Washington and on Wall Street have defined these issues in either/or
terms, and that is how they're portrayed in the news media.

Because there's no middle ground, the doors have been flung
open to products made around the world, often by workers whose
wages are counted in pennies—eliminating American jobs. Because
there's no middle ground, the progressive income tax—designed so
that the very rich would pay their appropriate share of the cost of
government—has been gutted. And because there's no middle
ground, the notion that government has a vital role in the economic
direction of the country has been shoved aside. Either you believe
in unfettered private enterprise or that the government should run
the economy.

But putting the issues in such a rigid way ignores what the federal government can do and has done in the past to bolster the
economic well-being of average Americans.

Throughout much of this century, government played a critical
role in development of American society—protecting the powerless, curbing the excesses of business and creating a regulatory
framework to safeguard the health and welfare of its citizens.
Equally important, the federal government has assured opportunities, evened out the economic playing field and tackled issues
that neither Wall Street nor the market deemed significant.

It was the federal government—not Wall Street or the market—that spurred the greatest wave of home building in American history after World War II with the Federal Housing Administration (FHA) program to insure mortgages for emerging middle-class families.

It was the federal government—not Wall Street or the market—that created the student aid program after World War II, enabling millions of servicemen and -women to attend college.

It was the federal government—not Wall Street or the market—that built the interstate highway system, linking small towns, rural areas and the nation's cities.

It was the federal government—not Wall Street or the market—that initiated development of the computer, the machine that has transformed everyone's life.

And it was the federal government—not Wall Street or the market—that financed the technology and underwrote the early costs of the Internet, the global information superhighway that is projected to become a $79 billion-a-year business by the turn of the century, generating enough revenue to place it among the 20 largest U.S. industrial and service corporations.

Writing Off People

All of which brings us full circle to Marion, Va., and the men and women who once worked for Harwood Industries and who lost their jobs, thanks to U.S. government trade policies.

Marion is in the heart of what Virginians call the Mountain Empire, a region of lovely rolling hills, pleasant valleys and gentle streams. It is a place where jobs have never been plentiful. But small manufacturing facilities, especially clothing plants, have dotted stretches of the countryside along Interstate 81, providing jobs for area women.

For more than half a century Harwood Industries, a maker of men's pajamas, robes and casual clothing, was one of the fixtures of the Marion economy. At its plant on the outskirts of town, Harwood employed several hundred seamstresses, cutters, warehousemen, packers, mechanics and office workers. By national standards, the pay was never good. In 1992, the average wage for women in the sewing department was $6.75 an hour, or roughly $14,000 a year. But Harwood did have a health plan, the women were close to family and friends, and at least it provided steady work.

Until August 31, 1992. On that day, Harwood announced it was closing the sewing operation, eliminating 120 jobs. In a statement all too familiar to American workers, Harwood officials said they regretted the decision but that it was "necessary because we were not competitive on most of the products we were producing." The company said it planned to keep open a distribution center and office "to maintain a substantial presence in Marion." But they, too, were phased out over the next 18 months.

For years, Harwood had been shuttering plants in the United States and, under pressure from retailers to cut costs, shifting production offshore—first to Puerto Rico, then Nicaragua, and finally to Honduras and Costa Rica. The employees at Marion had watched as the company closed other plants, and had seen other manufacturers in their area shut down. They knew the signs did not look good. Yet the layoff still came as a shock.

"It does something to your self-esteem," said Ann Williams, who closed out her 20 years at Harwood working in the office. "You don't get over it. I don't know anyone who has really gotten over it. Even those of us who have gone on and been fortunate enough to find work feel that way. We all knew we hadn't been singled out. Everybody had been let go. But you still take it personally. I don't think there is any one of us who didn't take it personally."

For Darlene Speer, the shutdown hurt, both personally and financially. "I loved my job, but after the way they treated us at the end, I was almost glad to get out of there," she said. "We all worked so hard. They didn't close it because of our work. I don't think there's any one of us now who is not glad to be away from there, even though we might not be making the same money."

Speer, who is divorced and the mother of two grown children, ultimately wound up with two jobs, with the furniture maker and the video store, and together, she said, the two equal roughly what she earned annually at Harwood. "But you can't look back," she said. "I've gone ahead with my life. And, for the most part, I'm happy. But I'll tell you it's hard to start over."

One of her coworkers, Nancy Anders, who worked in the sewing department for 25 years, recalled how she'd felt such a sense of responsibility toward the job. She went to work regardless—"when I was sick, when my family was sick," she said. At the company's request, she even went to Nicaragua in the late 1970s to help train new employees at a plant Harwood had built there. Anders spent six weeks showing Nicaraguan women how to operate sewing machines. At the time, she didn't think much about it. She felt sorry for the people, who were so poor. It was only years later, reflecting on the trip, that she realized she'd been "training them to take our jobs but didn't know it."

She did everything she was asked because that was her nature. "When I worked there, I thought this company can't get by without me," Anders said. "And when I found out they could, it hurt. I was bitter at first. It seemed like they shouldn't have closed it. But the more I thought about it, I thought, 'If they don't want me, then I can find a job somewhere.'"

Eventually, Anders did find one, for less money. "I have a good job now," she said. "It's a part-time job. I'm Wal-Mart's people-greeter, and I love it. And I think I'm the best people-greeter Wal-Mart's got."

Smiling and upbeat, Nancy Anders has gone on with her life, even though she earns less and must pay for her health coverage. Yet for her, the greatest loss can't be measured in dollars and cents. Harwood's closing cheated her out of a chapter of her life.

For 25 years, she had gone to festive dinners sponsored by the employees when fellow workers retired. On these occasions, employees chipped in to buy the retiree a finely crafted oak rocking chair made at a nearby furniture factory. It was a lasting gesture of affection from those who stayed to those who were departing, and the rocking chair came to symbolize not only a life of leisure but also a kind of closure to a life of working at the Harwood plant. "I went to the retirement dinners for 25 years and I couldn't wait to retire so I could get one of those great big rocking chairs," she said. "I just dreamed about that day. That was my goal, getting that rocking chair."

When Harwood announced the shutdown in 1992, Nancy Anders knew there would be no retirement dinner, no rocking chair. "I went home that night and I cried," she said. "My husband thought I was crazy being so upset over a rocking chair. He said, 'Go get one.' I could have bought the rocking chair. But it wouldn't have meant the same after all those years. I missed getting that rocking chair almost as much as I hated to lose my job."

Wendell Watkins, a Harwood vice-president and the last manager of the Marion plant, said the company regretted the closing but had no choice if it wanted to remain "competitive." "We have always manufactured private-label goods for big firms [department stores] who can shop the world and get the best price they can," Watkins said. "Now, that's great for the U.S. consumer, and they are the real beneficiaries. Our major customers always insist on having the lowest price. They tell us, 'We'll bring it in from the Orient if you can't do something to match the cost.' I think we did a great job of keeping it open as long as we did and we would have loved to have continued to operate it, but we just could not compete with the competition we had to meet and pay U.S. labor prices."

Watkins said he knew the closing was hard on many employees, but he felt it was the right decision—not just for Harwood but for the nation as a whole. "As much as this has hurt my industry, it is my belief and feeling that our government is going about this in the correct manner," Watkins said. "I think that they have to write the industry off and go for high-tech and let the less-expensive labor countries produce the apparel and other things. I have lived in the industry all my life and it has been good to me, and as much as I hate to admit it, I think we are taking the proper approach. I know it has hurt a lot of people, but it is also helping a lot of people in the long run, the consumers."

When Harwood shut Marion, the company ceased to manufacture in the United States. The gradual move of its plants offshore was complete to three new facilities—two in Honduras and one in Costa Rica. For many American apparel makers, Honduras has become the country of choice in recent years. The Central American nation of 5.3 million people has been highly successful in attracting U.S. plants because of cheap labor, no taxes and a solicitous government. American companies that manufacture products in specially created export zones are exempt from all import and export duties, from currency charges when they ship profits back to the United States, and from all Honduran taxes— a "Permanent Tax Holiday," as the Honduran government describes it.

Best of all, they are exempt from U.S.-style wages. The minimum wage of the Honduran factory worker, according to that government's statistics, is 48 cents an hour, including benefits—or less than $20 a week in take-home pay. Even by Latin American standards, that's low. Mexicans who work in American plants in the north of Mexico now earn, on average, $60 a week—three times the average pay of Hondurans. And Mexican wages, of course, are only a fraction of the $7 to $8 an hour that a U.S. worker would be paid. In short, for all the talk about the need to be "competitive," there is no way a plant in the United States paying minimum wages and no benefits could compete with a Honduran plant that pays 48 cents an hour and where profits are exempt from taxes.

Not surprisingly, many American companies have moved some operations to Honduras in recent years. The list includes such familiar names as Sara Lee, Bestform, U.S. Shoe, Fruit of the Loom, and Wrangler. One of those companies, Sara Lee, in turn announced plans in the summer of 1996 to acquire Harwood. "Harwood's manufacturing expertise complements Sara Lee's knowledge of the underwear [industry]," said Donald J. Franceschini, executive vice-president of Sara Lee.

Harwood was one of the first to capitalize on Honduran incentives; its first plant was built there in 1980. When Harwood's Watkins was asked if labor was the main reason for going to Central America, he answered: "It's the only benefit. And you do it only so you can compete, not because you want to."

Having successfully transferred all of Harwood's operations abroad, the company's chief executive officer and principal owner, Michael Rothbaum, subsequently offered some words of advice to American manufacturers who might be considering a Caribbean operation. After first warning that the process was not easy— think of it "as if you were starting a plant on the moon," he wrote in a trade journal—he then assured them it was worth it. If "approached correctly, the savings in labor costs can be significant."

Rothbaum went on to paint a picture of the average worker: "Caribbean employees work longer hours, from 44 to 48 per week, and they travel further to work, sometimes two hours by bus each way. Some also attend school at night. For many, the only decent meal they get each day is the one served in your cafeteria. Also remember that Caribbean employees are younger than your domestic workforce. The average age in a Caribbean plant may be 19 to 20.

"Medical care as we know it is not available, and people come to work when they're sick—because that is where they may find a doctor or nurse. To a great extent, you, the employer, must compensate for these differences in conditions through the social contract you make with your employees in order to achieve acceptable performance."

If Rothbaum believes U.S. employers must enter into a social contract with their Caribbean employees, it is just such a contract that their abandoned employees in the United States believe has been broken—by cutting off jobs, wiping out benefits, lowering their standard of living.

And the outlook for a long-term social contract in countries such as Honduras is not good, either, if history is any guide. Harwood's first offshore plant was in Puerto Rico. When wage rates rose there, the company moved its apparel production to a lower-wage country, Nicaragua. But after political upheaval there in the late 1970s, Harwood relocated to Honduras and Costa Rica.

One longtime Harwood employee at Marion, Garney Powers, after noticing how the company kept moving its operations from one developing country to the next to cut costs, said he once asked a Harwood manager if there was any chance, as wages rose in developing countries, that Harwood might shift some of its manufacturing back to the States. No way, he said the manager told him:

"There's too many countries out there."

CHAPTER • TWO

Global Trade— Sending Jobs Abroad

Importing Goods, Exporting Jobs

Ask a president of the United States how to create good-paying jobs for American workers. He will say: exports. That's what Bill Clinton says, and what every president before him, Republican and Democrat, has said for 30 years and more.

"Every time we sell $1 billion of American products and services overseas, we create about 20,000 jobs" at home. That's Clinton in 1993. "Each additional billion dollars in exports creates nearly 20,000 new jobs here in the United States." That's George Bush, in 1991. "Every billion dollars by which we increase exports, one hundred thousand new jobs will be created." That's Lyndon B. Johnson, in 1964, when a billion dollars went a little further.

It has become an enduring article of faith in Washington: If U.S. manufacturers can sell more goods through unrestricted global trade, the American factory worker will have a bright and secure future.

Just one problem: It doesn't work.

For the last 25 years, Washington has marched steadily in the direction of "free trade"—and the American worker has just as steadily lost ground. Blue-collar wages have eroded; high-paying manufacturing jobs, once the mainstay of the middle class, have dwindled. America is moving toward a two-class society of have-mores and have-lesses.

The problem with Washington's free trade-equals-jobs formula is that it ignores the other half of the equation—the negative impact of imports. For if $1 billion in exports creates 20,000 jobs, then $1 billion in imports eliminates a like number. That's the minus of free trade.

Under Washington's open-door policy, imports have far out-

Global Trade—Sending Jobs Abroad

paced U.S. exports. America is creating jobs, all right—in Malaysia, Taiwan, Honduras, Japan and China. In all the presidents' statements extolling global trade, you'd be hard pressed to find the number of American jobs lost because of imports. And here's the reason: Since 1979, a total of 2.6 million manufacturing jobs have been eliminated. That's equal to the entire workforce of the state of Maryland.

In the last two decades, Washington policy makers have thrown open the doors of the world's most lucrative consumer market to foreign products without adequate regard for the consequences—either for American workers or for the long-term health of American industry. While the dropping of most U.S. import restrictions has meant big profits for big companies, it has been a disaster for workers, their families and many small businesses.

Not that exports didn't account for new jobs. They did. From 1980 through 1995, the value of exports more than doubled to $576 billion, creating millions of jobs. But exports were swamped by imports, which tripled to $749 billion, thereby wiping out millions more jobs.

In the global economy, U.S.-based multinational corporations, with operations around the world, find it far more profitable to manufacture in low-wage countries than at home. Instead of employing U.S. workers to make the products in this country and then exporting them for sale abroad, they employ workers in other countries to make the products sold there.

Today, many U.S.-based global companies have barely a nodding acquaintance with the word *export*. General Motors Corp., the world's largest automaker, says it shipped 95,000 cars and trucks abroad from the United States in 1995—or 2 percent of the 4.3 million vehicles GM manufactured here. The rest of its worldwide sales were of vehicles made overseas. Ford Motor Co., the world's third-largest car and truck maker, says it shipped 104,000 cars and trucks abroad in 1995—or 3 percent of the 3.45 million vehicles it manufactured in the United States.

And then there's the Colgate-Palmolive Co., the giant household products company, headquartered in New York City. The cover of its 1994 annual report to stockholders sums up Colgate's goals: GLOBAL BRANDS. GLOBAL INVESTMENT. GLOBAL GROWTH.

From modest beginnings, peddling candles on Wall Street in 1806, the company has expanded so that it now sells toothpaste, soap, shampoo and other household products in nearly 200 countries. More than 70 percent of Colgate's $8 billion in annual sales comes from outside the United States. That means plenty of exports and thousands of export-generated American jobs, right?

Wrong.

Lynne and Ed Tevis can tell you why. One day in 1985, Colgate-Palmolive announced plans to close the factory in Jersey City where they worked. The Tevises could consider themselves fortunate, though, because Colgate was going to keep them on. True, they would have to move halfway across the country to Kansas City, Kan., where a small part of the Jersey City operation was to be transferred as part of a "restructuring." Unlike corporate executives who relocate, they would have to pay for the move out of their own pockets. That would cost $5,000 to $10,000.

But Lynne and Ed had each been with Colgate for 12 years. And while 1,200 others at the Jersey City plant were laid off, the Tevises were among the 80 or so families who had made the cut. So they sold their home, uprooted their family, and left relatives and friends behind to move 1,200 miles west to an area they had never seen. They reasoned that the short-term upheaval and expense would be worth the long-term security of remaining with Colgate, where they had accumulated pension credits and other benefits. All they would lose, they were told, was their seniority.

Job security: that's what the Tevises prized most. Ed Tevis, then 50, had 12 years to go until retirement, so his wife had asked a mid-level manager in Kansas City how safe their jobs would be there. "He reassured us about moving," she said. "He told us, 'Your husband will definitely retire from here.' He was less certain about me because I was younger. He said, 'Nobody knows what's down the road 20 years in the future, but more than likely you will retire from here, too.' So we came out here based on that."

Less than two years after arriving in Kansas City, the Tevises were thrown out of work. The reason? Another Colgate "restructuring." From 800 employees in 1988, the Kansas City workforce would be reduced to about 200. The first group laid off included many new arrivals from Jersey City who had relinquished their seniority. Some had worked for Colgate for more than 20 years, but that counted for nothing. Meanwhile, as the company was busily thinning out its American workforce, it was hiring by the thousands overseas, where it could pay employees far lower wages.

Look at the people who make Colgate products today—and remember the Tevises and their futile trek to Kansas City. From 1980 to 1996, a total of 15,390 Colgate workers in the United

Global Trade—Sending Jobs Abroad

States lost their jobs. The company cut its domestic workforce from 21,800 to 6,410, according to a company representative. During that period, Colgate added 4,490 workers overseas, bringing total employment in foreign countries to 30,890.

In short, the number of workers on Colgate's U.S. payroll plunged 71 percent while the number on its foreign payroll went up 17 percent. Looked at another way, U.S. workers accounted for 45 percent of Colgate's total workforce in 1980. By 1996, U.S. workers accounted for just 17 percent.

If Colgate's employees are faring none too well, the company itself is doing quite nicely, thank you. In the decade from 1986 to 1995, while Colgate was cutting its U.S. workforce:

- Dividends paid to holders of common stock went up 159 percent, from 68 cents to $1.76 a share.
- The stock price shot up 244 percent, from $20.44 to $70.25 a share.
- And profits soared 371 percent, from $115 million to $541 million, before a restructruing charge.

While it may seem strange to regard Colgate as a predominantly foreign manufacturer, consider this Customs Service list of products and materials the company imported over the last six months. Toothbrushes from Colombia and South Africa. Cashmere Bouquet soap from India and Guatemala. Dental cream from Panama. Cleaning products from Mexico. Household products from Barbados and Costa Rica. Dental floss from the United Kingdom. Perfumes from Guyana. Powder puffs and pads from China. Packaging material from El Salvador.

And what did Colgate manufacture in the United States and ship abroad for sale? When the question was first posed to a Colgate public affairs officer, she said she would contact the appropriate company official for an answer. After two weeks passed without a response, one of the authors who asked about the status of the inquiry was told, "It was kind of lost in the shuffle. I think the reason no one got back to me was we're a multinational company with operations on the ground and in many, many countries. That's probably why I was unable to get [an answer]."

As is increasingly the case with most foreign trade by U.S. multinationals, the flow of Colgate goods is largely in one direction. The company manufactures products abroad and ships them into this country, but it makes little here for sale overseas. Indeed, that applies even for Colgate products sold in neighboring Mexico. As the company put it with great pride in its 1994 annual report: "Virtually all the products we sell in Mexico are made there and do not have to be imported from the U.S.A. . . ."

That so many of the imports that kill American jobs are made by U.S. multinationals such as Colgate, which once manufactured most of their products here, is a grim irony. It was particularly grim for the small band of Colgate workers from Jersey City who demonstrated faith in their employer and trooped out to Kansas City, there to be terminated.

Stanley Darago was another Colgate worker who made the ill-fated trip with his wife, Terry. "A lot of families were destroyed by what happened," said Terry. "People split up. People got divorced. Some people had to sell their houses. Others had their cars repossessed. People struggled. They didn't have the income anymore."

Stanley Darago was out of work five years before he found another steady job. The family squeaked by only because Terry was employed. She was a Midwest manager of General Binding Corp., a global manufacturer and marketer of business machines and related supplies. A year after Stanley secured work again, though, Terry's company also restructured and eliminated her job. She could have accepted a position elsewhere with General Binding, but she, her husband and 15-year-old son would have had to move yet again.

"So I decided to go back to school," she said. "I'm studying to be a nurse. Three months I'm back in school and I wonder, am I doing the right thing? I've got so long to go before I become a nurse and build up the tenure and experience to bring me back to the level of income I was making."

She chose nursing because she felt the future was uncertain with most large corporations. "I wondered, what are the odds of me going to work for another company in corporate America and once I'm in my early 50s, winding up in the same boat I'm in now," said Terry. "Then where do I head after I've dedicated another 10 years to another company?"

As for her husband, he has suffered the kind of economic setback that is typical of blue-collar workers whose jobs are abolished. Stanley Darago made about $15 an hour at Colgate, not including overtime, which was often plentiful. Today, working the production line for a food-processing company, he earns $11.60 an hour, about 23 percent less than he made eight years ago.

The story of lower earnings is much the same for other former

Colgate employees in Kansas City. Ed Tevis has had three jobs since Colgate—the first for a glass-cutting company, which later closed; the second for a pharmaceutical maker, where he was laid off. He now is a production worker for a bottle maker.

Lynne Tevis went back to school and learned secretarial and bookkeeping skills. She briefly kept the books for a health care company until the firm closed the office. She has not worked since, and in the spring of 1996, Lynne, now 40, gave birth to her third child, a girl.

Gus Tillman, a pipe fitter who also transferred from Jersey City, was actually laid off twice by Colgate. The first time came in 1989, when his two daughters were in college. He found a job as a welder. Then Colgate hired him back in 1992, only to lay him off again—permanently—in 1994. He now repairs freight cars for the Union Pacific railroad at $12 an hour, or about two-thirds of what he earned at Colgate.

"What do they [corporations] expect people to do?" he asks. "I know productivity at Colgate has risen. I know at one time that was their major complaint. Well, productivity went up to the standard they wanted and they still are not satisfied. So I don't know what else people can do. That's the part that gets you. I was told by one of my supervisors—'It's not about work. What you do. They just want the profit.'"

For Darago, the Tevises and Tillman, Colgate-Palmolive's transformation into a global corporation has meant this: The more the company sells abroad, the less it makes at home; the more money it spends overseas, the less it invests in the United States; the more money that goes to shareholders, the less that goes to employees; the more work it farms out to lower-paid subcontractors, the less need for higher-paid employees; and the more plants it closes, the fewer jobs overall that are to be had.

In that, Colgate is representative of what is happening across much of corporate America.

The New Math of Free Trade

To better understand the magnitude of the problem, let's return to those presidential job projections—the estimates that every $1 billion in exports creates 20,000 jobs.

The way to encourage export sales, according to big business and Washington, is through "free trade": Every nation agrees to lower the tariffs that make imported products so expensive. Na-

Imports Have Cost the U.S. Manufacturing Jobs

In the 1970s, imports into the U.S. began their relentless climb, abetted by the nation's free-trade policies. As imports flooded the country, manufacturing jobs began to decline, with 2.6 million lost since 1979.

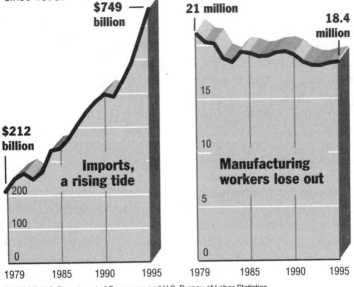

$749 billion

$212 billion

Imports, a rising tide

200

100

0

1979   1985   1990   1995

21 million

18.4 million

15

10

Manufacturing workers lose out

5

0

1979   1985   1990   1995

SOURCE: U.S. Department of Commerce and U.S. Bureau of Labor Statistics

tions no longer protect their key industries by keeping out rival products made by foreign competitors. Industries are free to grow worldwide, limited only by the quality of what they produce.

Free trade produces exports, which produce jobs—that's the mantra recited incessantly by big business and big government. But look at the numbers: If the Johnson-Bush-Clinton figures were the whole story, the United States today would be awash in manufacturing jobs. That, clearly, isn't the case.

Consider what has happened since 1979, the peak year for manufacturing employment. The United States exported $184 billion worth of goods that year. By 1995, exports had climbed to $576 billion. According to presidential arithmetic, that should have created nearly eight million new jobs.

In fact, manufacturing jobs went down, falling from 21 million in 1979 to 18.4 million in 1995. That was a loss of 2.6 million

Global Trade—Sending Jobs Abroad

jobs—not a gain of nearly 8 million. One reason for the drop: Since 1979, the United States has run up a merchandise trade deficit of $1.7 trillion—meaning Americans have bought that much more in foreign-made televisions, computers, clothing, autos and other products than we have sold abroad. Not all of the job loss was due to imports, of course. Technologies change, productivity improves, old industries die, new ones take their place. But in the past, the number of jobs created by new technologies traditionally went up—until the trade deficit began to soar.

The job loss actually was much worse than the figures suggest, because the number of manufacturing jobs was going down while the size of the overall workforce was going up—by 26.8 million. Among the biggest gainers: Retail trade and other low-paying service-sector jobs, and state and local governments. In 1979, 23.4 percent of American workers were in manufacturing. By 1995, it was down to 15.8 percent.

So the solution is obvious, you say: Control imports. Bring imports and exports into better balance.

Exactly.

You might call that "fair trade."

In other words, you don't close your borders to my products, and I won't close mine to you. But if you do choose to block certain imports—computer chips, let's say—in order to protect one of your key industries, then you balance the account by buying more of some other product from me—cars, for instance.

Free-traders oppose any restraints. They argue that any restrictions the United States might place on imports would bring on retaliation—that countries would close their borders to our products. The free-traders, who want the government to stand back and let market forces play out, have defined the debate. And their views have prevailed.

As is the case with so many government economic policies, on the issue of trade, there has been no middle ground. Washington, Wall Street and much of the news media have cast it as an either-or proposition: Either it's wide-open, unfettered imports or a wall around Fortress America.

Other nations haven't taken such a radical position. They have kept some barriers to protect their workers and their most important industries. Thus, Germany limits imports of cars from Japan. Japan restricts imports of telecommunications equipment. France limits imports of food products. Mexico bars imports of used cars from America.

America: Who Stole the Dream?

None of America's major overseas trading partners has run up trade deficits on the scale that has occurred here. Indeed, when it comes to letting in imports, the United States stands apart from most of the world. From 1980 to 1995, the United States compiled a perfect record—16 merchandise trade deficits in 16 years. The string of unmatched deficits added up to $1.7 trillion. It was the worst trade performance in the world.

During that same period, Sweden posted trade surpluses in 13 of the 16 years. Its last deficit year was 1982. The Netherlands recorded trade surpluses in 14 years. Its last deficit year was 1980. Germany achieved trade surpluses in all 16 years, for an overall surplus of $625 billion. And Japan had trade surpluses in 16 consecutive years for an overall surplus of $1.1 trillion.

Remember just two numbers: Over 16 years, the United States ran a trade deficit of $1.7 trillion, while Japan had a trade surplus of $1.1 trillion.

Meanwhile, the United States government, urged on by corporations that profit from global trade, refuses to impose tough trade restrictions, stands aside while the workforce is decimated by imports, and even sacrifices the jobs of its own citizens to create jobs for workers around the world. (More on that later.) The United States has allowed in just about anything that people in other countries know how to make. Sometimes, it even teaches them how to make it. More often than not, by paying lower wages, they can make it more cheaply than we can. They can sell it in this country cheaper. And very quickly, Americans who make those same products find themselves looking for work.

Is the problem that American businesses are somehow "unable to compete"? Judge for yourself. When the United States indiscriminately drops its trade barriers, as it has done:

- An American company that pays its workers, say, $12 an hour, must compete with foreign companies that pay their workers $12 *a week.*
- An American business that provides medical insurance for its workers must compete with foreign businesses that provide no medical coverage.
- An American business that is required to pay Social Security taxes to provide a basic retirement benefit for its workers must compete with foreign businesses that pay no such tax and provide no retirement benefits.

- An American business that receives no direct subsidies from local, state or federal governments must compete with foreign businesses that are subsidized by their governments.
- An American company that complies with environmental regulations to protect air and water quality must compete with foreign businesses that don't have to comply.
- An American company that is subjected to open-ended litigation and required to abide by endless government regulations—dealing with everything from employee and customer disabilities to labels on packages—must compete with foreign businesses that don't face any of those mandates.

Until recently, the global economy's heaviest impact was on blue-collar workers in manufacturing. Today, white-collar jobs, long thought to be immune to overseas competition, are being affected as well.

Just ask the women who once processed medical, disability and life insurance claims at the New York Life Insurance Company office in Gretna, La., across the Mississippi River from New Orleans. Most of the women were in their 30s or 40s. For some the job provided a second paycheck in the family; for others it was the only paycheck. On average they earned from $15,000 to $25,000 a year. In May of 1993, the company told them the office would close that summer. "They said there weren't enough claims, enough work to keep the office open," recalled Claudette Green, who had worked there 10 years.

She also remembered that a company official told them not to mention the upcoming closure to policyholders. "They told us to not tell the insureds—just carry on the business as usual," she recalled.

When the office closed, she said many women broke down and cried. "They did not have a job," she said, "and they did not know what to do." The final weeks were made all the more unpleasant as they were instructed to pack boxes of files for shipment to other New York Life offices.

In the beginning, the women couldn't understand why the office was closing—there were still plenty of claims to process. Then they realized what was happening. Sheryl Washington, a

13-year veteran, explained: "After a couple of weeks into it you started putting labels on boxes and they were going to Ireland. Booklets, claims, whatever they wanted to ship—to Ireland."

In 1989, New York Life opened a claims-processing office in the village of Castleisland, in rural southwestern Ireland. In recent years, Ireland, with its educated, English-speaking low-wage workforce, has become a favorite offshore site for large U.S. insurers and other corporations that process large volumes of paper and data.

Sheryl Washington went back to school, enrolling in a course to learn word processing and accounting skills on a computer. When she could not find a job in New Orleans, she relocated to Jacksonville, Fla., where she now works as a receptionist for a large company. Like a number of other women interviewed, she said the change, in some respects, was good for her personally. It spurred her to go back to school and learn new skills, and ultimately pointed her life in a new direction. But like many women interviewed who were forced out of longtime jobs, the positive personal aspects were offset by the ground they lost financially. "I'll never be exactly where I was when New York Life closed," she said.

A soft-spoken person who is resigned over the transfer of her job abroad, Sheryl Washington asked a question that was posed time and again by people who were interviewed: "You wonder why the smaller jobs are being transferred instead of the bigger jobs. It's fine to want to help Third World countries. But why are [we] putting our own people out of work?"

Added Claudette Green, who also went back to school, for training to become a physical therapist: "You hear how the country is doing all right but it's not. I think we are all going to be homeless."

Selling Jobs, for a Profit

Because there is no middle ground on trade, U.S. policy makers have thrown open the American market even to those countries that have imposed take-it-or-leave-it ultimatums on the government and on American business—ultimatums that, if agreed to, will cost the jobs of millions of American workers.

Take the case of the Boeing Co., the premier manufacturer of jet aircraft. Boeing ranks among the top half-dozen American companies in exports, and thus, if the claims about the benefits of export-driven jobs are accurate, should be providing good-paying jobs for Americans.

But look at what is happening to Boeing jobs. In January 1990,

Global Trade—Sending Jobs Abroad

Boeing employed 155,900 people, largely at its home plant in Seattle and at facilities in Wichita, Kan., and in the Philadelphia area. Over the next six years, Boeing slashed one-third of its workforce, bringing the number of employees to 103,600 in February 1996.

One reason for the shrinking workforce: Airplane parts once made here by Boeing employees now are manufactured by subcontractors in other countries and shipped back to the United States for assembly. On a 747 jumbo jet, for example, the nose gear, the landing gear, the outboard and inboard flaps and spoilers all contain parts made in Japan. At present, about 40 percent of the parts of a Boeing 777 are manufactured outside the United States. That number is expected to reach 50 percent over the next few years.

To sell planes in other countries, Boeing agreed to move a portion of its manufacturing to those countries, to provide employment for people there to make aircraft parts. That eliminated the jobs of U.S. workers.

Frank Shrontz, chairman of Boeing, explained this practice, albeit in a roundabout way, at a 1995 stockholders meeting. His comments came in response to a question about joint-production agreements with other countries. Said Shrontz: "It is necessary, as we sell into the world market, for us to have an access to that market, and in many cases that requires that we ask the countries, and companies within those countries, to participate in our aircraft production. We are trying to put those activities out in which they could do a better job than we can and it does not destroy our core technologies, but some of that market access is simply going to have to be a trade for putting work outside."

To that end, Boeing buys parts of the wings for its jumbo 747s and for its 737s from the Xian Aircraft Co., the Chinese company that built MIG fighter planes. China has imposed that requirement as a condition of the sale. Eventually, the Chinese factory will produce the tail section for the 737, which now is made at the Boeing plant in Wichita. Chinese engineers have visited Boeing facilities in the United States and Boeing engineers have visited China.

How did the Chinese factory secure the tooling and machinery required to build tail sections?

Easy.

Boeing supplied the tooling. When asked whether Boeing furnishes tooling to its subcontractors in the United States, a company representative replied: "Boeing provides tooling for some suppliers, and then some suppliers provide their own tooling. So it's both."

In addition to tooling, Boeing has provided flight and maintenance training, helped Chinese airlines establish safety departments, provided flight simulators and pilot training, and established a corporate office in China. The company also has opened what it describes as "one of the largest aircraft spare parts centers in the world" at Beijing's Capital Airport. The center stocks more than 30,000 parts.

For their part, Boeing officials view all this as good news. At least for the Chinese. Larry Clarkson, senior vice president of planning and international development, told a conference in Singapore early in 1996 that Western trade with China is "helping millions of Chinese obtain greater freedom to choose their work, their employer and their place of residence."

Now listen to another view, expressed by an American labor leader who has been an observer of the Boeing-China trade process close-up—both in the United States and China—and who is sympathetic to Boeing's predicament: "China has all these five-year plans for autos, aerospace, etc. They are going to develop these industries. They are going to be the basis of the new China. Because it's such a huge market, they say to Boeing or Airbus or whoever wants to sell in China: 'We'll buy thirty 737s. We'll want to produce the back end of the 737 in China. You give us the machinery. You give us the engineers. You give us the technology. You help us set up the facility. And then we'll buy the airplane. . . .

"It is the biggest foreign subcontracting order the Chinese have ever had. They see it as a blueprint for the development of their aerospace industry. You see a top Boeing executive saying, Boeing is committed to developing the Chinese aerospace industry. . . ."

The source, who has visited the Xian factory where the Chinese are making aircraft parts for the 737, went on: "There are more than 500,000 Chinese employed in the aerospace industry. The average wage rates are $50 a month. I saw Xian, which employs 20,000 workers who live in barracks. The government role is totally coordinated, totally subsidized."

Instructing China, step by step, on how to build its aircraft, Boeing is essentially setting a competitor up in business. The day may well come when China can supply to the world at least some of the planes that Boeing does now, and do it more cheaply. But like much of American business today—and most especially those

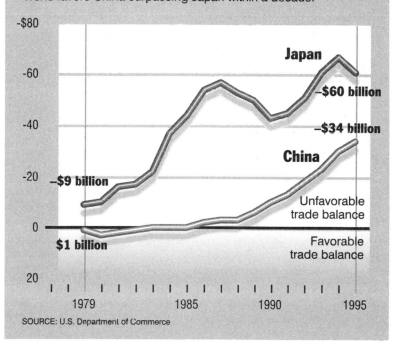

U.S. Deficit with China
Approaching Levels with Japan

Trend favors China surpassing Japan within a decade.

- -$80
- -60
- -40
- -20
- 0
- 20

Japan

–$60 billion

–$34 billion

China

–$9 billion

Unfavorable
trade balance

$1 billion

Favorable
trade balance

1979   1985   1990   1995

SOURCE: U.S. Department of Commerce

businesses that are publicly owned and susceptible to profit pressures from Wall Street—the Boeing-China deal was made for short-term gain, at the expense of any long-term commitment in America.

It was also made at the expense of the American taxpayer—on two counts. First, was the actual sale of planes to China. From 1993 to 1995, the Export-Import Bank of the United States guaranteed loans totaling $1.4 billion for China's purchase of Boeing aircraft. This made China the Ex-Im Bank's largest customer in Asia.

The Ex-Im Bank is an independent agency of the U.S. government which, in its own words, "has one mission: to help the private sector create and maintain American jobs by financing exports." Thus, a U.S. government agency backed by American tax-payers helped finance the sale of planes in China that will be built, in part, by workers in China. Or, if you will, U.S. government financing will create jobs in China.

Second, Boeing and the rest of the civilian aviation industry, perhaps more than any other industry, owe their technology leadership to the tens of billions of taxpayer dollars spent on research and development of military aircraft. Now some of Boeing's technology is being given away to the Chinese.

Boeing is not the first American corporation to follow this path. It is merely doing what the American electronics industry did many years ago: selling off the technology and manufacturing processes that made the companies and contributed to the overall health and wealth of the nation, its workers and communities.

Back in the 1960s, Japan blocked imports of American-made television sets and instead required U.S. companies to license their technology to Japanese manufacturers. That's one reason why foreign suppliers today control the American market for television sets—as well as a variety of other products, including radios, VCRs and portable computer display panels. And why no American companies manufacture television sets in the United States today.

More significant, Boeing's role in the global economy underscores why Washington's trade policies have been such a failure for the ordinary working American—and why the worst is yet to come: While Boeing cannot sell aircraft to China unless it builds part of its planes in that country, the United States does not impose any similar requirements on China or other countries.

If it did, here's how it might work: The U.S. government would tell Tokyo Widget Corp. that if it wanted to sell widgets in the United States, it would have to manufacture 20 percent of the parts in this country and ship them back to Japan for assembly and sale there. That eventually would grow to 100 percent and the U.S. government would then own Tokyo Widget's technology and manufacturing processes.

That would never happen, naturally, because the U.S. government refuses to impose requirements that other countries demand. This practice of U.S. companies acceding to joint production agreements requiring "local content" labor will translate into the loss of millions of U.S. jobs in coming years.

The point is, American corporations hungry for sales routinely agree to all manner of conditions set by foreign governments—while Washington asks little or nothing from foreign producers wanting to crack this, the largest consumer market in the world. Call it one-way free trade, but it's not fair trade. And the numbers show it.

Ten years ago, in 1986, China exported $4.7 billion worth of goods to the United States. In 1995, imports from China totaled $45.5 billion. U.S. exports trailed far behind. So the U.S. trade deficit with China jumped from $1.6 billion in 1986 to $33.8 billion in 1995—an increase of 2,012 percent. That's a huge number. You might want to think of it this way: If personal incomes had gone up at the same rate, the average American family in 1996 would earn more than $600,000.

In any case, if the deficit trend continues, China will replace Japan as the United States' most unequal trading partner shortly after the turn of the century. The United States then will have massive, structural trade deficits with two countries, instead of one.

Endangered Label: "Made in the U.S.A."

Look at almost anything you buy today and note where it was made. The hammer and screwdriver in the garage were manufactured in China. The notebook on the desk is from Indonesia. The windshield wipers on the car were made in Mexico.

In your closet, the Bugle Boy blue jeans came from Nicaragua. The Speedo swimming trunks were made in China and Malaysia. The Reeboks in Thailand and Indonesia. The Ralph Lauren Chaps sweatshirt in Pakistan. The Starter official U.S. Olympic baseball cap—inscribed "Bringing America Together"—was made in the Dominican Republic. The great American leisure-time uniform: sweatshirt, blue jeans, baseball cap, sneakers. All made offshore: all American jobs lost.

This is not to say that the United States should erect walls around the country to keep out all imported goods. Imports give consumers more choices and keep the pressure on American manufacturers to improve their products. Quality-built, stylish cars from Japan forced Detroit automakers to build better cars and to listen more closely to the wishes of American car buyers.

Imports also have benefited consumers through lower prices. But not all consumers benefit equally. A consumer who lives off stock dividends of companies that shift their manufacturing abroad to exploit cheap labor benefits twice from imports—because the increased dividends provide more money to buy more lower-priced imported products. But for a factory worker or white-collar employee whose job has been eliminated, or sent abroad, imported products at a lower price are no bargain, if the worker can't afford to buy them.

For much of its history, the United States had a healthy balance between exports and imports, with exports usually running ahead. Like other nations, the United States controlled the flow of foreign goods into the country through tariffs. By adjusting import duties, the government shielded some industries and encouraged trade in others.

Tariffs were viewed as a way to protect the national interest, ensuring the survival of industries, such as steel and autos, required for day-to-day living and vital in times of war. Without a strong manufacturing sector, the United States could not have won World War II. But since 1945, whole industries that were pivotal to the Allied victory, such as shipbuilding, have disappeared.

Emerging from the war as the world's dominant economic power, the United States began promoting lower trade barriers to encourage commerce among nations and to help rebuild shattered economies. Foreign policy concerns also were a major consideration. For these and many other reasons, the United States became the world's free-trade cheerleader. Washington was the prime mover behind the General Agreement on Tariffs and Trade (GATT), a pact reached by the world's leading industrialized nations in 1947, that has served as a vehicle to lower trade barriers ever since. And Washington became the principal force behind regional pacts such as the North American Free Trade Agreement (NAFTA), which lowered U.S. tariffs with Mexico and Canada after it went into effect in 1994.

Over the years, to spur others, the United States has generally taken the lead in lowering tariffs and reducing nontariff trade barriers. Other countries, Japan for one, have lowered tariffs, too. But they have kept the trade barriers in place— government regulations, red tape and collusive business practices that stymie American companies seeking to sell products there. The result: Japanese companies have essentially unlimited access to American consumers, while U.S. companies have only limited access to Japanese consumers.

As might be expected, when the United States gradually relaxed its trade barriers, exports and imports fell out of balance as more foreign-made goods surged into the country. In 1971, the nation recorded its first significant trade deficit of $2.2 billion.

Global Trade—Sending Jobs Abroad

Four years of mixed results followed—with deficits in 1972 and 1974, and surpluses in 1973 and 1975. The 1975 surplus would be the last for this century, as the country ran up a seemingly never-ending streak of deficits, beginning at $9.5 billion in 1976.

In response, Congress, usually with the cooperation of the White House, enacted one trade bill after another—each aimed at reducing the deficits. Yet they continued to grow. Along with them went jobs.

Still—in the face of clear evidence that imports were hurting the American worker—each successive administration held to the same course, right up to the present day. For all the tough talk embodied in trade bills through the years, no administration could bring itself to take retaliatory measures against other nations for fear it would set back the cause of free trade. It has been a bipartisan policy that has united politicians who otherwise have little in common.

President Lyndon Johnson in 1968: "Under international rules of trade, a nation restricts imports at the risk of its own exports. Restriction begets restriction."

President Richard Nixon in 1973: "Proposals to close American markets or raise barriers to goods abroad in order to save jobs here, that is terribly shortsighted. . . . If we close our markets in order to save jobs here, we are going to lose jobs for those products that otherwise would be sold abroad."

President Clinton's trade representative, Mickey Kantor, in 1994, when asked if Congress should retaliate against Japan for blocking access to its market: "I am a little worried when we start shutting down our markets, because what we are doing is shooting ourselves somewhere below the knees for doing it."

Oddly, the restrictive practices that these administrations claimed would be detrimental to the United States have proved enormously successful for Japan. The Japanese haven't just limited imports from the United States. They have chosen certain crucial U.S. products, such as televisions and machine tools, and subsidized their own factories to make those products, then inundated the American market with them—all the while blocking similar products made in the United States from entry into Japan.

As the office of the United States trade representative explained in a 1994 report: "Japan imports relatively fewer manufactured goods than any other [developed] country." Japan's imports have "failed to rise substantially over the past twenty years, despite the lowering of tariffs and other formal trade barriers. . . . Japan's domestic market still remains significantly less open to imports and foreign direct investment, despite years of market-opening efforts."

So, contrary to Lyndon Johnson's theory, restrictions do not beget restrictions—at least not when they are imposed on the United States. Realizing that the United States likely will not retaliate—in large part because powerful special interests profit from maintaining the existing system—countries such as Japan and China ignore the threats from Washington and continue business as usual.

The result: Industry after industry has been hammered. Few pitched battles have marked this war. Rather, it is a series of skirmishes that, except for a celebrated battle or two over autos, has rarely attracted much attention. The list of products invented or developed in the United States but made here no longer, or in trifling numbers, is endless. From telephones to reading glasses, from bicycles to irons, from sewing machines to cameras, from jeans to baseballs.

Other than the American worker, the biggest loser in this has been the small business. Unlike multinational corporations that have closed factories in the United States and shifted production abroad to take advantage of cheap labor, small companies seldom have that option. It is these businesses, employing from a few to a few dozen workers, that suffer most. Individually, they barely register a blip on the economic indicators. Taken together, they provide a livelihood for millions.

Small businesses have scant access to the people in Congress who write the laws, little influence in the White House, and rarely receive a favorable hearing from regulatory authorities. With few exceptions, their appeals for help go unheard when imports of competing products from low-wage countries begin flooding the United States. U.S. presidents and trade authorities from both parties conclude—most often incorrectly—that the industries are not endangered. Afterward, the industries slowly decline, gradually close plants and lay off workers.

That's what happened to the American flatware business. In the early 1980s, when stainless steel knives, forks and spoons suddenly surged into the United States from Japan, Korea and Taiwan in response to lowered tariffs and cutthroat foreign pricing, the domestic industry—one of the nation's oldest—found itself in trouble.

American producers, contending it was unfair competition,

appealed to the U.S. International Trade Commission (ITC) to impose higher tariffs on imported flatware. The trade commission is an independent government agency whose main job is to monitor the impact of imports on U.S. industries. If the ITC agrees with an industry's complaint, the presidentially appointed commissioners may recommend that duties be imposed. Even so, there is no assurance the duties will actually be assessed. And in most cases they are not. The final decision rests with the White House, which, historically, has refused to impose additional duties.

After five months of study, the commission ruled on May 1, 1984, that stainless steel flatware was "not being imported into the United States in such increased quantities as to be a substantial cause of serious injury, or the threat thereof, to the domestic industry." On the contrary, the ITC held that the "economic data on the performance of this industry fail to demonstrate the required degree of serious injury mandated by the statute. Rather, the industry is doing reasonably well."

According to ITC findings, nine companies produced flatware in the United States in 1982. Today, most of those companies are either out of business or purchasing flatware from foreign sources. Except for two plants of Oneida Ltd. in Oneida, N.Y., there is virtually no stainless steel flatware production in the United States.

War of the Roses

To ardent free-traders, the collapse of the domestic flatware industry, with its consequent job losses, was inevitable—a case of cheaper foreign products replacing those made in a country where wages, benefits and living standards are higher. It was inevitable, though, only because the people in Washington have created an unequal playing field. Contrary to the notion that government is powerless to affect economic forces, government action—or inaction, in this case—can and does change the destiny of American businesses and families. The federal government stood by and watched the flatware industry sink.

Sometimes, though, Washington does get involved—on behalf of foreign competitors. Just ask the people who grow roses in this country.

Twenty years ago, a bouquet of long-stemmed roses delivered on Valentine's Day more than likely came from a greenhouse in the United States. Today, most roses sold in this country are grown on the high plateau outside Bogotá, Colombia. And many of those American greenhouses are out of business.

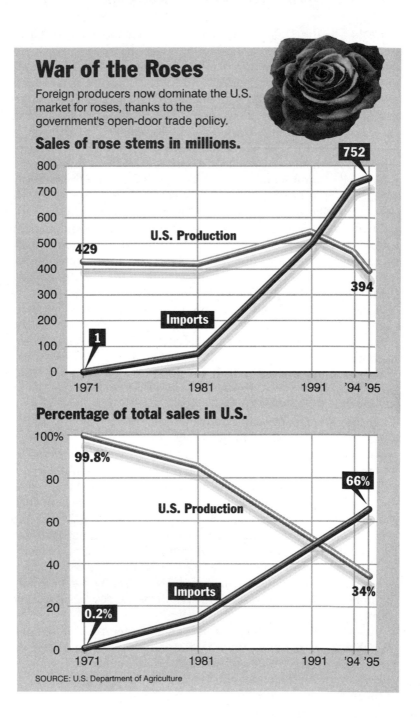

War of the Roses

Foreign producers now dominate the U.S. market for roses, thanks to the government's open-door trade policy.

Sales of rose stems in millions.

U.S. Production

429

Imports

1

752

394

1971   1981   1991   '94 '95

Percentage of total sales in U.S.

99.8%

U.S. Production

66%

Imports

0.2%

34%

1971   1981   1991   '94 '95

SOURCE: U.S. Department of Agriculture

Global Trade—Sending Jobs Abroad

What happened? The most common explanation is that Colombia merely exploited certain natural advantages to corner the market. As the *Wall Street Journal* reported on February 15, 1996: "The oil crisis of the '70s drove up heating costs at greenhouses, and business shifted south. Colombia and Ecuador, with their cheap labor and ideal climate, took over the market."

Not quite.

Colombia's strongest advantage was not climate, energy costs or even cheap labor. It was the U.S. government.

Colombia began growing flowers for export in the 1960s. The U.S. Agency for International Development (AID), the arm of the State Department that is assigned to encourage economic growth among poor nations, provided technical assistance to the Colombian growers. Technicians funded by the U.S. government helped Colombian growers cultivate their crops and create a distribution network to get the flowers to market.

In this period—the height of the Cold War—export development by poor countries was a high priority of U.S. foreign policy, and an important part of the American gospel of free trade. As early as 1959, according to congressional reports, AID "determined that Colombia must embark on an aggressive export promotion program."

Concluding that the country was much too dependent on coffee, its principal export, AID decided that Colombia should "diversify and develop other exports," so it channeled foreign-aid dollars to encourage the growth of fresh-cut flowers and other industries. Thus, U.S. taxpayers helped pay the start-up costs for an industry that eventually would undermine one of America's own.

Once Colombia's flower industry was on its feet, producing ever-greater quantities for export, the State Department made certain that the roses could be imported into this country free of high tariffs. At the time, the United States, Western Europe and Japan were the world's largest markets for fresh-cut flowers. Per capita, the European and Japanese markets were actually larger than the U.S. market. But Europe and Japan were essentially closed to imported flowers to protect their own producers. So the Colombian growers focused on this country as the place to send their flowers.

And send them they did.

In 1971, one million rose stems were imported, mostly from Colombia. That represented just two-tenths of 1 percent of sales in the United States. A decade later, in 1981, imported rose shipments soared to 72 million stems. More important, imported roses now claimed 15 percent of the U.S. market. Again, most came from Colombia. By 1991, imports had reached 504 million stems, giving foreign growers 48 percent of the American market. And by 1995, imports had climbed to 752 million stems, giving foreign growers control of the American market. They enjoyed 66 percent of all rose sales.

U.S. rose growers—whose profits plummeted as they tried to compete with the cheap imports—did not simply sit and watch it happen. Although they might as well have. The reason: They took their case to a U.S. government that exhibited more concern for the welfare of Colombians than for American employers and workers.

Beginning in the 1970s, the floral industry filed a series of complaints with U.S. trade agencies. In most of these cases, the U.S. government sided with the Colombian exporters, saying that U.S. growers were not at risk. A typical ruling was issued in 1984 by the U.S. International Trade Commission: "Imports of fresh-cut roses from Colombia have had no material impact on the domestic industry. . . . The domestic industry is in a healthy condition; domestic production, shipments, profits and productivity have all increased. . . . Potential imports from Colombia present no threat of material injury to the domestic industry because the industry has exhibited the strength to withstand import competition, and the projected increase in imports is small relative to the domestic market and past increases."

In 1984, when this ruling was made, imports accounted for 22 percent of the roses sold in the United States. Today, 12 years later, imports account for 66 percent. As you might expect, U.S. growers have been going out of business or have switched production to other flowers. Among them: White Brothers in Medina, N.Y.; A.N. Pierson in Cromwell, Conn.; Joseph H. Hill Co. in Richmond, Ind.; Desarose in Layton, Utah; Carl Dreisbach Inc. in Louisville, Ky.

The Pittsburgh Cut Flower Co., which will observe its 100th anniversary in 1998, once had 15 acres of greenhouses at Bakerstown, about 15 miles north of downtown Pittsburgh, and Zelienople, about 27 miles northwest of the city. Donald E. Hook, the company's president, said the Bakerstown greenhouses once had 250,000 plants, which yielded 5 million roses, and the Zelienople greenhouses had about 110,000 plants, which yielded 2.5 million roses, making Pittsburgh Cut Flower Pennsylvania's largest rose grower.

But no more.

Throughout the late 1970s and '80s, Hook said, U.S. growers complained to the federal government that foreign growers were dumping flowers in this country. "But it's like everything else, whether shoes or steel," Hook said. "In the time it takes to get a decision out of Washington, you are out of business. You can't get an immediate response. Some of these lobbying efforts have gone on for years."

Unable to compete with the cheaper Colombian roses, Pittsburgh Cut Flower closed its greenhouses in 1991 and went from about 140 workers to 35. Many were longtime employees, Hook said, because "a greenhouse is really a farm with glass over the land, and it requires some farming skills."

That left Dillon Floral Corp. of Bloomsburg, 120 miles northwest of Philadelphia, as the state's largest rose grower. Dillon Floral is now in its 121st year. Rob Dillon, the president, represents the fourth generation of the family in the business, which sells about 3 million roses a year. He has set for himself one goal: "To get it to the fifth generation successfully."

It won't be easy.

Dillon said the company's profit per rose has been declining steadily. "It's a free market," he said, "and there's definitely a supply-and-demand effect on that price. So what happens when there's a lot more South American roses on the market. . . . we can only vary that supply by reducing our rose production."

Like most of his colleagues in the industry, Dillon believes that "dumping [by foreign countries] has occurred and that it's been pretty blatant." In fact, he said, "the feeling that many of us have is that the [government] determination that they weren't dumping was somewhat political and not necessarily a truthful, objective decision."

Dillon has good reason to see politics in Washington's handling of the rose import issue. The State Department early on threw its backing to Colombia. And in a $7 trillion U.S. economy, rose growing is comparatively insignificant. Officials in Washington, who tend to be solicitous of multinational corporations, treat the rose growers and their employees with indifference—or worse.

In September 1993, David L. Pruitt, chairman of the board of the California Cut Flower Commission, testified before the trade subcommittee of the House Ways and Means Committee. After expressing the industry's concern over imports, Pruitt had this exchange with Rep. Sam M. Gibbons, the Florida Democrat who headed the trade subcommittee:

GIBBONS: I have some fresh-cut flower growers in my area, too. I know there are some problems. Let me ask you a personal question. Do you all produce this lily which has become so popular in floral arrangements?

PRUITT: Alstroemeria?

GIBBONS: I don't know the name of it. It is kind of a yellowish or whitish lily, throws off a very pungent odor.

PRUITT: Stargazer, possibly.

GIBBONS: Whatever it is, I got to tell you it so excites my allergies that I have to pull those things out of the arrangements and get them out of the house or out of the office real quick. And my plea to you is, can you all do something about that plant? I don't mean not sell it, but can you do whatever you do to it?. . . The lilies are very pretty, but they not only set my allergies off, but they set everybody else's allergies off that comes in. And I thought I would give you a little marketing hint: If there is some scientist out there that can get that odor out of them, it would sure be appreciated.

As Gibbons fretted about his allergies, thousands of workers in U.S. greenhouses worried about their jobs, and whether Congress would come to their aid.

It didn't.

While Colombian imports have idled American rose growers, they have also made Miami International the busiest airport for international cargo in the United States. Every day, especially in peak periods such as Valentine's Day, huge 747s loaded with long-stemmed roses touch down around the clock. Thousands of boxes of flowers are unloaded and transferred to more than 50 massive warehouses the size of small hangars on the western fringe of the airport. There, federal inspectors conduct random tests for pesticides and drugs, usually examining fewer than 2 percent of the imports, and then clear the roses for entry into the United States.

In the warehouse of a large importer, Sunburst Farms, incoming boxes of roses were stacked briefly on tall shelves in refrigerated rooms by one group of workers. Soon another group arrived to transfer the flowers to a truck waiting at a loading dock to take them to Indiana.

Sunburst and other big importers employ many temporary workers during peak periods to supplement full-time employees. Most of the jobs involve warehouse work—one of the principal low-tech, low-paid occupations, you may remember, that will dominate the import-based American economy of the 21st century as foreign-made goods continue to supplant domestic-made goods. In other words, instead of American workers in a variety of occupations making things with their hands, or growing things, they will take the same products produced by foreign workers, move them around warehouses and ship them to markets.

Nevertheless, every time domestic rose growers have sought tariffs or quotas on Colombian flowers, South Florida politicians invariably claim that thousands of jobs would be jeopardized. This was spelled out most recently in a February 16, 1996, letter to President Clinton from five Florida members of Congress, who feared that the U.S. government might impose punitive sanctions against Colombia because of that nation's failure to end the illicit drug trade there. "Such sanctions would cause major harm to Florida," the lawmakers warned, "particularly the economy of South Florida, where more than 7,000 persons are currently employed by the flower importers, who supply over two-thirds of all flowers consumed in the United States."

Without a doubt, the imports have created jobs. But most of them are not in South Florida. They are in rural Colombia, where an estimated 100,000 people cultivate roses and other flowers.

They work for 65 cents an hour. Or less.

When the Rules Don't Apply

Low wages paid to workers abroad are just one reason why small American manufacturers find it impossible to compete in the era of global trade. But there is more at stake than the standard of living of America's workers. Also at risk is the intricately crafted system of regulations that the United States has fashioned this century to protect its citizens.

To be sure, the government has been overzealous in enacting and enforcing some regulations. But the intent of the rules, put in place by a succession of Congresses and presidents, has been to ensure safety and enhance Americans' quality of life in everything from toys to auto emissions, land conservation to pure food and drugs.

A case in point: tomatoes. As recently as five years ago, the tomatoes you bought at the local market during the winter probably came from Florida, a product of that state's multibillion-dollar winter vegetable industry. Today, chances are that they were grown in the Culiacán Valley in remote west-central Mexico. The gradual lowering of duties on all types of products from Mexico has made this possible.

Unlike a shirt, pair of shoes, child's toy or some other manufactured product imported into the United States, which must carry a country-of-origin label, no "Made in Mexico" sign hangs over the produce bin at your supermarket. Federal law requires such a label, but the Department of Agriculture has never enforced it for fresh fruits, vegetables or flowers, maintaining that it would be too difficult to administer. For years, it made little difference. The United States grew virtually all its own winter tomatoes.

No more.

A surge in imported winter tomatoes and other vegetables from Mexico has displaced produce once grown in Florida. Mexican growers have certain cost advantages. The most obvious is wages. Mexican laborers earn about 25 cents an hour for picking the crop, versus $4.50 or more for pickers in Florida.

But consider, too, the federal and state laws that apply to a Florida grower and not to a Mexican producer: prohibitions against employing child labor, against the use of certain pesticides, and against the overapplication of chemicals during the growing season. Chemicals that are banned in the United States can be used freely in Mexico, and there is little regulation of chemical spraying of vegetable crops in that country.

For that reason, you might think that produce from Mexico is carefully inspected at the border before it is sent on to supermarkets in the United States.

You would be wrong.

The tomatoes shipped during the winter months receive only a cursory inspection. Most all Mexican imports come through U.S. Customs at Nogales, Ariz., about 60 miles south of Tucson. Each day from December through March, more than 300 trucks loaded with tomatoes cross the border at Nogales, where U.S. Customs, the U.S. Department of Agriculture, and the U.S. Food and Drug Administration, among other agencies, clear them for entry into this country. Hundreds more trucks arrive each day bearing other types of produce.

The FDA, which checks fruits and vegetables for pesticide residues, has three inspectors at Nogales. They must examine roughly 75 vegetable trucks an hour—less than one minute per truck. This means only a small fraction of the estimated 2.5 billion tomatoes that Mexico ships into the United States during the winter are actually sampled. Most of the trucks are waved through after a quick visual inspection. Federal officials, in fact, admit that only about 1 percent of imported produce is inspected.

Not to worry, says the FDA, because Mexican farmers meet high standards in growing and processing their tomato crop. "You've got state-of-the-art manufacturing down there and in the preparation of the commodities that come up here," said Gil Meza, a spokesman for the FDA in Phoenix. "They put some American factories to shame when you look at the quality control and the processing of the shipments that come into the States."

State of the art?

This rosy view of Mexican food production is not shared by everyone. Listen to this employee of an American food service firm that was forced to discontinue serving certain meals in cafeterias at American-owned plants in Mexico when workers became ill after eating contaminated chicken.

Octavio Galindo, a district manager for ARAMARK, which provides food for maquiladora plants along the U.S.-Mexico border, told the *Twin Plant News*, the magazine of the maquiladora industry: "Probably the worse problem we have had to face is with the raw materials we use for cooking. In Mexico, there is very little, if any, quality control, so for example, in the sacks of beans, we often find dead insects and pebbles. . . . There isn't one company that will guarantee quality, so we have to make do with what we've got."

By contrast, Florida producers who grow winter tomatoes must pay U.S. minimum wage, abide by child labor statutes, and conform to U.S. environmental and pure-food regulations. Growers in Mexico need not.

How can U.S. growers be competitive given those regulatory differences?

They can't.

Which is why Florida tomato growers are fast disappearing, and taking jobs with them. In 1970, the state had an estimated 500 growers in business. Today, there are fewer than 100.

America: Who Stole the Dream?

Free trade rewards those producers who incur the lowest costs. It punishes producers who try to ensure a decent wage for their employees. There's always someone willing to pay his laborers less to grow tomatoes or make shoes. And because of that—because an even cheaper competitor is forever just around the next corner—sometimes in the free-trade game, what goes around comes around.

In the late 1960s, U.S. retailers turned to Brazil to supply them with low-cost shoes, mainly women's, for sale in the huge American market. At the time, Brazil had a large domestic industry but little export capacity.

The plan was in line with Washington's theory that encouraging imports into the United States would give poor countries an opportunity to develop, a crucial tenet of American foreign policy. "Trade, not aid" was a popular slogan then among diplomats and international economists. Rather than simply giving foreign-aid dollars to developing nations, the United States would guarantee a market for a certain percentage of their manufactured goods, spurring job creation and economic growth. To do this required that the United States relax tariffs.

As Rep. Richardson Preyer, a Democrat from North Carolina, told House members on December 20, 1974: "Our fervent hopes for peace and improved living standards in the underdeveloped nations would be doomed if we strangled them with barriers to their exports. It would be particularly foolish to inhibit growth of those whom we have been assisting with our foreign-aid programs over the past 25 years."

So, to U.S. economists and Latin America experts, Brazil's willingness to gear up its shoe-manufacturing industry and become an exporter was something to celebrate. Here was a developing country progressing to the next stage: shipping out not just raw materials, such as coffee and other commodities—the traditional foreign trade of poor nations—but manufactured goods, which would produce domestic jobs and more export income.

Guaranteed a market in the United States, Brazilian shoemakers built plants, ordered machinery and licensed designs from North America. The industry grew up in southern Brazil around the town of Novo Hamburgo, which had been settled by German immigrants in the 19th century. The region was still largely rural but shoe plants rapidly multiplied.

By 1971, only Italy, Japan and Spain were sending more shoes than Brazil to the United States. And, as the *New York Times* put it, Brazil was poised to overtake those rivals "because of the wage and cost advantages enjoyed by the [Brazilian] footwear industry."

What Brazil gained, someone else had to lose. That someone was the American shoemaker. Hundreds of American plants closed. The shoe manufacturers filed a complaint with the U.S. International Trade Commission. They charged that their industry was being victimized by shoes priced artificially low by the Brazilians, whose costs were subsidized by the Brazilian government. After investigating, the commission recommended in 1976 that the U.S. government place a 35 percent tariff on Brazilian shoes.

When the recommendation was sent to President Gerald Ford for action, he declined to impose the duties, saying that such a move "would be contrary to U.S. policy of promoting the development of an open, nondiscriminatory and fair world economic system."

What's more, Ford, in what turned out to be one of many presidential misreadings of the health of an American industry battered by cheap imports, said the U.S. shoe industry had seen its darkest days and that it was well on the road to recovery. In his order refusing to act, Ford said:

> The U.S. footwear industry is benefiting from a substantial increase in production, shipments, and employment as a result of the economic recovery. Additionally, a number of plants have reopened, order backlogs of domestic manufacturers have increased, and profitability has improved.
>
> U.S. employment in the industry, which has been steadily declining over recent years, also shows signs of picking up. The total average monthly employment for the industry was 163,000 workers, compared to 178,000 for the year 1974. For the first two months of 1976, the monthly average is 172,000, the highest since July 1974.
>
> Meanwhile, imports of the nonrubber footwear covered by the [U.S. Trade Commission] recommendation. . . have been leveling off. In February 1976, they were 29,238,000 pairs, down from 32,200,000 in January.

But mostly, the president said that imposing higher tariffs on Brazilian shoes would run counter to America's free-trade policy, the aim of which was "to expand domestic employment and living standards through increased economic efficiency."

Expand domestic employment?

Sixteen years earlier, in 1960, shoe imports averaged 2.2 million pairs a month. By 1980, rather than "leveling off" as predicted by President Ford, imports rose to a monthly average of 30.5 million pairs. That number shot up to 74.8 million in 1990 and to 90 million in 1995.

Since Ford's claim that imports were holding steady, they have climbed from 29.2 million pairs a month to 90 million pairs—an increase of 208 percent. Since 1960, shoe imports have spiraled a whopping 3,991 percent. More significant, in 1960 foreign shoe manufacturers held just 4 percent of the U.S. market. By 1995, they controlled 89 percent. Ford also was wrong about employment in the industry. The number of jobs fell from the 172,000 he reported in 1976 to 146,000 in 1981 and then to 57,900 in 1994.

After Ford refused to act on Brazilian imports, American shoe companies continued to go back to trade authorities, seeking relief. But a new president from a different political party, Jimmy Carter, also declined to help. Thus unimpeded, the Brazilian shoe industry boomed, becoming, year-in and year-out, one of the three largest exporters of shoes to the United States. It soon had more than 3,000 shoe plants, employing upwards of 300,000 people.

And then, just as rapidly as they had grown, Brazil's shoe exports began to decline. There was a new kid on the export block: mainland China. Exploiting the same low-tariff policies that had fostered the Brazilian industry, the Chinese replicated the Brazilian model—only cheaper. By 1993, the Brazilians were quite alarmed at this upstart. An industry trade journal, *Footwear News*, reported on December 6, 1993:

"Despite gains in export dollars, Brazilian footwear exporters expressed growing concern about China's capturing a greater slice of the leather-footwear market, especially in the United States. . . . [For] the first time China has sold more leather-upper shoes to the United States than Brazil."

In its peak years, Brazil shipped $1.8 billion worth of shoes annually to the American market. Today, according to Heitor Klein, executive director of the Brazilian shoe industry association, shipments are $1.2 billion.

The decline in exports has devastated the shoe industry in southern Brazil. Klein says about 200 shoe plants have closed and 55,000 shoe workers have lost their jobs in the last two years. The speed with which China surpassed Brazil and went on to become the chief shoe exporter to the United States was "very dramatic," he said.

Brazil is fast losing a market it only recently captured. And it's not likely to win back that market. Why?

What goes around comes around: Brazilian shoe workers earn too much money to compete with Chinese shoe workers. The pay of the average Brazilian shoe worker is less than a dollar an hour; about $150 a month. That's big bucks compared to the average pay of Chinese shoe workers.

Their earnings: 25 cents an hour, or $50 a month.

CHAPTER • THREE

The Foreign Link

Americans Need Not Apply

Help wanted: Auto mechanic for a service station in Alexandria, Va.; pays $17.57 an hour. Accountant for an investment firm in Wilmington, Del.; pays $40,000 a year. Carpet layer for a rug company in Laurel, Md.; pays $16.40 an hour. Pharmacist for a drugstore in Huntington, W.Va.; pays $55,000. Software engineer for phone company in Murray Hill, N.J.; pays $45,700. Manager of a savings and loan in York, Pa.; pays $25,000.

Don't feel especially qualified for any of those openings? Well, then, how about one of these: Supervisor for a cab company in Philadelphia, Pa.; pays $21,000. Secretary for a church in Washington, D.C.; $13.22 an hour. Cook at a hamburger joint in Gaithersburg, Md.; $10.77 an hour. Management trainee at a hotel in Arlington, Va.; $22,685. Kitchen helper at a country club in Vienna, Va.; $5.36 an hour. Veterinary technician at an animal clinic in New Hope, Pa.; $10 an hour.

Any of those jobs appeal to you? Do you think someone, somewhere in America is capable of handling one of them?

The U.S. government doesn't think so.

It approved applications filed by businesses in 1995 so they could hire foreign workers to fill those and other positions. The businesses claimed—and the government agreed—that no qualified Americans could be found. At a time when countless Americans have lost their jobs due to imports and corporate layoffs, U.S. companies have been recruiting tens of thousands of workers from around the world. All with the blessing of Congress.

As a result, too many workers are chasing too few good-paying jobs. This, in turn, has helped force down wages in many fields, held increases to a minimum in others and contributed to the overall decline in the standard of living for many middle-class families. The recruiting of foreign workers even goes beyond U.S. businesses and corporations. Individuals—largely affluent people— also bring in workers from other countries to perform household and child-care tasks that they say no American is willing to do for the wages offered.

In each case, the businesses or individuals have filed applications with the U.S. Department of Labor stating that they need to hire foreign workers because "there are not sufficient U.S. workers who are able, willing, qualified, and available at the place where the alien is to perform the skilled or unskilled labor." Under what is called the Permanent Labor Certification Program, the Labor Department, in turn, is required—by law—to essentially rubber-stamp the applications if several general requirements are fulfilled.

Once the Labor Department issues a certification, the foreign national can file a petition with the U.S. Immigration and Naturalization Service (INS) for permanent residency, and eventual U.S. citizenship. So far in the 1990s, INS has approved upward of 90 percent of such petitions.

Who are some of these businesses and individuals, and what are the jobs they said only foreign workers could do? Here's a sampling from Labor Department records for the year 1995:

Salon Cristophe in Washington, D.C., whose owner, Cristophe Schatteman, has styled the hair of First Lady Hillary Clinton and President Clinton. You may recall, it was Cristophe who cut Clinton's hair while *Air Force One* sat on the tarmac at Los Angeles International Airport in May 1993, tying up air traffic.

Cristophe needed a hair stylist who would be able to "apply up-do and other French hair styling techniques" and to "study facial features of client and arrange, shape, and trim hair to achieve desired effect, using fingers, combs, scissors, hair-waving solutions, hairpins, and other accessories." The job paid $5.25 an hour, plus 50 percent commission for revenue generated in excess of $360 a week. A survey in 1994 showed that Cristophe charged women $250 and men $150 for his services.

In any event, after Cristophe said no qualified Americans were available—and the Labor Department agreed—the salon received permission in March 1995 to hire a woman who was a French citizen. According to documents filed with the Labor Department, she was in this country on an exchange visa, meaning that she was not entitled to permanent residency or U.S. citizenship. That, to be sure, would change if INS approved her petition.

71

Perot Systems Corp. of Reston, Va., the computer consulting company started in 1988 by Ross Perot, the Reform Party presidential candidate. Perot Systems requested permission to hire a foreign worker as a computer "systems analyst."

The company said that the special requirements for the job included these: "Exp. in C/C++, UNIX, Novel Network, ORACLE case tools, ORACLE FORMS & other tools, Informix database & development tools. . . ." The foreign national the company was seeking to hire just happened to have precisely the same qualifications: "Exp. in C/C++, UNIX, Novel Network, ORACLE case tools, ORACLE FORMS & other tools, Informix database & development tools. . . ."

Perot Systems advised the Labor Department that as a result of recruitment efforts, including a help-wanted ad in the *Washington Times*, four American workers applied for the job, but "we concluded that they are not qualified for the position."

In October 1995, the company received approval to hire a citizen of India who was in the country on an H-1B visa. That's a temporary work visa, meaning the person holding it is not entitled to remain in the United States permanently or to become a citizen. That situation would change under the Permanent Labor Certification Program.

Angela M. Buchanan of Oakton, Va., the sister of erstwhile candidate for the Republican Party presidential nomination, Pat Buchanan. When President Reagan named her U.S. treasurer in 1981, she was the youngest person, at 32, ever to hold that post. She managed her brother's campaign for the GOP presidential nomination in 1996. During the campaign, Pat Buchanan called for a moratorium on legal immigration. While he lost the bid, parts of the party platform reflected his views and those of his sister.

Angela Buchanan requested permission in October 1994 to hire a foreign worker as a "professional tutor for her three children." She explained the need this way: "As a single mom with a busy career which involves considerable traveling, I require professional assistance to see to the educational progress and success of my children. . . . The position I am seeking to fill does not involve everyday care of the boys or housekeeping and is not live-in; this is strictly an educational position. . . . In general I desire approximately six hours of tutoring each school day. Each boy should receive about two hours of concentrated attention from the tutor each day."

The Foreign Link

Buchanan added that the "position requires a professional with strong academic background and experience" and that "I have been unable to find a qualified U.S. worker willing and able to perform these duties."

In December 1995, she received permission to hire a native of Finland at a pay rate of $13.54 an hour, or $28,200 a year, assuming a 40-hour week. Labor Department records show she was in the United States on a B-2 visa, which is issued to temporary visitors who come to this country for pleasure. Indeed, in an affidavit, Buchanan said she met the prospective tutor when the woman was on "a trip to the United States to visit her sister."

Once more, when the Labor Department authorized Buchanan to hire the native of Finland, that qualified her for permanent residency, pending final approval by INS.

American Red Cross of Rockville, Md., headed by Elizabeth Dole, wife of 1996 Republican presidential candidate Robert J. Dole, sought a research assistant to work in its blood research laboratory.

According to the Red Cross's application for alien employment certification, the job required someone who could "perform research in blood coagulation proteins to steady [cq] the molecular basis of hemophilia A . . . perform tests on blood from individuals with hemophilia." Among the requirements: "Must be willing to work with contagious diseases including hepatitis & AIDS. . . ."

Again, no American workers were available. In the agency's application, the Red Cross personnel manager stated: "I have spoken to employees & business associates, placed an advertisement in the newspaper, and posted a job notice, but I have been unable to find a citizen or legally employable alien to fill this position."

The Labor Department authorized the Red Cross in July 1995 to hire a citizen of India who just happened to have precisely the same skills the agency was looking for: "ability to use spectrophometer HPLC, gel electrophoresis, immuno & electroblotting equipment. . . ."

The Indian native, like the foreign national hired by Perot Systems, was in this country on an H-1B visa, meaning he could work here temporarily, but was not permitted to remain in the United States permanently or to become a citizen.

Richard Ben-Veniste, a Washington lawyer who was a member of the Watergate prosecution team that forced President Nixon from office. He also was the Democratic counsel on the Senate

Whitewater Committee that probed President Clinton's involvement with assorted real estate and banking deals in Arkansas.

In November 1995, Ben-Veniste requested permission to hire a foreign national as a houseworker. His application described the job opening this way: "General housework, including laundry and ironing of clothes, dust, vacuum, clean baths and light outdoor cleaning. Perform marketing and cooking, and help with child care and employers' personal and business entertaining." The job paid $9.11 an hour, or $18,950, assuming a 40-hour work week.

Once more, no Americans were available. In a letter to the Labor Department, an attorney representing Ben-Veniste said that no one responded to a help-wanted ad placed in the *Washington Times*. The ad stated: "DOMESTIC/GHW—Child care, cooking, F/T job, good pay. US citizen or green card ONLY."

In December 1995, the Labor Department gave Ben-Veniste approval to hire a woman who was a native of the Philippines. She was in this country on a G-5 visa, according to Labor Department records, meaning that she was here as an employee of a foreign government representative. As such, she was not entitled to permanent residency or citizenship.

Denny's Restaurant in Fairfax, Va. In August 1994, Denny's filed an application with the Labor Department to hire a foreign worker as a manager. The restaurant's human resource manager described the job requirements this way: "Monitor daily operations to ensure that expenses are within budget. Account for cashflow and make bank deposits. Order food supplies and establish food costs. Inventory. Hire and fire personnel. Conduct personnel review, employee work schedules. Responsible for local advertising and business strategy." The job paid $26,600 a year.

Once again, no qualified Americans were available. Denny's said help-wanted ads were run regularly in the *Washington Post* or the *Washington Times*, and "the last advertisement produced three applicants who were not hired due to lack of qualified experience in restaurant management."

The Labor Department authorized Denny's in April 1995 to hire a citizen of Pakistan for the job.

The Permanent Labor Certification Program under which all these foreign workers were hired is but one of several government programs that keep a supply of foreign labor moving into the United States.

The Foreign Link

Consider the numbers for the years 1990 through 1995:

- Nearly 600,000 foreign workers and family members were admitted to fill certain jobs, including 332,646 positions under the Permanent Labor Certification Program. The jobs ranged across the economy, from fast-food cooks to computer systems analysts. All were immigrants entitled to become U.S. citizens.
- Some 1.1 million visas were issued to foreign workers to fill short-term positions, in such fields as computer software engineering. They are aliens—citizens of another country—and by law are allowed to remain in this country only six months, working for foreign companies. Many stayed permanently.
- More than 225,000 visas were granted to foreign workers to fill so-called "specialty occupations." These jobs ranged from restaurant manager to financial analyst, from piano teacher to assistant professor. They were limited to a maximum stay of six years. Again, many stayed permanently.
- Nearly 35,000 visas were issued to foreign registered nurses. This at a time when nurses in the United States are having trouble finding permanent jobs as hospitals trim their staffs under managed care.
- More than one million visas were issued to foreign students. While many completed their education and returned home, others stayed on and went to work here.

The foreign-worker programs are just one small part of the story of the impact of immigration—and the globalization of work—on American jobs. The bigger picture is this: From 1990 to 1995, legal immigrants entered the United States at an annual rate higher than in any decade in American history—in even greater numbers than those that washed over Ellis Island at the turn of the century.

They arrived at a rate of 1.1 million a year. That's nearly one-and-a-half times the record 820,000 immigrants a year set in the first decade of this century. More immigrants arrived in the 16 years from 1980 to 1995—13.1 million—than in the previous half-century, from 1930 to 1979—11.6 million.

Thus far in the 1990s, immigration is running three times greater than in the decade of the 1890s, five times greater than in the good-times decade of the 1950s, and 16 times greater than in the hard-times decade of the 1930s. And that's *legal* immigration—it has nothing to do with the tens of thousands of people who cross the borders illegally every year.

What all these numbers—permanent immigrants and alien workers here under jobs programs—add up to is this: Since 1990, at least six million foreign workers have been thrown into the competition for U.S. jobs. No other developed country in the world has asked its labor force to absorb so large a number of new workers. Or to put it in another context: The number of alien and immigrant workers exceeds the number of out-of-work Americans in 46 of the 50 states.

Thanks to a combination of U.S. government policies—the world's most generous immigration policies and the world's most open-ended trade policies—the people in Washington have created a labor surplus. It has been good for corporations and Wall Street—and bad for working Americans.

In fact, in a little-noted report issued in May 1996 by the Inspector General's Office of the Labor Department, investigators evaluating the Permanent Labor Certification Program concluded: "The program does not currently protect U.S. workers' jobs; instead, it allows aliens to immigrate based on their attachment to a specific job and then shop their services in competition with equally or more qualified U.S. workers without regard to prevailing wage."

This is not to suggest that the United States should close its borders, or that by halting immigration the living standard of middle-class America would improve dramatically over night. It is to suggest that what is lacking in Washington is moderation—an absence of balance, as is the case with most of Washington's economic policies. With that in mind, let's return to some of the businesses and individuals who asked for—and received—permission from the Labor Department to hire foreign workers.

The Monocle Restaurant in Washington, D.C., is a Capitol Hill hangout for lawmakers and lobbyists. It is located in a building owned by Congress. In October 1995, the Labor Department authorized the restaurant to hire two foreign workers as cooks for $8.46 an hour. Assuming a 40-hour week, that's $17,600 a year.

The U.S. Congress Office of Technology received approval to employ a foreign worker as a project director for $47,000.

Baltimore Veterans Affairs of Baltimore, Md., received permission to hire a foreign pathologist for $70,200.

Coopers & Lybrand of Philadelphia, the accounting firm, re-

Employment-Based Programs for Immigrants and Foreign Workers

Total number of immigrants or aliens brought to the U.S. under four jobs programs since 1990, when immigration laws were revised.

H-1B Specialty Occupation (Temporary)

227,459 aliens have been hired under a U.S. foreign-labor program (H-1B) that allows companies to recruit "the best and the brightest in the international labor market" for work in "specialty occupations." Workers may stay up to 6 years.

Permanent Immigrant Workers

589,554 permanent immigrants and their families were admitted to fill certain jobs, including 332,646 jobs for which the government certified "there are not sufficient U.S. workers who are able, willing, qualified and available" where the work is. They gain permanent residency status, qualify for citizenship after 5 years.

Short-Term Workers (Temporary)

1,114,358 visas were issued to foreign workers to fill short-term positions, in such fields as computer-software engineering. They are allowed to remain six months and may work only for foreign companies in the U.S.

Registered Nurses

34,912 visas were issued to foreign registered nurses. Workers may stay up to 6 years.

SOURCE: U.S. State Department

ceived authorization to employ a foreign worker as a systems analyst for $100,000.

Steptoe & Johnson of Washington, D.C., a law firm, received permission to hire a foreign lawyer for $77,000.

The University of Virginia received permission to employ 11 foreign workers as faculty members and professionals, from a botanist to a physiologist, for salaries from $23,500 to $54,000.

Prudential Insurance Co. in Fairfax, Va., received authorization to hire a foreign worker as an insurance sales agent for $33,700.

The Women's Club of Chantilly, Va., received approval to employ a foreign worker as a cosmetologist for $5.56 an hour. Assuming a 40-hour work week, that would be $11,600 a year.

The Maryland Department of Housing and Community Development received authorization to hire a foreign worker as an archaeologist for $21.89 an hour, or $45,500 a year for a 40-hour week.

Logical Concepts in Washington, D.C. received approval to employ a bookkeeper for $24,320.

Keating Building Corp. in Bala Cynwyd, Pa., received authorization to hire a foreign worker as an estimator for $35,000.

Labor World USA in Washington, D.C., received permission to employ a foreign worker as a kitchen helper for $5.36 an hour, or $11,100 a year for a 40-hour week.

The University of Maryland received permission to hire eight foreign workers as faculty members and professionals, from a pathologist to a job analyst, for salaries from $20,378 to $64,500.

First USA Bank in Wilmington, Del., received permission to employ a foreign worker as a market research analyst for $50,000.

The Hard Rock Café in Washington, D.C., received authorization to hire a foreign worker as a cook for $10.77 an hour, or $22,400 a year.

Hershey Foods Corp. in Hershey, Pa., received approval to employ a foreign worker as a corporate lawyer for $120,000.

Oakton Quality Services Co. of Oakton, Va., received authorization to hire a foreign worker as a roofer for $11.10 an hour, or $23,100 a year for a 40-hour week.

The Ramada Hotel in Falls Church, Va., received approval to employ a foreign worker as a bell captain for $7.00 an hour, or $14,600 a year for a 40-hour week.

Ramesh C. Batta Associates of Wilmington, Del., received permission to hire a foreign worker as a civil engineer for $48,500.

The Philadelphia School District received permission to employ a foreign worker as a counselor for $27,300.

The Foreign Link

A number of Washington think tanks and study groups sought and received permission to hire foreign workers. The Center for Strategic & International Studies wanted a public relations representative at $30,000. The National Council on Crime and Delinquency wanted a sociologist at $16 an hour, or $33,300 a year, assuming a 40-hour week. The Center for Women Policy Studies wanted a research assistant for $36,000. The Institute for Public-Private Partnerships wanted a consultant for $55,000. The National Organization for Victim Assistance wanted a training representative for $538.46 per week, or $28,000 annually.

Some businesses in the Labor Department files say the foreign workers who were certified have yet to show up.

That was the case with Dumont Export Corp. of Philadelphia. Dumont is a clothing recycler that collects used clothing, sorts and sells it in this country and to more than two dozen other countries. It is a family business that was started by Harry Usatch a half-century ago and is now run by his son, Jerald. In 1985, the company and the Usatches pleaded guilty in U.S. District Court in Philadelphia to charges involving kickbacks paid to Salvation Army employees for supplying used clothing.

Labor Department records show that from July through November 1995, Dumont received permission to hire 22 foreign workers at $3.92 an hour—or 33 cents below the minimum wage at that time.

When asked about the foreign workers, who were being recruited to sort the incoming used clothing, Jerald Usatch said: "Somebody asked us if we would give jobs to foreign workers who came in. Nothing happens very quickly. This is something that we started several years ago, about four or five years ago. And I haven't seen the first employee."

Q: Who asked—
A: There was a fellow in Washington. And we just have not seen them. We have had various times when we've had great difficulty getting workers. We're basically a minimum-wage, starting type of company.
Q: The Labor Department record showed the wage listed as $3.92. Does that make—
A: Again, I think it's because it was prior to the last minimum wage increase. . . . The last wage increase was '91. Okay, this was prior to that. We're now, like, a quarter an hour above minimum starting and we run

up to about $7 or $8 or $9 because we try to tie it into incentives. . . . We start at $4.50.

Q: Who in Washington was doing this?

A: It was a company asked us if we would hire, you know, if they would give us qualified Korean employees, would we be willing to give them a job. And at the time we were very desperate for employees. In fact today, we're hiring a lot of people from halfway houses. . . . We tried Cambodians. We caught one of them stealing. The whole group quit. We're sort of like a United Nations.

Q: Do you remember the name of the company in Washington?

A: I don't recall.

Q: Was it specifically Koreans?

A: Yeah, I think they were Koreans.

Another company that says it is still awaiting the arrival of its foreign workers is Robzen's Inc., a Scranton, Pa., meatpacking plant. At various times, Robzen's has received U.S. government contracts to provide meat to the Defense Department and to the school lunch program for needy children.

In December 1994, agents of the U.S. Immigration and Naturalization Service (INS) raided the Scranton slaughterhouse and rounded up more than 125 suspected illegal aliens from Mexico, Honduras and El Salvador who were working at the plant. Later that day, many of the workers were put on a plane for Mexico. Some were packed off to a Texas jail. Deportation hearings were scheduled for the rest. Robzen's later pleaded guilty to employing illegal aliens.

Sidney Robzen, the company president, said the process to bring in foreign workers was started before the INS raid and was not connected with it in any way. One of the authors had the following exchange with Robzen:

AUTHOR: Would these people be in the country or would they be coming from—

ROBZEN: It could be either. Some may be in the country already. Some may not be. Some may be in the country not eligible to work yet. And a good number of them may not even be here.

Q: How do you find them?

The Foreign Link

A: Well, we deal with a service that —
Q: Can you tell me who that is?
A: Well, I'd really rather not. We have an independent service that we've engaged to help with that process.

Robzen's had, indeed, started the recruiting process before the INS raid. But the company stepped up its efforts after losing a large part of its workforce.

Robert M. Foley, a Washington lawyer representing the company, wrote to the Labor Department on February 9, 1995: "The reason for the current request [to expedite proceedings] stems from the fact that the INS has recently raided the company, devastating the company's workforce. Nearly two-thirds of the staff were removed.

"Apparently these employees had obtained what appear on their face to be legitimate INS and Social Security documents, but in fact, according to the government, were fraudulent. The company has endeavored to fill the positions vacated by its alien workers, but has been unable to do so. It currently needs over 120 more workers."

Foley went on to explain that Robzen's was "chronically under-staffed" and that "apparently no one wants to enter the meat industry anymore . . . despite the fact that the industry is heavily unionized and well paid."

Well paid? In its application seeking permission to hire foreign workers, Robzen's listed the starting pay at $5.50 an hour. Assuming a 40-hour week, that's $11,440 a year—a poverty-level income for a family of three.

When Sidney Robzen was asked about the company's ability to find workers in the area, he replied: "It's not particularly easy to do that. Oftentimes, people just don't find it very appealing working in a beef slaughtering and boning facility. By and large, a good number of the local labor force just does not like to do it."

As for the pay rate of $5.50 an hour, Robzen said that was starting pay. "We're talking about somebody green off the street, who's never seen a knife or never done anything before," he said.

What could a more experienced worker expect to earn?

"I would rather not discuss that," he said.

In any event, two months after one federal agency (INS) rounded up illegal aliens at the meat-packing plant, another federal agency (the Labor Department) authorized Robzen's to hire 30 aliens to work as meat boners at an hourly pay of $5.50. The certification was issued on February 10, 1995—one day after Robzen's Washington lawyer requested the Labor Department to advance its screening process.

"Manipulated and Abused"

On March 27, 1996, the office of Pennsylvania's Republican governor, Tom Ridge, distributed the following news release about Empire Kosher Poultry Inc. of Mifflintown, Pa.:

> On behalf of Pennsylvania Governor Tom Ridge, Pennsylvania Commerce Secretary Thomas B. Hagen today visited Mifflintown to announce that Juniata County's largest employer, Empire Kosher Poultry, will create 150 new jobs in their state-of-the-art processing plant. Empire Kosher Poultry is the largest kosher poultry facility and largest kosher poultry producer in the world.
>
> "Empire Kosher Poultry's superior dedication, hard work and commitment to provide family-sustaining jobs for Pennsylvanians and economic growth for the community is to be commended," Hagen said. "This expansion in Pennsylvania is a clear indication of Empire Kosher Poultry's faith in the Ridge Administration's new job-friendly climate."

The governor's press release went on to quote David Wiggins, president of Empire Kosher Poultry, as saying: "We are fortunate to draw from Pennsylvania's dedicated workforce. There is no better place to work. Our ability to offer new jobs through continued growth and expansion, means greater opportunity and quality employment for future generations."

What neither Empire Kosher Poultry's president nor the governor's office mentioned was this: Just months earlier, between July and December 1995, the company received approval to employ 23 foreign workers as poultry eviscerators, U.S. Labor Department records show. Their pay, described by the commerce secretary as "family-sustaining," was put at $4.75 an hour, or $9,900 a year if they worked regular 40-hour weeks. That's a poverty-level income for families.

As was the case with Robzen's, the company says the foreign workers have not yet arrived at Empire Kosher Poultry, although their hiring has been authorized by the Labor Department. A company representative said she was unfamiliar with the government certifications. "I know we had talked about doing something with Koreans," she said. "But I don't think we ever did. I bet that's what it is."

In fact, the company had filed an application for alien employment certification in July 1995, one in a series seeking approval to hire Korean workers. The company stated that it was "unable to secure willing U.S. workers."

The application described the jobs to be filled this way: "Receiving, eviscerating, dressing, packing, cut-ups, and deboning of poultry." Starting pay was $4.75 an hour. That could go to $6.40 after six months. Again, assuming a 40-hour week, that would amount to $13,300 a year—a poverty-level income for a family of four.

Misplaced foreign workers are not uncommon. In fact, during the audit of the Permanent Labor Certification Program conducted by the Labor Department's Inspector General's Office, investigators found that "7 percent [of the aliens] never worked for the employer at all." What's more, the Inspector General's Office reported, "our findings indicate that the [program] is being used to satisfy the needs of aliens—the attainment of the green card. . . ."

Some companies insist they have no choice but to look overseas for workers. One of them is RCG Information Technology Inc. of New York, a computer consulting firm that provides programming solutions to *Fortune* 500 companies, large banks and other businesses. The company is a subsidiary of Reliance Group Holdings, which also owns the Reliance Insurance Co. and is controlled by Saul Steinberg, a perennial entry on *Forbes* magazine's list of 400 richest Americans. *Forbes* estimated his worth in 1995 at $380 million.

The Labor Department authorized RCG Information Technology to hire 25 foreign workers as programmer analysts in 1995. A spokesman for the company explained: "There is a tremendous demand [for programmers] and the company recruits aggressively both domestically and then supplements that with overseas recruiting. And, you know, quite a bit's been written about curbing this kind of immigration and one risk of doing that is the business itself will go to foreign countries, which, as some of this becomes more portable, is not inconceivable."

Keep in mind that all these foreign workers came into the United States because the employers stated that no local workers were qualified or available. But was that true? And if it was, how did the Labor Department arrive at that conclusion?

When an employer seeks to hire a foreign worker under this

program, the U.S. Labor Department and the State Employment Security Agency where the job is located are required to test the local labor market to make certain there are no Americans "able, willing, qualified and available" to fill the job. The state employment agencies are supposed to refer qualified applicants to the employer, who also is required to advertise the opening for three consecutive days. If local applicants are rejected, the employer must give the state a job-related reason.

And most *are* rejected. Why? Here's the blunt answer from the Labor Department's Inspector General's report: The program is being "manipulated and abused. For the most part, employers use the program to obtain permanent resident visas for aliens who already work for them, some illegally. Others use the program to obtain the green card for friends or relatives for jobs that may or may not actually exist."

Furthermore, the Inspector General's investigators determined that "the required labor market test is ineffective in ensuring that qualified, willing and available U.S. workers are given a fair opportunity to compete for the jobs for which aliens are hired." Based on their survey, the investigators concluded that 136,400 Americans applied for jobs in three-fourths of the 23,400 cases requiring a labor market test. Of that number, only 104 were hired. That worked out to a hire rate of eight-hundredths of 1 percent.

In the other one-fourth of the cases, the employers received no local applicants from the advertisements, no referrals from the state employment agencies. That's because, as the investigators learned, state employment personnel "are reluctant to waste their own and the applicants' time on referrals for job interviews when they know there is no real job opening." The employer is just going through the motions; the job is reserved for an alien. To discourage American applicants, "employers bury advertisements in the smallest available print, mislabel the jobs being advertised, and fill advertisements with baffling abbreviations making the job requirements unclear," the audit found.

In short, the labor market test is a sham. Of the "immigrants" hired under this program, 99 percent already were in the United States at the time of application and 74 percent already were working for the petitioning employer. The system, the inspector general concluded, "is being used to determine which students or temporary workers will be allowed to remain in, rather than enter, the United States."

Many businesses and organizations that made use of the immigrant worker program in 1995 sought—and received—permission to hire from several to several dozen foreign workers, again, on the basis that "there are not sufficient U.S. workers who are able, willing, qualified, and available at the place where the alien is to perform the skilled or unskilled labor." A sampling:

United States Service Industries of Washington, D.C., a janitorial and building maintenance firm that cleans office and commercial buildings in and around the nation's capital, received approval to employ 21 foreign workers as janitorial cleaners and supervisors. Wages ranged from $5.40 to $6.96 an hour, or $11,200 to $14,500 a year. A U.S. Appeals Court ruled in 1996 that the company had failed to pay some of its workers the required overtime.

Americana Grocery Inc. of Washington, D.C., and its surrounding suburbs, received approval to hire seven foreign workers as meat cutters at wages from $10.46 to $12.00 an hour, or $21,800 to $25,000 a year.

Pittsburgh Business Consultants Inc. of Pittsburgh, Pa., received authorization to employ six foreign workers as software engineers and programmer analysts at salaries from $40,000 to $55,000.

Burger King of Bethesda, Md., received authorization to hire 22 foreign workers as fast-food employees at wages from $5.00 to $5.50 an hour, or $10,400 to $11,400 a year.

Merrifield Garden Center of Merrifield, Va., received approval to employ nine foreign workers as landscape gardeners at wages from $9.22 to $9.50 an hour, or $19,200 to $19,800 a year.

DeLoitte & Touche Consulting Group in Chadds Ford, Pa., received permission to hire four foreign workers as systems analysts for $60,000.

Hartz & Company Inc. of Frederick, Md., received authorization to employ seven foreign workers as tailors and stitchers at wages from $7.10 to $9.73 an hour, or $14,800 to $20,200 a year.

Rite-Aid Pharmacy in Finksburg, Md., and Huntington, W. Va., received permission to hire five foreign workers as pharmacists at salaries from $47,200 to $56,200.

The WEFA Group Inc., an economic consulting firm in Bala Cynwyd, Pa., received approval to employ four foreign workers as economists at salaries from $23,800 to $38,000.

Showell Farms Inc. of Showell, Md., a poultry processor acquired by Perdue Farms in 1995, received authorization to hire 45 poultry dressers for $5.50 to $5.90 an hour, or $11,400 to $12,300 a year.

Vie de France Yamazaki Inc. of Vienna, Va., a Japanese-owned French bakery, received approval to employ 23 foreign workers as counter attendants, bakers and cooks at wages from $4.04 to $10.77 an hour, or $8,400 to $22,400 a year.

Price Waterhouse in Washington, D.C., received authorization to hire two foreign workers as consultants, one for $52,000, one for $100,000.

In addition to all the businesses and organizations that received permission from the Labor Department to hire foreign nationals, hundreds of individuals also sought—and received—similar authorizations to fill a variety of jobs—houseworker, child monitor, butler, tutor, and horse trainer, among others.

Again, this was under the Permanent Labor Certification Program, which, at least in theory, says that a prospective employer must test the labor market for the availability of U.S. workers at the time the foreign worker seeks a visa.

In reality, the foreign nationals are usually in the United States on another type of visa when they seek employment. Such was the case with those aliens who were authorized to go to work for families in the Washington, D.C., area.

Among the families were Brett Esber and Eva Petko Esber of Arlington, Va. He's a lawyer with the Washington firm of Dyer, Ellis & Joseph. She's a lawyer with Williams & Connolly, the high-powered criminal law firm in the nation's capital.

She was a member of the defense team that represented Leona Helmsley, the outspoken, self-styled New York hotel queen who spent 18 months in prison after she was convicted on income tax fraud charges. One of her more memorable observations in better times: "Only little people pay taxes."

In November 1994, the Esbers sought permission to hire a foreign citizen to be a "houseworker." An application for alien employment certification, carrying the signature Eva Petko Esber, described the job to be performed this way: "General housekeeping duties, including vacuuming of carpets, dusting, washing floors, laundering, ironing, general babysitting for two children, including preparation and serving of nutritionally balance [cq] meals."

The application also listed these "other special requirements": "Non-smoking/drinking. Willing to work some weekends. Must have valid driver's license and clean driving record. Must have experience caring for infants."

The Foreign Link

The job paid $8.84 an hour. Assuming a 40-hour work week, that would amount to a yearly salary of $18,400.

The Esber's candidate for the job, a woman who was a Bolivian national, recited her previous work experience as evidence that she qualified for the position: "General housekeeping duties, including vacuuming of carpets, dusting, washing floors, laundering, ironing, and general babysitting for two children."

According to documents filed with the Labor Department, she was in the United States on a B-2 visa. That visa is issued to a temporary visitor for pleasure. The person is not entitled to remain in the United States or become a U.S. citizen.

All that changed in July 1995, when the Labor Department gave permission to the Esbers to hire the alien housekeeper under the Permanent Labor Certification Program. Now the Bolivian woman would qualify for permanent residency and eventual citizenship, if she received final approval from the Immigration and Naturalization Service.

Another Washington professional couple seeking to hire a foreign national were Karen Judd Lewis and Jeffrey Lewis of McLean, Va. She's lawyer with Williams & Jensen, a Washington law firm. He's an aide to John F. Kerry, the Democratic senator from Massachusetts. He formerly was an aide to a pair of Republican senators, the late John Heinz of Pennsylvania and Bob Packwood of Oregon.

In November 1994, the Lewises sought permission to hire a "houseworker, live in." In the application for alien employment certification, carrying the signature of Karen Judd Lewis, the job was described as calling for "light housework including housekeeping, laundry, cooking, ironing and child care."

The job also paid $8.84 an hour, or $18,400 a year, assuming a 40-hour work week. In addition, the Lewises offered free room and board.

The agent that handled the application process for the Lewises was Associated Catholic Charities of Washington. In an earlier letter to that agency explaining their need for a housekeeper, the Lewises wrote: "It is necessary for us to have a live-in employee who can take care of our toddler-aged child and help with various activities including laundry, light housekeeping and cooking. I am a practicing attorney with a D.C. law firm and a very full, five-day per week schedule. My husband, Jeffrey Lewis, is Chief of Staff to an individual who is extremely involved in political and philanthropic activities. While my job does not often require business-related travel, my husband, who is based in D.C., must travel out-of-town approximately three days every week. . . ."

The Lewises' candidate for the job was a woman who was a citizen of the Philippines. Again, according to documents filed with the Labor Department, she was in the United States on a G-5 visa. This visa is issued to persons employed by official representatives of foreign governments. It does not entitle the holder to remain in this country permanently, or to become a U.S. citizen.

Once more, that status changed when the Labor Department, in March 1995, gave the Lewises permission to hire the alien housekeeper under the Permanent Labor Certification Program. Pending final approval by INS, she now qualified for permanent residency and eventual U.S. citizenship.

And lastly, David M. Feitel of Rockville, Md., a member of the Baltimore law firm of Miles & Stockbridge, and staff counsel for the Senate Select Ethics Committee panel that investigated Senator Bob Packwood, sought permission to hire a foreign national as a children's tutor.

In a three-page, single-spaced, typewritten letter explaining the need to hire a woman who was a citizen of China and had been a kindergarten teacher there before coming to the United States, Feitel wrote: "Like many other young American couples nowadays, both my wife and I have professional careers that demand full and uninterrupted devotion. The fact that we are both lawyers makes it more uncompromising in terms of time and attention allowed to family matters, particularly child education.

"My wife is a corporate lawyer employed at Patton Boggs L.L.P. Her work schedule is presently about 40 hours a week, which is considered 'part-time.' She was granted this status on a temporary basis after the birth of our first child. . . .When she is required to return to full time status, her time commitment will be approximately an average of 55 to 60 hours per week. . . .

"My job as a government attorney is no less demanding. I work as a Staff Counsel to the United States Senate Ethics Committee. . . . My normal working week easily runs from 55 to 60 hours. . . ."

Feitel went on to say that the couple had tried to hire a "'loving nanny' to solve the problem," but the applicants seeking that job "lacked minimum professional skills in child education. . . . We did not hire any of them. This is because we do not want to entrust our daughter's early education to a house keeper or babysitter.

The Foreign Link

"We decided that what we want is an early childhood educator. . . . We understand that this decision means that we have to look for somebody with professional skills and we have to pay more for the service. We decided to make a long-term commitment and offer $8.15 per hour for the job."

As it turned out, the $8.15-an-hour offer fell below the government guidelines for such work, and was increased to $9.11. That amounted to $18,950, assuming a 40-hour week.

In his letter, Feitel said they had selected the Chinese national for the job because she "had been working as a kindergarten teacher since 1988 in China before she came to this country about two years ago."

Labor Department records fail to show the type of visa the Chinese woman held. In any event, Feitel received permission from the Labor Department in August 1995 to hire her as a children's tutor under the Permanent Labor Certification Program. She then qualified for permanent residency and eventual U.S. citizenship.

All the individuals who hired foreign workers either failed to respond to requests for interviews or declined to talk.

Karen Judd Lewis told one of the authors: "You know what, I don't have anything to say to you."

And Ben-Veniste, the former Watergate prosecutor, said: "Why would you want to talk to me about that? . . . I regard my public life as separate from my private life since I am an individual not in government and not in the cross-hairs of this tabloid mentality. So my personal life is separate, and if this had something to do with my involvement in public life, I would talk to you about it."

While many job openings seemingly could be filled by any number of American workers, in some cases only the alien worker already in line for the opening can meet the qualifications fixed by the employer. Such was the case at DuBois Business College in DuBois, Pa., a community of 8,900 people in western Pennsylvania, about 105 miles northeast of Pittsburgh. The college, which has an enrollment of 250 students, received permission in June 1995 to hire a foreign worker as an educational program director. Francis Kenawell, president of the two-year business college, explained why only the alien—and not any U.S. citizens—qualified for the job.

A Chinese student, Xuiwen Wang, who graduated from Pennsylvania State University with a doctorate in education, had asked Kenawell if the business college would be interested in establishing a branch in China. Kenawell liked the idea. With Xuiwen's assistance, he opened a branch campus in Canton, China. At the same time, he began to recruit Chinese students to come to the United States to attend DuBois Business College.

He offered the job as education director to Xuiwen. But to meet the Labor Department requirements, he also advertised the position. Although he received a number of applications, Kenawell said, "no one could do both parts of the job. You know, going over there [to China] to recruit you need to have some pretty good connections. And also, keeping the branch over there rolling, the branch was basically set up because of [Xuiwen's] connections. So it wasn't the kind of job that I could have filled by anybody else."

When the Labor Department certified that no qualified Americans were available, Xuiwen got the job, thereby allowing him to establish permanent residency in the United States. "He still has not received his completed green card," Kenawell said. "He's received a notification saying that it's coming now, he's been approved, everything's okay."

Kenawell said that Xuiwen divides his time between DuBois and China. "He travels all over China for us. The recruiting part takes him—and it's not just China—it started out to be just China because that's what he was most familiar with. But now, it's been Taiwan, Vietnam."

How many students have come to the DuBois campus from Asia? "Since this whole thing has started up," Kenawell said, "I've had maybe 30 or 32 students come through our program. I don't ever have more than about 10 at a time. . . . We're a small school and I didn't really want to change the face of our school by having it become 20 or 30 or 40 percent Asian."

Kenawell said that as part of the advertising process, he listed the job's pay at $36,000. But the figure, in Kenawell's words, was "not real accurate" because there was no way to take into account other sources of income related to the position. As he explained, Xuiwen receives not only his $36,000 salary from DuBois Business College, but "he's being compensated for by the branch [in China] and by other entities over there."

Since 1990, nearly more than 330,000 foreign workers have come to the United States under the Permanent Labor Certification Program. All were guaranteed U.S. citizenship.

A quarter-million more workers were brought into the country under yet another program called H-1B, which allows businesses to hire foreign workers for up to six years. At the end of that period, the workers—at least in theory and in law—are required to return to their home countries. Many stay.

Why did the U.S. government establish this program? Because big business convinced Congress it was needed to compete in the global economy. U.S. corporations lobbied hard for it when Congress revised the immigration laws in 1990. And not without reason.

Foreign workers often are paid less than U.S. workers in the same positions. They are willing—sometimes forced—to work longer hours without overtime pay. Sometimes there are no fringe benefits. They can be dismissed when a specific project is completed, so companies need not be burdened by full-time employees. Sometimes foreign workers are treated as independent contractors, so companies don't pay federal income taxes or Social Security taxes. And sometimes the workers themselves pay no U.S. income tax on their earnings in this country.

How is it possible for a full-time foreign worker in the United States to escape payment of federal income taxes that working U.S. citizens must pay—indeed have withheld from their paychecks?

Easy.

The salaries of the foreign workers are deposited in bank accounts in their home countries. They receive allowances to live on while in the United States. Rent for apartments is paid directly, as are insurance costs. As a result, some foreign workers pay no U.S. income tax or state and local taxes on their earnings here.

The tax question was posed during an unrelated legal proceeding to one Indian computer specialist who worked both for American International Group and Firemen's Fund Insurance.

LAWYER: Do you pay taxes here in the United States?
INDIAN COMPUTER WORKER: No.
LAWYER: Only in India?
INDIAN COMPUTER WORKER: Yes.

Under the H-1B program, employers are not required to show that there is a shortage of American workers. They merely fill out a form describing the job, the pay rate and how long the alien will be employed. The only supposed protection for Americans is that employers must agree to pay the prevailing wage. It's a promise often ignored, the inspector general's audit found.

By law, the Labor Department is allowed to review the applications only "for completeness and obvious inaccuracies." Congress set up the program in such a way that the Labor Department has no say in whether a particular job opening meets the definition of a "specialty occupation." That task falls to the Immigration and Naturalization Service (INS).

So what are some of the "specialty occupations" that INS has authorized foreign workers to fill—positions defined as requiring "theoretical and practical application of a body of highly specialized knowledge"? Well, Pizza Hut in Marlboro, Mass., wanted a manager for $30,000. Page One Italian Ristorante in New York needed a food service worker at $29,120. Office Depot in Chicago wanted an assistant manager for $27,500. Denny's restaurant in Danvers, Mass., wanted a manager for $25,000. Circle K Corp. in Phoenix wanted an assistant marketing director for $24,000. Intercontinental Hotel in New York sought a marketing representative for $23,000. The Ritz-Carlton Hotel in Boston wanted an assistant manager for $23,000. And Howard University in Washington, D.C., sought a swimming coach for $10,000.

As the Inspector General's Office observed, with some understatement: "Not all types of jobs being filled by H-1B aliens necessarily represent jobs that would enhance U.S. employers' abilities to compete in a global economy."

But many of the H-1B jobs are indeed in technical fields. Throw a dart at the *Fortune* 500 and you'll most likely hit a company that has filed requests with the Labor Department to hire foreign workers. Among the recruiting companies: Chrysler, Cigna, First National Bank of Chicago, Ford, General Electric, General Mills, Georgia-Pacific Corp., Hewlett-Packard Co., IBM, Intel, J.C. Penney Co., Metropolitan Life Insurance Co., Microsoft, Motorola, Pacific Bell, Procter & Gamble, and Unisys Corp.

Some companies that received permission to employ foreign labor have even laid off American workers. AT&T received approval in 1995 to hire a foreign electrical engineer to work in Murray Hill, N.J., for $50,000 a year; a computer systems engineer in North Andover, Mass., at $40,000; and a computer scientist in East Brunswick, N.J., at $65,000. In January 1996, AT&T announced it would cut 40,000 jobs (13 percent of its workforce), most through layoffs, as part of its plan to break into three separate companies.

Chase Manhattan Bank got permission to hire foreign workers to fill openings in New York for a derivatives analyst at $40,000, a financial analyst at $36,000, and a Latin American financial officer at $60,000. Following its merger with Chemical Bank, the banks said that the jobs of 12,000 workers would be eliminated.

The demand for workers under H-1B has become so great that employment agents have set up job shops supplying foreign labor to U.S. companies. The agents secure visas and arrange jobs for thousands from abroad each year.

One such company is Tata Consultancy Services, a Bombay, India, company with satellite offices in a number of U.S. cities, including Detroit, Dallas, Houston, Cincinnati and Silver Spring, Md. Tata, which, as you might expect, recruits computer workers in India, received government approval to bring in software specialists, largely design engineers, to fill jobs in Poughkeepsie, Schenectady and Hawthorne, N.Y.; in New York City; and in Neptune, Roseland, Murray Hill, Cranbury and Jersey City, N.J.; among other locations. Most of the jobs paid $28,500.

Mastech Corp. in Pittsburgh, another employment firm specializing in computer engineers and programmers from India, received permission to fill at least 750 jobs in about two dozen U.S. cities with foreign nationals, according to a sampling by the authors. The reported salaries ranged from $30,000 to $45,000.

Mastech, which advertises that "its base of over 300 clients includes the White House," also uses the Permanent Labor Certification Program to recruit foreign workers. In 1995, the company received Labor Department approval to bring into the United States more than 50 software engineers, programmer analysts and systems analysts because there were no U.S. workers "able, willing, qualified and available at the place where the alien is to perform the skilled or unskilled labor." Mastech said the salaries ranged from $38,000 to $51,100.

The country that supplies the most people for H-1B visa jobs: India. During 1994 and 1995, a total of 16,948 H-1B visas—or 16 percent of the 105,925 such visas issued—went to Indian citizens, primarily in the computer field. Runner-up: the United Kingdom, with 13,696 visas. Japan was third, with 7,317.

Passage to India

Not only are U.S. companies bringing in foreign workers; they're eliminating the jobs of Americans and shipping their tasks overseas.

In the global economy, job-shifting can be done with a computer keystroke—as Patricia Yancey discovered. Yancey, a native of Cincinnati, earned a master's degree in information science and worked briefly for a library in Wyoming before joining a promising company in Denver called Information Handling Services (IHS).

Founded in 1959, IHS became the world's largest provider of technical and engineering databases. The company converts reams of court records and printed materials on engineering, government procurement, and U.S. and international technical standards into sophisticated electronic databases for access by corporate and government clients. A privately held company, IHS serves diverse industries—pharmaceuticals, chemicals, financial services, transportation, communications, human resources and engineering. It had 1995 sales of $257 million.

Yancey worked on IHS indexing projects, from state government documents to court briefs, for nearly 17 years. She was promoted to senior director of the Indexing Department, overseeing a staff of 70. In time, the salaries of Yancey and her senior indexers rose to between $40,000 and $50,000 a year.

Then, on May 12, 1994, Yancey was called into a meeting with IHS's vice president for manufacturing and a human resources official. "I walked into an office and I was told I was being laid off," she recalled. "I didn't have any idea. . . . Basically, my manager told me, 'As you know, we have been looking for ways to reduce costs in your area. And this is the way we have chosen to do that.' That was it." Yancey, two senior indexers and seven others in the 70-member department lost their jobs that day.

IHS had chosen to cut costs by shedding some of its higher-paid U.S. employees—mostly women—and transferring a portion of their duties to India. Like many companies in the United States, IHS over the years had sent some data to low-wage countries for keypunching. "But they had never done anything in the area of the kind of work we were doing, the intellectual processes," Yancey said.

The reason her department was targeted, she believes, was that "the people we had were a little more expensive than other people in the manufacturing process. Many had master's degrees. That wasn't a requirement, but it just helped in understanding some of the literature we were indexing."

Months before the employees were dismissed, IHS had brought in a consultant to study their department and recommend ways that costs could be cut. The consultant was from Vetri Systems Inc. Vetri is one of those companies that supplies the

The Foreign Link

U.S. market with workers or services from India. It has an office staff in Troy, Mich., a suburb of Detroit, but the bulk of the company's 600-person staff is in Madras, India, where Vetri provides document and data-conversion services for clients in the United States, Asia and Europe.

Vetri, a private company, outlined its business philosophy on its World Wide Web site on the Internet, where it tries to interest potential customers: "Our mission is to build partnerships with our clients by creatively applying technology, with a low-cost global workforce, to improve their competitive positions in their marketplaces. By applying the latest developments in technology and offering outstanding outsourcing services, Vetri has consistently increased our clients' profitability." Calling itself one of the industry's "largest globally based conversion businesses," Vetri said: "Scanned document images are routed to Vetri's offshore conversion facilities in India, via a live satellite line."

Yancey said that in January 1994, a Vetri representative had come to Denver to spend a month with her indexing group, "learning the processes and seeing if they could come up with anything to streamline the operation." She remembered being uneasy about the visit. "I knew they had this facility in India and I could see what their recommendation might be," she recalled. "Just that whole idea of American workers and shipping jobs overseas, I was really uncomfortable with the idea of doing that."

Little did she know it would be *her* job. Vetri ultimately recommended cutting back the Indexing Department staff and farming out some of the work to its subsidiary in India, which IHS did. An IHS spokesman, Miles Baldwin, senior director of corporate development, explained: "The reason it was downsized was that . . .we had essentially completed the development of a major engineering thesaurus, and we were reducing because the ongoing maintenance of that was going to be a lot less than the cost of building the original database."

Saying it was a "relatively small number of people" who lost their jobs, Baldwin said part of the indexing was "outsourced to India." When asked how that had fared, he said: "I think it has been very successful."

A Vetri official, Bill Cox, painted a different picture. Cox, a senior vice president who conducted the study at IHS and recommended the layoffs, said that after work was sent to India, the remaining Indexing Department employees complained about the quality.

"It was sort of a pilot to see if somebody else could do [the work]," Cox said. "And the people who are there basically . . . contrived together and made it so anything which came in from India was inappropriate . . . Basically what happened was, I cleaned house and there were certainly sore feelings around all that."

But India is still very much in IHS's future. The company has established its own subsidiary in New Delhi to convert data for a new division dealing with U.S. federal and state regulatory laws. "We looked at the options," said Baldwin, the IHS spokesman. "We had never actually done much in the way of full-text databases in-house, and outsourcing seemed to be rather expensive. So we took a look at the option of building a staff up in India. Which is what we ended up doing, and it's proven to be a lot more efficient and a lot cheaper than the alternatives."

As for Patricia Yancey, she—like increasing numbers of people laid off by large corporations—went into business for herself. "I've been doing a lot of back-of-the-book indexing and some of the larger projects, like database management," she said. "Some thesaurus development. A little bit of consulting."

But it's been hard. Starting your own business means being subject to ups and downs—work, followed by fallow periods, followed by bursts of work. "It's a real adjustment doing this," she said, "after you've had a regular paycheck and your insurance taken care of."

For many companies, the engine that is driving this relentless push to hold down costs is a Wall Street clamoring for ever-greater returns. In the case of IHS, the pressure is coming from a different source.

The company that laid off Patricia Yancey and the others is owned by one of the world's richest men, Baron Hans Heinrich Thyssen-Bornemisza. Heini, as his friends call him, is worth an estimated $1.7 billion, according to *Forbes* magazine. The baron presides over a business empire of a type that is becoming commonplace—one with operations in many countries but which owes allegiance to none. And unlike companies such as General Electric and Exxon, which have to answer to thousands of stockholders, the baron's company essentially answers to one man: him.

The corporation is TBG Inc.—the Thyssen-Bornemisza Group. It has operations in glass, plastics, auto parts, shipping, trading, precision metalworks, agricultural machines and information systems. Information Handling Services, Yancey's former employer, is wholly owned by TBG.

The Foreign Link

As befits someone with global reach, the baron is a true citizen of the world. He was born in the Netherlands, raised in Switzerland, owes his noble title to Hungary, and is officially, for tax purposes, a resident of Monaco. The baron prides himself on being a tough businessman and is fiercely competitive. Over the years, he has collected companies, wives (he is now married to number five, a Spanish beauty queen) and some of the world's finest art.

His deal-making abilities were exhibited some years ago in an arrangement that still has the art world talking. In what caused museum curators around the globe to cry foul, the baron leased—rather than loaned, as is customary—his art collection to Spain for nine years before deciding where it would be permanently housed. "Collectors don't rent out their art—it's unheard of," said John Caldwell of the San Francisco Museum of Art. "It exposes every institution to the risk of having to pay for a loan of art." And yet, such is the baron's business craftiness that he was able to convince the Spanish government to spend $50 million to house the collection.

In going offshore, the baron's company, IHS, was merely doing what scores of companies in the United States have been doing to reduce costs and improve profits. Many software-development tasks that once would have been done in this country are now transferred to India, where salaries are a fraction of what professionals in the United States earn.

India ranks high among labor suppliers for several reasons. The world's second most populous country, India is also the world's second largest English-speaking nation, behind the United States. And it is one of the world's poorest, with per capita income of about $350. But the poverty numbers disguise the fact that India has a growing class of well-educated professionals.

The nation has aggressively promoted technical training and has more than 1,600 engineering colleges, technical institutes and polytechnic schools that train more than 55,000 people a year, many of whom work for the burgeoning Indian software industry. "Just as the Gulf has its natural resources in crude oil, and South Africa its diamonds, India's natural resource lies in its abundant technically skilled manpower," says an Indian report on the country's software industry. "And this natural resource easily transforms India into a software superpower."

Indeed it has. In 1985, when the information age was beginning to take off in the United States, India exported a negligible amount of computer software, less than $10 million a year. By

1995, India's software exports had soared to $485 million—58 percent of which went to the United States. More significantly, India's software industry is growing at an annual rate of more than 45 percent—or double the growth rate in the United States.

That dramatic increase is directly attributable to a decision made by the Indian government in 1986, when it identified "information technology" as a high-priority industry with tremendous growth potential. To encourage its development, the government enacted a broad program of incentives to foster training, foreign investment and industrial development to "enable the software industries to commence their operation with a minimum gestation period," as an Indian government report put it.

In 1990, India went a step further, establishing what were called software technology parks. The Department of Electronics of India has since created software parks in seven Indian cities. Much like traditional industrial parks, they are geared to attract companies to produce software for export. The Indian government provides office space, electrical power, satellite hookups to the West, streamlined procedures for importing and exporting, and tax exemptions for software companies.

The software technology parks are much like the export zones found in poor countries, such as Honduras or the Dominican Republic—except for one big difference: The jobs created in those Latin American nations replace labor-intensive, low-wage U.S. jobs in industries such as apparel and shoes. The high-tech jobs created in India draw work away from computer programmers, software engineers and information specialists in the United States—all good-paying jobs.

India's technology know-how and its technology parks have attracted many of America's largest multinational corporations, which have set up operations in India to take advantage of its vast pool of low-cost skilled labor. From the standpoint of an American employer, why pay a computer specialist $50,000 to $70,000 when you can hire someone in India with a master's degree for $5,000 or $6,000?

Most major U.S. computer- or software-related companies now have operations in India—under their own name, through an Indian partner or by contract with an Indian company. Hewlett-Packard, Digital Equipment, Motorola, Novell, Texas Instruments, Oracle, IBM, Zenith, Microsoft and Apple, to name a few, have a large presence there. The southern Indian city of Bangalore has become known as the Silicon Valley of India for its heavy concentration of information-technology companies.

Using high-speed satellite links, programmers in India can be in constant communication with a client in the United States. Notes the annual review of the National Association of Software and Service Companies in New Delhi: "Even if the client is situated 10,000 miles away from the software company in India, the client is still able to monitor the software development on a minute-by-minute basis, ensure quality checks, communicate with the programmers as if they were just next door and get efficient software developed."

That's what the General Electric Company did. GE decided to begin using Indian programmers following a trip to that country in 1989 by Jack Welch, the company's chief executive officer. That's the same Jack Welch, you may recall, who has terminated GE employees by the tens of thousands on his way to becoming one of corporate America's most revered cost cutters and highest paid bosses. As the decision was explained in a report to GE employees: "The outsourcing of information systems work is not an uncommon practice at GE. . . . The cost of living in India, about one-sixth that of the United States, provides capability for extremely cost-effective solutions."

The report continued: "To evaluate the feasibility of working with Indian firms, pilot activities were conducted during 1990 at several GE businesses. Approximately 50 person-years of work was outsourced to five firms in order to assess their ability. . . . By year end, there were more than 37 contractors at eight GE businesses."

The report noted that about 30 percent of the work was completed on-site, and "the project is then moved to India. . . . The cost savings were impressive. Even with the mix of on-site and offshore labor, project savings ranged from 50–66 percent. The average development cost per work year of effort was $41,000 (over 60 percent less than typical GE costs)." Translation: Indians work for considerably less money than Americans.

As for managing a computer project in both the United States and India, it "was not a major issue," the GE report said. "In most cases, work was monitored through weekly project reports faxed to the United States. All firms have individuals located in the United States to facilitate handling of questions or problems."

GE is but one U.S. company. Multiply that experience by the dozens and you begin to understand why exports of software and information services from India to the United States are booming. They are expected to easily top $1 billion by the turn of the century.

How a Scarcity Became a Glut

While highly skilled workers like Patricia Yancey worry about computer jobs going offshore, other Americans must compete with millions of immigrants here.

The record volume of immigrants coming to America is traceable to the Immigration Act of 1990. The first major rewrite of immigration law in 25 years, the 1990 act greatly increased the number who could enter the country each year and made it much easier for companies to bring in temporary foreign workers.

Even before those changes, the United States was more open to immigrants than any other nation. For much of American history, immigration has been a controversial issue, as the nation has tried to balance the interests of domestic labor with the desires of foreigners to come here. But never before were the doors opened as wide as they were under the 1990 law. The peak year for immigration in all of U.S. history was 1991, when 1,827,167 immigrants arrived.

Just as important was a change in the type of immigrant who would be admitted. The 1990 law quadrupled the number of skilled workers allowed, from 27,000 to 110,000 a year. Since 1990, American companies have brought in aliens under work visas by the tens of thousands, many of them well-educated computer scientists and programmers.

What was the rationale for increasing the number of work visas? The answer is found in a curious place—the National Science Foundation. A series of internal papers within the agency in the late 1980s put forth the theory that the United States, by the early 21st century, would face an acute shortage of scientists and engineers.

In a paper titled "Future Scarcities of Scientists and Engineers: Problems and Solutions," requested by then–NSF director Erich Bloch, the foundation's Division of Policy Research and Analysis predicted a "shortfall" of scientists and engineers that would grow to 675,000 by early in the next century. Bloch used the coming-scarcity theme over and over in speeches and in testimony before Congress to try to obtain more funding for the science foundation.

While appearing before then-senator Albert Gore Jr.'s Senate

Immigration Running at an All-Time High

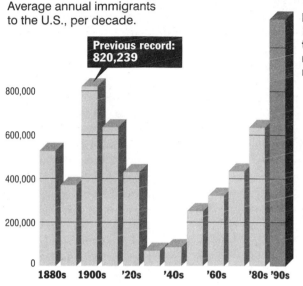

Average annual immigrants to the U.S., per decade.

Previous record: 820,239

From 1990 to 1995, immigration averaged more than 1.1 million a year.

800,000

600,000

400,000

200,000

0

1880s 1900s '20s '40s '60s '80s '90s

SOURCE: U.S. Immigration and Naturalization Service

subcommittee on science, technology and space on May 8, 1990, Bloch was asked about the accuracy of the numbers forecasting a shortage: "If you were a betting man," Gore asked Bloch, "what kind of odds would you give that there will, in fact, be—without changes in current policy—a serious shortage of well-qualified scientists and engineers by the year 2000?"

> BLOCH: Two to one.
> GORE: Two to one. Did you win on the Derby last Saturday?
> BLOCH: No, I do not bet on horses; I only bet on people.

In 1989, when Congress held hearings on revising immigration law, a stream of corporate witnesses paraded before House and Senate committees calling for changes to allow corporations to bring in more foreign workers.

Said Frank D. Kittredge, speaking for the Business Immigration Coalition, a group of *Fortune* 500 companies, immigration lawyers and foreign trade interests: "We must be able to have the right person with the necessary international capability and experience in the right place at the right time. Otherwise, we face a serious lack of competitiveness."

Said the American Immigration Lawyers Association, representing large corporations: "The present low number of available visas for employer-sponsored immigrants translates into harmful delays for U.S. business and industry, causing delays in projects, delays in production, and decreased economic competitiveness."

Said Phyllis Eisen, director of risk management for the National Association of Manufacturers: "Increasingly, America faces new challenges from foreign economic powers. There is a growing pressure on U.S. industries to compete efficiently and effectively in the international marketplace. One of the tools necessary to do so are our immigration laws that provide for the transfer of international personnel and the entry of employer-sponsored immigrants. Unfortunately, these laws and procedures are outdated and do not reflect the needs of U.S.-based corporations that operate in a global marketplace."

President George Bush's economic report to Congress in 1990 sounded the same alarm: "As the U.S. economy enters the 1990s, concerns are growing about the effects of possible labor shortages on production and wages. . . . With projections of a rising demand for skilled workers in coming years, the nation can achieve even greater benefits from immigration. . . with policies designed to increase the number of skilled immigrants. Immigrants with more education or training will likely make the greatest contributions to the U.S. economy. . . ."

Newspapers, magazines and television picked up on the story, repeating as gospel the notion that the United States was on the verge of an acute shortage of scientists and engineers: *Science* magazine, on June 30, 1989, warned about the shortfall in an article titled "Wanted: 675,000 Future Scientists and Engineers." A *Wall Street Journal* story on September 17, 1990, was headlined, "Shortage of Scientists Approaches a Crisis as More Students Drop Out of the Field."

Fueled by this ongoing drumbeat about the impending shortage, Congress enacted the Immigration Act of 1990. Lawmakers cited the looming skill shortage as a reason for approving the bill:

"The bill allows 75,000 principals to enter the United States for employment in order to remedy critical labor shortages in specific fields," said Rep. Jack Brooks (D., Tex.).

"The Department of Labor projects 6.7 million new professional and managerial jobs will be created in the 1990s across the country. Unfortunately, the education and skills of the U.S. labor force will be unable to match labor market needs. This legislation's employment-based immigration provisions will supplement the threatening labor supply shortage," said Rep. Ted Weiss (D., N.Y.).

A real labor crisis, right? Wrong.

The National Science Foundation prediction was flatly erroneous.

So, too, were the speeches on the floors of the U.S. Senate and House of Representatives. And the testimony before congressional committees, the speeches by representatives of professional organizations, the newspaper and magazine articles, the radio and television reports.

The much-touted skills shortage never materialized. Indeed, the opposite occurred. Between 1990 and 1993, according to the Bureau of Labor Statistics, 146,000 engineering jobs disappeared, as employment fell from 1.862 million to 1.716 million. Two new engineers were graduated from American universities for every job that opened up. And the unemployment rate for engineers doubled, rising from 2.1 percent to 4.1 percent. Yet during this period, the United States admitted nearly 190,000 engineers as immigrants or temporary workers.

While engineering employment has recovered somewhat since 1993, consider this: From 1990 to 1995, the total number of engineers employed in the United States increased by 72,000. During those same years, 388,000 students were graduated from American colleges and universities with bachelor's degrees in engineering. A total of 178,000 received master's degrees in engineering. A total of 36,000 received doctorates. And 237,200 foreign engineers came into this country to work "temporarily."

Not only was the "shortfall" prediction off base, but the methodology by which the National Science Foundation arrived at the numbers has since been discredited by other scientists, who said it was based on faulty assumptions and weak data. By then, of course, the damage had been done. Foreign engineers and computer programmers were streaming into the United States, courtesy of the new immigration law designed to accommodate multinational corporations.

While the law proved bad for ordinary U.S. workers, it was quite good for the employment-placement firms that brought foreign workers here. Just how good can be found buried in court records in Detroit, where a director of one such company, Tata

Consultancy Services, a division of Tata Sons Ltd. of Bombay, testified about the profits of his business.

In April 1991, F.C. Kohli, a director of Tata, testified in a legal proceeding that his company employed 2,700 people in India, the United States and other countries, and had more than 500 clients, including many U.S. multinational corporations. Indeed, one of its affiliates was Tata Unisys in Blue Bell, Pa.

But the profits from the company's computer-related projects came largely from outside India, and especially from the United States. Kohli explained:

Two-thirds of Tata employees work in India, but generate only one-third of the company's revenue. The "one-third who work abroad [generate] two-thirds. So the profits are mainly coming from the jobs abroad. Indian jobs serve as a training ground for people."

Aliens who come in on special work visas are allowed into the United States only on the condition that they leave after a specified time—six years at most. But it's always possible for "temporary" workers to get around such restrictions. American companies that want such workers, and agents that supply them, use a variety of subcontracting arrangements that allow foreign nationals on temporary work visas to remain permanently.

Anyone who tries to follow this paper trail can end up sounding like a character in an Abbott and Costello routine. Listen to this inadvertently comic exchange between a lawyer in Tallahassee, Fla., and a computer specialist from India brought into the country on a temporary work visa by Syntel Inc., a placement firm. The worker was questioned during a legal proceeding in March 1991.

ATTORNEY: You are working here in Tallahassee now?
WORKER: Yes.
Q.: On a project?
A.: Yes.
Q.: And what project is that?
A.: It's a [welfare] project for the state of Florida.
Q.: Okay. Is it in any way affiliated with Deloitte & Touche?
A.: It is.
Q.: How?
A.: The state of Florida subcontracted the project to EDS

and EDS subcontracted a part of the project to Deloitte Touche.

Q.: EDS—Electronic Data Systems from Dallas?

A.: Yes. And then Deloitte & Touche subcontracted a
part of the project to Syntel, and we're part of it.

Translation: The state of Florida subcontracted a welfare computer project to Electronic Data Systems, which subcontracted a
part of the project to Deloitte Touche, which subcontracted a part of
its part to Syntel, the firm that brings in computer engineers from
India. But all that's the easy part. In fact, the worker began her corporate sojourn through yet another company. Listen some more:

Q.: How long have you been working on [the Florida
project]?

A.: I've been working on it for one-and-a-half years now.

Q.: One-and-a-half years? But you've been working for
Syntel five-and-a-half months?

A.: I've been employed by Syntel for five-and-a-half
months.

Q.: Who were you employed with before?

A.: A company called Mascon.

Q.: And anybody before Mascon?

A.: TCS.

Q.: So you've been with Syntel for five-and-a-half
months working on the Deloitte project?

A.: Uh-huh.

Q.: Prior to that, for approximately a year, a little bit
more than a year, you were working for Mascon on
this same project?

A.: Through Syntel.

Q.: Through Syntel? Tell me about that. How did, how
did you work through Syntel via Mascon and work
for Deloitte?

A.: Like, TCS works for Tata Inc.

Q.: Well, explain the whole thing. Imagine I don't know
anything. Tell me about it.

A.: Like, for example, if TCS is a company in India and
they can't really send people here to work. So we
have to send the people to work for a company
which is based in the United States, which is Tata
Inc. So, like, when I first came through TCS, I be-

longed to Tata Inc.; as long as I was in the United
States, though, my employment was TCS.

As the questioning wore on, the puzzled lawyer finally asked
her why she had switched from Mascon to Syntel after about a
year. She replied: "Because I felt it would be nice to be employed
in the United States."

Q.: Why?
A.: Why? Because I like the life here and I would like to
live here for some time.
Q.: But you were living here in Tallahassee?
A.: That's not a permanent kind of agreement.
Q.: So Syntel is permanent?
A.: Permanent, more permanent than, let's say, coming
here through an Indian company.
Q.: Are they sponsoring you for an H-1 visa?
A.: I'm already on H-1.

A Glimpse at the Future?

The challenge of labor competition from places like India is a recent phenomenon, a high-tech development. Its low-tech coun-
terpart, under way for years, is a steady drain of blue-collar jobs
out of the United States into, among other places, Mexico. This,
too, is a direct result of U.S. policy.

It began in 1965 when, with the encouragement of the U.S.
government, Mexico adopted something called the Border Industrialization Program. Its aim was to create work for impover-
ished Mexicans in the region closest to the United States.

As with the erroneous National Science Foundation report
that led to thousands of foreign computer engineers pouring into
the United States, a faulty premise was used to sell the Mexican
program to the American public. It went like this: If Washington
helped create jobs in Mexico, it would reduce unemployment
there and stem the tide of illegal immigrants seeking work in the
United States. Best of all, Washington said, not a single American
company would be hurt.

Adding tax breaks to the promise of cheap labor, the U.S. government encouraged American companies to establish subsidiary
Mexican operations called *maquiladoras*. Under the program, a
U.S. corporation could set up an assembly plant in Mexico, for
electronics, apparel, appliances, automobile components, toys

and other products. Parts would be shipped into Mexico for assembly, then the finished goods would be exported back to this country for sale.

An obscure provision in U.S. tariff law, which allowed companies to bring the finished product back across the border virtually duty-free, made it all possible. The section had been on the books for years and a few companies had built plants in the Far East to make use of it. But Mexico would elevate the practice to another level.

The primary attraction: a cheap labor pool. At the time, the minimum wage for unskilled work in the border city of Juarez, Mexico, was 30 cents an hour. Trainees received 15 cents an hour. The U.S. minimum wage then was $1.25 an hour.

Needless to say, the maquiladora idea sounded pretty good to corporate America. So many U.S. companies moved across the border that the Nixon administration, pressed by organized labor and political leaders in industrial states, called for a review of tariff policy to determine if the program should be scaled back. A succession of witnesses appeared before the U.S. Tariff Commission in the spring of 1970 to testify that the program was relieving Mexican poverty. If it were abolished, they warned, a flood of poor Mexicans surely would sweep into the United States.

A typical comment came from Mark T. Miles, director of plans and programs for the Chamber of Commerce in El Paso, Tex., across the border from Juarez: "The location of large numbers of diversified manufacturing operations, and the relatively high wages paid in these operations within the border zone of the Republic of Mexico, is beneficial for the United States in relieving conditions of poverty and unemployment in that zone, thereby reducing the pressure for legal and illegal immigration in the U.S."

The mayor of El Paso, Peter De Wetter, echoed this view. "The poverty problem of U.S. cities on the Mexican border is further complicated by tremendous pressures for immigration to the United States from Mexico. Economic opportunity must be provided on both sides of the border if we are to ease the immigration situation and improve the lot of our own. . . residents."

Other witnesses disputed contentions that the program was putting Americans out of work. Ignacio Garcia Batista of the Commission of the Californias testified: "Not one United States factory has been known to close its doors as a consequence of the program."

With such assurances, and backing from major U.S. corporations that had begun moving operations to Mexico, the tariff commission decided to let stand the duty-free provision of the Border Industrialization Program.

Twenty-three years later, Congress debated the North American Free Trade Agreement (NAFTA), which essentially made permanent the border program—and expanded it to all of Mexico. By then, immigration from Mexico into the United States—legal and illegal—was running at record levels. As for the factories in the United States that would never close—they closed in record numbers.

Nevertheless, the arguments for NAFTA in 1993 sounded eerily like those advanced on behalf of the Border Industrialization Program in 1970. NAFTA would create jobs, raise incomes and reduce illegal immigration.

President Clinton in June 1993: "If you have more growth on both sides, then you'll have less illegal immigration from Mexico, more people will be able to get jobs at home and stay with their families, their incomes will rise and they'll buy more American products."

Rep. Joan Kelly Horn (D., Mo.), in September 1993: "Turn down NAFTA and there will not only be thousands more illegal immigrants every night, there might well be tens of thousands every night."

Sen. Max Baucus (D., Mont.), in October 1993: "Creating jobs in Mexico will help the Mexican economy and will decrease the likelihood of illegal immigration from Mexico to the United States."

Sen. George J. Mitchell (D., Maine), in November 1993: "NAFTA provides the United States with significant new opportunities for the future: expanded markets for American products in this hemisphere, more American jobs from higher export levels and the growth of prosperity in the hemisphere, which will ultimately reduce illegal immigration as a problem."

They were as wrong in 1993 as their predecessors had been in 1970. Mexicans continue to stream across the border. The reason: Enough jobs can never be created to sustain Mexico's population growth. To understand that growth, think of it this way:

If the U.S. population had increased at the same rate as the Mexican population since 1960, there would be 483 million people living in this country in 1996.

As it is, there are not enough good-paying jobs to support the current population of 264 million. Now add 219 million people to that number and imagine the effect on your weekly paycheck as companies awarded jobs to whoever would work for the least amount of money.

Without fundamental changes in U.S. policy, what's on the horizon for the American worker? Make a visit to El Paso, a brisk walk across the bridge from Juarez. Because of its long experience with having a low-wage workforce next door, El Paso offers a glimpse into the future of America's emerging two-class society— from job prospects and wages to housing opportunities and living standards. In this city of 515,000 people, the middle class is disappearing. In its place are a few very rich people and a lot of poor.

Thousands of Mexicans come across the border each day to work in low-wage jobs—convenience store clerks, manual labor, whatever they can get. Wages generally are so low that comparatively few people have enough money to buy houses. That's why El Paso ranks near the bottom on the annual lists of American cities in terms of affordable housing.

For the last quarter of 1995, the National Association of Home Builders ranked El Paso 185 out of 192 cities on housing affordability. The median selling price of houses was $88,000. By the home builders' calculations, people with the average El Paso household's income could afford to buy only 37.5 percent of the homes. At the other end of the economic scale, growing enclaves of homes—many enclosed behind walls and gates—sell for a half-million dollars and up.

Duane Sanders, who works for the Salvation Army in El Paso, has watched these changes occur, including a decline in contributions to his and other social service agencies. "People don't have the money they used to," he said. "In my church, we're constantly having to ask people to fill up the food pantry. . . . For every job [opening in El Paso], there are 100 applicants. . . .This town is northern Juarez."

At the same time, Sanders said, there are "157 millionaires in this county. There are million-dollar homes on the west side of town. A lot of half-million-dollar homes and quarter-million-dollar homes. I was in one the other day; the bathroom was bigger than this office."

The homes that poor people do buy often are purchased from affluent families, who own large tracts of desert land. Michael R. Wyatt, an attorney with Texas Rural Legal Aid, says that two types of *colonias*, or poor developments, have grown up around El Paso.

The first type of *colonia* has existed for years, Wyatt said. In it, the farmer subdivided fields and sold off lots without plotting roads or providing standard services. One water meter may service 30 houses. A one-inch pipeline runs off the meter and eventually branches into garden hoses that serve the individual houses. "They pay the owner $25 a month," Wyatt said. "In El Paso County, that's a pretty good deal. There's no sewerage. They run off septic systems."

And then there's the other *colonia*. "The second type of *colonia* is more desperate," Wyatt said. "These people are living in the middle of the desert in shanties, tar-paper houses. They are never going to get water. There's no realistic way for them to get water. The lots are being sold on land contracts. If after 30 years you make all the payments and if you are never late, you will get the land. If late, and paid faithfully for 20 years, they can forfeit the contract and kick you off. There are people buying this land for $5,995 for about one acre. They pay $30 a month for 30 years."

When someone is late with a payment, Wyatt says, the costs add up quickly:

$ 13.82	-	interest
16.08	-	principal
3.00	-	escrow tax
1.50	-	late fee
2.50	-	service fee
302.29	-	attorney's fee
$339.19	-	TOTAL

One other real estate item worth mentioning about those land contracts. Do you remember when you purchased your home and the deed was recorded in the county courthouse to show that you owned the property? Well, many people buying on land contracts are not permitted to record the contracts. In fact, if they do so, they can lose the land. Read carefully this provision from one agreement: "This contract shall not be filed for record and to do so shall be a breach on Purchaser's part for which Seller may terminate."

So where do people work who buy lots without running water or sewer systems? One place is El Paso's garment industry, which turns out clothing bearing well-known labels—from Levi's to Calvin Klein.

The Foreign Link

Wherever they may live, workers don't share much in the big profits from the designer labels.

Hilda Mata was a sewing machine operator at Sonia's Apparel. Her pay rate: $4.25 an hour. She quit, she said, because "I did not want to work without getting paid anymore." She and her co-workers were owed a total of $25,000 in back pay, according to Gutberto Martinez of the U.S. Labor Department.

Anita Gasca was a sewing machine operator at Generation Apparel, which produced clothing carrying the Calvin Klein label. She went to work at the factory on May 18, 1994, and was making $4.25 an hour when she left in October of that year. Why did she leave? "Because we were not paid for three weeks," Gasca said.

The man behind Generation Apparel was Jose C. Salas. He was not available to be interviewed. But let Martinez, a Labor Department investigator, tell you about him. Martinez described the Salas operation during a court proceeding.

He said that Salas has operated several garment factories—Jose Salas Sportswear, Montview, El Dorado and Romie's. At one, called El Dorado, "We found that Mr. Salas owed 77 employees about $20,000 in unpaid wages." Martinez was asked about another factory, Salas Sportswear: "We did an investigation in 1985, where we found that 20 employees were due about $3,000." And still another: "Montview was an investigation we conducted in 1988 which revealed that about 44 employees were owed about $8,000."

Then Martinez was asked whether the Department of Labor ever had attempted to take legal action against Jose Salas, other than trying to recover the back wages. Said Martinez: "We attempted to take him to litigation," after the last investigation in 1990. "But we've never found him to serve him." The losers, once again, were working people.

Most Americans, of course, don't live on the border, in a city like El Paso. But that doesn't mean they're not in competition with Mexicans—and Indians and Brazilians and Hondurans.

Because the U.S. government has failed to cushion the impact of global competition through its import and immigration policies, an increasing number of American workers are seeing their livelihoods at risk. Foreigners flood in, jobs flood out.

In the global economy constructed by Washington and Wall Street, all Americans live next door to a low-wage country.

111

CHAPTER • FOUR

The Decline and Fall of Manufacturing

From Making Things to Selling Things

This is a Washington morality tale. Or, how the people who run the country can label you poor one day, and rich the next.

Once upon a time (in 1975, to be exact), the people in Washington enacted a new law to help poor working folks. They called it the earned-income tax credit. They said that those workers who were struggling at the bottom of the economic pile should receive some financial assistance from the federal government to encourage them to continue working. To do that, the people in Washington said, they would return to the working poor a portion of the Social Security taxes that had been withheld from their paychecks.

Then they patted themselves, collectively, on their backs. "This provides needed tax relief to a hard-pressed group in the population—the lower-income worker," the people in Washington (in this case, Congress) said. Over the years, as the cost of living went up, so, too, did the amount that the poor could earn and still keep the tax credit.

Then one day (April 23, 1996, to be precise), one of the people in Washington (the president) declared that new studies showed his good works had resulted in the creation of many jobs that pay high wages. The news was so good that the president's advisers held a press conference and announced that more than half the jobs created were "high-wage" jobs.

The news media rushed to report the good news. "Two-thirds of [new] jobs pay above-average wages," reported CNN. "Newly created jobs pay well, report says," said the *New York Times*. "White House says most new jobs pay well," said the *Los Angeles Times*. "Two-thirds of the jobs created in the last two years have come in occupations paying more than the $480 per week median wage," said the *Washington Post*.

112

The Decline and Fall of Manufacturing

Four hundred and eighty dollars a week? That's $24,960 a year. High wage?

In 1995, a working mother or father with two children who earned $24,960 received an earned-income credit of $343 because they were among the working poor.

Or, if you will, they were "high-wage" and "working poor"— at one and the same time.

How is it possible to be both? It's not, of course. But that's the kind of statistical sleight of hand Washington practices year in and year out to assure Americans that good jobs are being created.

To be sure, President Clinton's Council of Economic Advisers, which issued the happy-news study, was only doing what its predecessors have done for three decades or more: putting the best possible face on economic statistics. Every administration, Democratic or Republican, boasts of the jobs created on its watch as evidence of wise stewardship of the economy. President Ronald Reagan talked of 20 million new jobs added during his two terms. The Clinton administration claims credit for 9.7 million.

But behind the numbers is a stark reality that doesn't show up in the press releases: Overall, the new jobs do not match the pay of the old manufacturing jobs that many Americans have lost.

Where have those manufacturing jobs gone? Government policies, especially on global trade, have crippled whole industries that were the lifeblood for generations of production workers. Two and a half million manufacturing jobs have been lost in the United States since 1979, the peak year for manufacturing employment. As a share of all jobs, manufacturing has dropped from 23 percent to 16 percent.

These were the kinds of good-paying jobs that boosted millions of blue-collar families into the middle class in the 1950s, '60s and '70s. As manufacturing jobs have been eliminated, wages have stagnated. Measured in constant dollars, the average weekly wages of manufacturing workers in 1995 were the same as three decades earlier, in 1965.

In 1955, 16.9 million people were employed in manufacturing, where the pay averaged $3,916 a year. That was 89 percent of median family income, enough to maintain a middle-class lifestyle. An additional 7.6 million people worked in the lower-paying retail-trade field, where wages averaged $2,535 a year—or 57 percent of median family income. That means 9.3 million more people were employed in higher-paying jobs making things than in lower-paying jobs selling things.

By 1995, that pattern had been reversed, as 20.8 million people worked in retail trades, 18.4 million in manufacturing. Now, 2.4 million more people were employed selling things than making things. Even worse, the average manufacturing pay of $26,652 a year now was only 67 percent of median family income and was not enough to maintain a middle-class lifestyle in many parts of the country. As for retail trade pay of $11,532, it had plunged to only 29 percent of median family income, meaning that it would require the incomes of two working spouses and one child to bring a family near the median income level.

Many of the people who lost those manufacturing jobs—or would have held them if they had been created—now work in service industries that pay only slightly above minimum wage, between $5 and $9 an hour. At the high end, that's $18,720 a year—before taxes. They are people like the security guard at your bank, the aide who works in the nursing home caring for your aged parent, the custodian who maintains the classrooms where your children attend college.

People like Roger Brockert, who worked eight years at a machine-tool plant in Lima, Ohio. Once he earned $11 an hour as a material handler. But that job came to an abrupt end in 1992, when the plant's last owner, Giddings & Lewis, closed the facility, putting Brockert and 75 others out of work.

After looking for months, he took a job as a shipping clerk for an auto parts supplier that paid $5.50 an hour—or $11,440 a year. Brockert, 55, has since moved up to $8 an hour—still 27 percent less than he earned in 1992. "It's been quite a drop," Brockert says. "What you would call a progression. A progression down."

And Roger Brockert isn't an exception. In fact, 50,000 former workers in the machine-tool industry could tell the same basic story. When they looked to Washington for help in keeping their jobs, Washington turned its back. The jobs went to another hemisphere. And America surrendered its leadership in yet one more manufacturing industry.

Tool and Die: How a Great Industry Was Lost

For most of this century, the United States had the world's largest, most innovative machine-tool industry. As manufactured products go, machine tools lack the sex appeal of automobiles or electronics, yet they are indispensable to a nation's manufacturing capability.

Before companies can make cars, refrigerators, washers, dial-

The Decline and Fall of Manufacturing

ysis machines or hair dryers, they must have custom-made machine tools to cut, shape, drill, polish or mill the parts that form the finished products. A nation with a weak machine-tool industry is dependent on foreign suppliers to underpin its manufacturing base.

Unlike autos and steel—high-profile industries with thousands of workers in one plant—the machine-tool industry was made up of thousands of small tool-and-die shops, many of them family-owned, with a few to a few dozen workers. Nevertheless, the American industry possessed a technological flair that made it unique. Most major advances in machine-tool design originated in the United States, including the development of computer-driven models that are now the foundation of the modern machine-tool industry worldwide.

More important, the industry was a steady source of good-paying jobs. All through the 1950s, '60s and '70s, the number of engineers, machinists, salesmen and others employed by machine-tool companies grew, rising to a peak of 108,000 in 1980. As the 1980s dawned, the U.S. machine-tool industry stood atop the world.

Then, with remarkable speed, the industry unraveled. Orders collapsed from $5.6 billion in 1979 to $1.7 billion in 1983—a falloff of 70 percent. As hundreds of shops closed or merged with other companies, the number of jobs plunged from 108,000 in 1980 to 69,000 in 1983. What happened?

Many factors were at work—a severe recession in the early 1980s, an inability to fully respond to new demands and consolidation. Yet the chief cause of the industry's troubles was not domestic. It was, rather, a dramatic increase in imports from Japan—and the response to that surge from the U.S. government. Washington's tireless advocacy of free trade has flooded the American marketplace with imported products of all kinds from all nations, endangering—and frequently ruining—U.S. companies that make the same goods.

During the 1950s, the golden era of American middle-class growth, U.S. imports averaged $11.8 billion a year. In the 1960s, annual imports nearly doubled, to $22.4 billion, then soared 381 percent to $107.8 billion during the 1970s. The upward spiral continued in the 1980s, as imports shot up by an additional 216 percent, averaging $340.5 billion a year. So far in the 1990s, they have climbed 73 percent more, to $588.9 billion a year.

Other countries have not been nearly as receptive to imports.

115

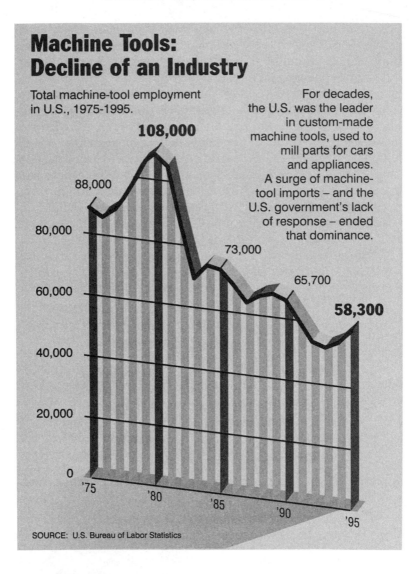

Machine Tools: Decline of an Industry

Total machine-tool employment in U.S., 1975-1995.

For decades, the U.S. was the leader in custom-made machine tools, used to mill parts for cars and appliances. A surge of machine-tool imports – and the U.S. government's lack of response – ended that dominance.

108,000

88,000

73,000

65,700

58,300

80,000

60,000

40,000

20,000

0

'75 '80 '85 '90 '95

SOURCE: U.S. Bureau of Labor Statistics

And so exports from American manufacturers have fallen behind—as has the living standard of the American worker.

But you may judge for yourself by looking at trade with one country—Japan. In 1995, the United States' single largest commodity export to Japan was semiconductors. Total value: $3.8 billion. Think that sounds good?

Think again.

The Decline and Fall of Manufacturing

During that same year, the United States imported semiconductors from Japan valued at $10.6 billion. That meant a trade deficit of $6.8 billion. And the loss of thousands of American jobs.

The United States' second largest commodity export to Japan was computers. Total value: $3.6 billion. But there was the same problem: the United States imported computers from Japan valued at $6 billion—meaning a trade deficit of $2.4 billion. And the loss of more thousands of jobs.

The United States' third largest commodity export to Japan was motor vehicles and passenger car bodies. Total value: $3.1 billion. Again, there was an imbalance. The United States imported motor vehicles and passenger car bodies from Japan valued at $23 billion. That added up to a trade deficit of $19.9 billion. And the loss of tens of thousands of jobs.

By now you get the idea. We sold semiconductors to Japan. They sold more to us. We sold computers to Japan. They sold more to us. We sold motor vehicles and passenger car bodies to Japan. They sold a lot more to us.

And that's exactly how the Japanese took over the machine-tool industry, step by step. They began by exporting small quantities to the United States in the 1960s. A trickle of machine-tool imports suddenly became a torrent, rising from $300,000 in 1961 to $854 million in 1985.

"Imports are beginning to look more and more like the cat that swallowed the canary," reported an article in a machine-tool trade journal, *Purchasing*, in October 1985. "Foreign penetration of the domestic market continues to increase. . . . Imports now exceed exports by five times."

To free-traders and other critics of American industry, it was simply a case of the Japanese being more competitive—producing high-quality goods at rock-bottom prices. But there was more to the Japanese success than efficiency. There was the government of Japan.

Starting in the 1950s, Japan's Ministry of International Trade and Industry (MITI) encouraged the growth of a large, export-oriented machine-tool industry. MITI did this with a few tools of its own: government-backed incentives, including low-cost loans, subsidies, loan guarantees and export assistance.

In the meantime, to protect this fledgling industry, Japan sealed off its home market to machine-tool imports from abroad. Thus shut out, American companies found that the only avenue open to them was to license their technology for a fee to Japanese companies. This generated short-term income for U.S. toolmakers, and devastating long-term consequences.

All through the 1960s, Japanese companies acquired licenses giving them the right to manufacture American-designed machine tools in Japan. Before long, those U.S.-designed tools began showing up in this country as Japanese imports. While every industrialized nation requires machine tools, Japan targeted the United States for its export thrust. It was not only the largest market; thanks to U.S. government trade policy, it was also the one most open to imports.

In 1982, the American machine-tool industry tried to fight back, seeking help from the U.S. government. Charges of unfair trade practices were filed before U.S. trade authorities, with the industry contending that Japanese manufacturers had benefited from Japanese-government subsidies and a closed market at home in Japan that enabled them to price their export products at below-market value. The Japanese government had helped fashion a global machine-tool colossus. And what did Washington do for its industry?

Very little.

The industry's petitions for relief provoked a controversy within the Reagan administration. On one side were those who maintained that a vital industry was at stake and some curbs should be placed on imported machine tools. On the other side were free-traders who opposed any constraints on imports.

The media lined up mostly on the side of the free-traders. Typical was this editorial from the *New York Times* on November 8, 1982: "The reason the Japanese are succeeding is that they make fine tools and sell them at competitive prices. There is no good legal or economic case for invoking protectionist measures. . . . American exporters, including machine-tool exporters, could end up the losers."

The head of one major machine-tool company that had sought relief complained that no one in Washington would listen to the industry's plight. "They treat us like second-class citizens with dirty fingernails," said Phillip A. O'Reilly, president and chief executive officer of Houdaille Industries of Buffalo, N.Y., then a leading machine-tool maker.

O'Reilly was correct on more than one level. Not only did Washington turn its back on his industry, but a new generation of corporate managers, Wall Street, economists and even the American education establishment looked down on people who earned a living by getting their hands dirty. After all, in the new America, all the good jobs would be high-tech and white collar.

Never mind that no nation will remain a world power if it is unable to build the machines that build the machines. And never mind that, within one decade, Washington and Wall Street—through corporate restructuring that ran out of control—managed to wipe out centuries worth of skills.

In any case, no one disputed the quality of the Japanese-made machine tools. It was the Japanese business practices, underwritten and supported by government policy, that were at issue. American toolmakers provided extensive documentation showing that Japanese tools were selling for less in the United States than in Japan, a violation of international trade rules, and that the government of Japan had subsidized the industry, further driving down the selling price and making it more difficult for American companies to earn a profit.

In the end, the free-traders, backed by intense lobbying by Japanese importers and the Japanese government, prevailed. President Reagan, in February 1984, declined to impose trade sanctions on the Japanese tool industry, saying that such a move would be a blow to free trade. "I remain committed to the principle of free trade as the best way to bring the benefits of competition to American consumers and businesses," Reagan said.

The industry proceeded to go into such a slide that the U.S. Department of Defense became concerned about the implications for national security if machine tools were no longer produced domestically. As a result, the Reagan administration negotiated a so-called Voluntary Restraint Agreement that placed a cap on Japanese machine-tool imports into the United States for five years. (A similar agreement was negotiated with Taiwan, a much smaller machine-tool exporter.)

As trade protection measures go, Voluntary Restraint Agreements are about as mild as they come. This one did nothing to roll back the volume of Japanese imports. It merely limited future growth. The idea was to give U.S. toolmakers time to regroup.

In 1991, the Voluntary Restraint Agreement was extended for two years. It expired at the end of 1993. At that point, the U.S. machine-tool industry's trade group, the Association for Manufacturing Technology, told Congress that the American team was once again competitive and "ready to take on the world in fairly traded products."

What kind of an industry has emerged to "take on the world"?

The U.S. machine-tool industry—the world leader in the 1970s—now is a distant third in production, behind Japan and Germany. And it jockeys with Italy, a nation one-fourth its size, for third place on the list.

Machine-tool orders for 1995 totaled $4.9 billion—well below the peak orders of $5.6 billion recorded 16 years earlier in 1979. Measured in constant dollars, the 1995 tool orders were little more than half the value of orders three decades before, in 1965.

Far more telling are the trade statistics with individual countries over the 10 years from 1986 to 1995. The United States recorded machine-tool trade deficits in nine of those 10 years with the United Kingdom, another onetime world power in steep decline. The United States shipped machine tools worth $602 million to the United Kingdom. But the United Kingdom shipped tools to this country worth $1.025 billion. That produced total deficits of $423 million.

The United States registered machine-tool trade deficits in all ten years with Italy. The 1995 deficit alone—when the industry supposedly was ready to tackle the world—came in at a record $118.5 million. Total deficits for 10 years: $692 million.

Then there was Taiwan, a nation with a population smaller than the state of California. Again, U.S. deficits in all 10 years, with a record $195 million deficit in 1995. Total deficits for 10 years: $1.2 billion.

The United States logged machine-tool trade deficits in all 10 years with Switzerland, a nation with a population that is smaller than New York City. Once more, the 1995 deficit was a record at $209 million. Total deficits for 10 years: $1.3 billion.

The United States ran up machine-tool trade deficits in all 10 years with Germany. Once again, 1995 came in at a record deficit of $454 million. Total deficits for 10 years: $3.2 billion.

And finally, of course, Japan. The machine-tool deficits, naturally, extended over the 10 years. In fact, the deficits exceeded $1 billion in six of the 10 years. Again, 1995, when the United States was ready to face the world, the deficit with Japan hit a record $1.7 billion. Total deficits for 10 years: $10.9 billion.

Let us summarize: One industry, six countries, 59 years of trade deficits out of a possible 60, adding up to a total deficit for the United States of $17.7 billion.

And more bad news may be on the way. For nine of the last 10 years, the United States maintained a trade surplus in machine tools with South Korea. That surplus came in at a record $118.5

million in 1992. Three years later, in 1995, the United States incurred its first machine-tool trade deficit with South Korea. It totaled $40 million.

All those trade deficits, also as you might guess, were accompanied by a sharp decline in employment. Nearly half the machine-tool workforce has vanished, as the number of jobs plummeted from 108,000 in 1980 to 58,000 in 1995.

And as is the case with most middle-class Americans, the wages of machine-tool workers have trailed behind the rising cost of living. The industry has traditionally paid solid middle-class wages. A machine-tool worker in 1995 earned $34,083 a year. But counted in constant dollars, that was $1,332 less than workers earned 20 years earlier.

A Way of Life, Gone

Just about anyone in Lima, Ohio, could direct you to the machine-tool plant on North Baxter Street. It has been there since 1916. Inside its brick walls, generations of men manufactured tools and dies, molds and special machinery for the auto and electrical industries. The factory was typical of small manufacturers throughout the industrial Middle West. It never had more than 300 workers at a time. But they were steady, good-paying jobs.

Gary Reese went to work there operating a milling machine after he graduated from high school in 1959. He was trained at the plant, a practice common in the machine-tool industry of the time.

Over the next 30 years, the plant would have a succession of owners. All through the 1980s, as Japanese imports surged into America, the plant lost orders and jobs. In 1992, the last owner, Giddings & Lewis, the nation's largest machine-tool company, shut it down and laid off Gary Reese and the 75 remaining workers.

Reese was earning $12.31 an hour, a little less than $26,000 a year. After the layoff, he found work—and was let go again—at three other machine-tool plants in west-central Ohio. None paid what he had earned at Lima, a town of 45,000 in the western part of the state. The first, in Sidney, paid $10.41 an hour. The second, in Minster, paid $8.25. The third, also in Sidney, paid $9.50. Finally, in February 1996, he found work again, at a machine shop in Cridersville, Ohio. The hourly pay was $8.25 an hour—or a third less than what he had been making four years before.

Reese had to drive 75 miles a day round-trip to Sidney and 80 miles round-trip to Minster. The last job is closer to home, requiring a 15-mile-a-day round-trip. None of the jobs had health coverage or benefits the equal of those at Lima.

Although he's glad to be back at work, Reese wonders what the future holds. "When you get to be my age [56] a lot of places don't want you," he says.

That's a lesson he's learned every time he's been out of work since the Giddings & Lewis plant closed. "I tried for work at a couple of places that pay good wages, and I was turned down because of my age," Reese said. "They didn't say this, of course. But they sent me a letter and said they found somebody who was more qualified. That isn't what they meant. They meant they found somebody who was younger.

"At one place, I went so far as to get two or three interviews, and they sent me for a physical examination. And I thought, 'I've got the job. I've got the job!' And then I turned around and got a letter from them. I'm at the age they don't want you. They want the younger fellows." For the time being, Reese simply hopes he can hold out until he retires.

By ceding leadership of the machine-tool industry to Japan, Washington undermined the prospects of thousands of young workers who had hoped to find a future in the business—workers like Reese's grown son: "I sent him through precision machining at a vocational school here for two years, and that's what he's in now," Reese said. "But he's not making a big wage, either. He's probably making $6.50 to $7 an hour."

Machine tools are only one example. The current generation of young blue-collar workers has lost the option their parents and grandparents had to pick and choose jobs from a variety of manufacturing plants in their hometowns.

If conditions prevailed as they were in the 1950s and 1960s, when manufacturing employment averaged 31 percent of all jobs across the two decades, factories today would employ 34.5 million men and women. Instead, manufacturing employment in the 1990s has averaged 18.4 million people a year. That's 16.1 million fewer jobs in a workforce of more than 110 million people.

As a result of unrestrained imports, the American machine-tool industry has lost—most likely forever—its place as the number-one global producer of machine tools. But you would never know that reading news stories about the industry. Business pages of newspapers and magazines invariably, when they report on the industry, tend to dwell on the positive side of its activities.

On January 29, 1996, the *Wall Street Journal* reported that

Losing the Jobs That Paid Well

In 1955, manufacturing jobs paid almost as much as the median family income, so one wage-earner could support a middle-class family. By 1995, low-paying retail jobs were dominant — meaning two incomes were needed to have a middle-class lifestyle.

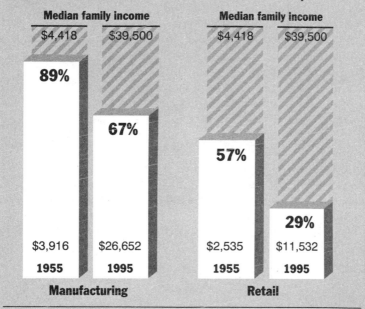

Median family income		Median family income	
$4,418	$39,500	$4,418	$39,500
89%			
	67%	57%	
			29%
$3,916	$26,652	$2,535	$11,532
1955	**1995**	**1955**	**1995**
Manufacturing		**Retail**	

By 1995, retail jobs had surpassed manufacturing jobs.

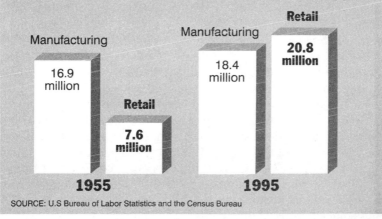

Manufacturing
16.9 million

Retail
7.6 million

1955

Manufacturing
18.4 million

Retail
20.8 million

1995

SOURCE: U.S Bureau of Labor Statistics and the Census Bureau "machine-tool orders hit a 16-year high in 1995 amid signs that deteriorating domestic demand is finally beginning to over-shadow strong gains in the export market. . . . Export orders more than doubled to $687.2 million from $333.7 million in 1994." The *New York Times*, in a similar story that same day, reported that "exports fueled much of last year's gain, surging 106 percent even as domestic orders slipped 4.3 percent."

Missing from both news accounts was any mention of imports. In 1995, the United States racked up the largest trade deficit ever in machine tools—$2.3 billion—as imports swamped exports nearly three-to-one.

Such stories help explain why, in part, a growing number of people are so skeptical about the news media. In interview after interview over the last two years, workers and their families questioned the economic reports that they read in newspapers and magazines, watched on television and heard on radio. They saw little relation between those reports and their own lives, or those of other family members and friends, neighbors and co-workers, and they sensed that something was amiss in the "good news" stories.

They had every right to be skeptical. Consider just two articles from thousands of comparable news accounts published or broad-cast over the last five years.

In April 1991, *Forbes* magazine offered this assessment of U.S. trade: "Better informed protectionists know that the trade issue is being defanged. The U.S. merchandise trade deficit is falling steadily (to a present level of around $100 billion). It is now widely accepted that it should be in rough balance within three years."

In rough balance?

In 1994, the year by which *Forbes* predicted a balance in trade, the deficit hit an all-time record: $166.1 billion. And in 1995 it reached $173.4 billion.

Or *Newsweek* magazine's ringing defense of unrestricted trade, published in July 1993 under the headline: "The Trashing of Free Trade: The new gospel argues that an open global economy is bad for America; don't believe it." While allowing that imports "have wiped out a lot of U.S. jobs," the article said that "even for indus-tries that are supposedly being battered by foreign competition, the international economy is looking unusually friendly."

As one example of the positive side of free trade, the magazine cited Timberland Co., the manufacturer of boots, shoes, sandals and accessories: "Timberland's plants in Tennessee, North Carolina and Puerto Rico rack up 40 percent of their shoe sales in Europe and Asia; executive Jeffrey Swartz says that lower U.S. costs for transportation and materials make up for higher U.S. wages."

That was July 1993. Two years later, in June 1995, Timberland closed its manufacturing plant in Mountain City, Tenn., throwing 340 people out of work, and shuttered its Boone, N.C., plant, eliminating the jobs of 200 employees.

The company no longer makes any footwear in the United States. Contrary to the claims put forth in the *Newsweek* article that other advantages offset higher U.S. wages, Timberland decided that wages were all that counted. Or as Roger Rydell, Timberland's vice president for corporate communications, put it at the time:

"Manufacturing is a global commodity. We will go where we can obtain the highest quality for the most competitive price." Today, all the company's products are made in Europe, Asia, Puerto Rico or the Caribbean.

While the company shut down its manufacturing plants in Tennessee and North Carolina, and closed distribution facilities in New Hampshire and Massachusetts, it did open two new offices. As Timberland executives explained in a report to stockholders:

"In 1995, the company also opened offices in Bangkok, Thailand, and Taichung, Taiwan, in order to more closely supervise the company's sourcing activities conducted in the Asia-Pacific region."

Washington Did It

There once was a time when the United States offered enough employment variety so that most everyone could find a job to match his or her skills. Not everyone who graduates from high school can—or should—go to college. Not everyone can—or should—be employed in a high-tech industry. And no one should be forced into a low-paying job simply because it is a job of last resort.

In years gone by, government policies encouraged creation of a diversity of jobs that for decades contributed to social stability in towns and cities, large and small.

No longer. And here is why.

U.S. Policy No. 1: Eliminating Manufacturing Jobs. By the late 1970s, the American microwave-oven industry, one of the nation's newest and fastest-growing sectors, was hard hit by imports. Companies were reducing workforces. Profit margins were slipping. And plants that had only recently operated at capacity were cutting back production.

The appliance that is a fixture today in 84 million American homes was invented in the United States. The Raytheon Corp. developed microwave technology as a defense contractor in the 1940s. The first microwave ovens appeared in homes in the 1950s, but it was not until 1967, when Amana Refrigeration introduced a countertop model, that the industry really took off. From a mere 60,000 units sold in the United States in 1970, the number jumped to 1.1 million in 1975 and hit 3.6 million in 1980. Today an average of 8.5 million are sold every year.

Following Amana's lead, General Electric, Tappan, Litton, Roper, Magic Chef and Whirlpool also began making countertop models to capitalize on the popular item. For a short while, American companies had the market mostly to themselves. Then the Japanese, led by Matsushita, Hitachi, Toshiba, Sanyo and Sharp, began exporting in volume to the United States, often selling microwaves at prices lower than similar models were priced in Japan.

It was the patented Japanese formula to dominate sales of an array of consumer products in the world's richest market—the United States. It would be repeated time and again as the Japanese government supported Japanese business in a variety of ways, including by permitting products to be sold more cheaply abroad than at home. Imports of microwave ovens rose through the 1970s, starting from a minuscule number in the late 1960s and rising to 35 percent of the domestic market by 1980.

In 1972, Amana Refrigeration filed a complaint with the Commerce Department contending that the Japanese were "dumping" countertop microwaves in America—selling them at less than similar models sold for in Japan, a violation of international trading rules. The U.S. Treasury Department rejected the complaint, saying there was no evidence that the U.S. industry was being harmed by imports.

In 1979, when imports had climbed to more than a third of the U.S. microwave market, the Association of Home Appliance Manufacturers, the trade group for domestic microwave makers, filed a similar complaint with the U.S. International Trade Commission (ITC). Once again, the Japanese companies were accused of violating trade laws. Once again, the requested remedy was higher tariffs.

Although the trade commission made a preliminary finding

agreeing with the domestic industry, the Treasury Department—the agency then responsible for imposing additional duties on imported items—declined to levy a higher tariff. Treasury's position was summed up in an August 24, 1979, letter to the ITC on the microwave investigation by the department's acting general counsel, David R. Brennan: "You are hereby advised that the information developed during our preliminary investigation has led me to the conclusion that there is substantial doubt that an industry in the United States is being, or is likely to be, injured by reason of the importation of this merchandise into the United States."

What happened to the industry that the Treasury Department claimed was not being injured by imports? Of the 19 plants that manufactured microwave ovens in the United States in 1980, only four are left. And just two of those are owned by U.S. companies. In 1980, when U.S. policy makers foresaw no harm to domestic producers, imports accounted for 35 percent of microwave sales in this country. In 1995, imports made up 85 percent of microwaves sold.

As for jobs, about 4,500 U.S. production workers made microwaves in 1976, the peak year for employment. Today, fewer than 1,000 make them. But the most significant number does not show up on any employment balance sheet. It is the number of jobs that should have been—but weren't—created in this industry.

In the last 20 years, sales of microwave ovens increased from 1.8 million in 1976 to 8.6 million in 1995. But during that time, the number of microwave ovens manufactured in the United States remained about the same, averaging 1.5 million units a year. At a time when microwave sales went up 378 percent, employment in the industry went down 78 percent. Potential jobs eliminated by U.S. government policy decisions: upward of 6,000.

U.S. Policy No. 2: Protecting Manufacturing Jobs in Foreign Countries. As corporations have closed plants and slashed jobs in the United States, the federal government has stood by and watched. Time and again, Washington has adopted the position of Wall Street: There is little that government can do. It is the market at work.

There have been, to be sure, some exceptions. On occasion, government is moved to action. In 1994, when the jobs of thousands of phone workers who were making cordless telephones for AT&T were imperiled by trade regulations, the U.S. government rushed to their rescue. But the jobs on the line were not in

West Chicago; Shreveport, La.; Baltimore; San Leandro, Calif.; or any other U.S. city where AT&T has closed a factory or reduced jobs in the last decade.

They were in Malaysia.

The tropical peninsula in Southeast Asia is home for a growing volume of offshore manufacturing by AT&T and other U.S. multinational corporations. Over the last decade, AT&T, by its own estimate, has eliminated about 25,000 manufacturing jobs in the United States and transferred much of the work to plants or suppliers in Asia and Latin America.

Like many global corporations, AT&T often no longer owns the foreign manufacturing plants that make products bearing the AT&T label. Rather, it contracts out the work and has the company logo affixed. Such was the case with AT&T's manufacturing of cordless telephones in Malaysia. The corporation contracted with a company called S. Megga Telecommunications Ltd., whose principal investors have included a businessman in China and the city government of Dongguan, China, to manufacture the phones at a plant near the capital, Kuala Lumpur. The phones were shipped to the United States for sale.

Under U.S. trade laws, AT&T and other communications companies are permitted to import cordless telephones from Malaysia duty-free so long as they do not exceed a specified limit. When that limit was surpassed in 1993, AT&T and other importers sought an exemption from the Office of the U.S. Trade Representative to allow them to import more phones duty-free.

Without the waiver, AT&T warned, the Malaysian manufacturing industry would suffer. In other words, thousands of Malaysians would lose their jobs. As Gerard G. Nelson, government affairs director of AT&T Consumer Products, explained in a March 2, 1994, letter to the U.S. trade representative: "In order to compete in the United States consumer electronics market, AT&T and its competitors must aggressively manage the costs of their products.

"One of the options available to AT&T and its competitors to compensate for an increase in product costs resulting from the imposition of import duties on cordless telephones manufactured in Malaysia would be to shift production of cordless telephones now occurring in Malaysia to other locations to take advantage of opportunities to achieve lower costs of production. Should such a shift occur, the nascent electronic manufacturing industry in Malaysia could suffer a material loss in revenues and employment."

Another cordless telephone importer, Thomson Consumer Electronics Inc., was more blunt about the consequences to Malaysians if the U.S. government did not grant the waiver: "Malaysian employment in this industry will suffer a significant decline. . . . Manufacturing facilities will be forced to seek other locations. . . . This outflow of investment will deter the growth of Malaysia's manufacturing sector."

Both importers assured the U.S. trade representative that no U.S. jobs would be lost by granting the waiver. "AT&T is unaware of any significant United States manufacturing facilities devoted to the production of cordless telephones," wrote AT&T's Nelson. "Thus, no United States employment opportunities would be jeopardized by granting the waiver."

But if the waiver wasn't approved, AT&T warned, some U.S. jobs might be jeopardized. The company claimed that the Malaysian imports provided a "significant product line" for AT&T's Consumer Products unit, which employed 6,000 people in the United States, ranging from product managers and engineers to sales managers and representatives.

"The jobs held by these people in the United States are ultimately dependent upon profitable product lines, including profitable cordless telephones," Nelson wrote. "For these reasons, AT&T believes that granting the requested waiver. . . . will benefit all parties concerned—Malaysian workers and employers and United States consumers, businesses, and employees. . . ."

And on July 1, 1994, the U.S. Trade Representative's Office approved the waiver.

A year and a half later, AT&T wiped out nearly half the 6,000 jobs in the United States that the company had said were dependent on securing the waiver. On January 24, 1996, AT&T's Consumer Products unit announced it would close all 338 AT&T Phone Center stores nationwide, throwing about 2,500 sales people and managers out of work.

"We have decided to focus our business on what we do best, the design and manufacture of high-quality consumer communications products," said Homa Firouztash, Consumer Products' vice president of marketing, sales and product management. "We believe larger retailers can distribute our products more efficiently than we can."

America: Who Stole the Dream?

Let's run through this one more time—slowly: Since AT&T had contracted out the work and no longer manufactured the phones in the United States, the company said, additional imports from Malaysia would not take away American manufacturing jobs. They had been taken away some time ago. But if the government didn't approve the waiver allowing more phones into the country, AT&T might be forced to eliminate the jobs of the people who sold the phones. After AT&T received the government waiver, it eliminated the jobs of the people who sold the phones anyway.

U.S. Policy No. 3: The Legislation That Makes Policies No. 1 and 2 Possible. For the last 25 years, policy makers from both parties periodically have expressed alarm about the nation's deteriorating international trade balance.

As the excess of imports over exports grows, a great hue and cry arises from the White House and Capitol Hill about the need for tough measures to open foreign markets for American goods and to stiffen America's backbone in negotiations with its trading partners. Over the years, lawmakers have enacted one bill after another to "open markets." Each time, when the legislation failed to achieve the promised results, they returned for another round of lawmaking.

In 1973, with the nation's trade balance deteriorating, Rep. Bill Frenzel, a Republican congressman from Minnesota, urged his House colleagues to approve a new trade bill that he said would open foreign markets and create jobs at home: "The Trade Reform Act of 1973 provides both the incentives for expanded fair and mutually beneficial trade and the authority to take action to correct or defend against unfair treatment. The bill is calculated to expand trade and is therefore, for us, a job-creation bill."

It didn't work out that way. The trade reform package was approved and signed into law in 1974, but the nation's merchandise trade deficit continued to worsen, moving from a surplus of $900 million in 1973 to a deficit of $27.6 billion in 1979. So Congress once again took up the cause, passing the Trade Agreements Act of 1979.

"This legislation. . . . will open up vast new opportunities for American exports," said President Jimmy Carter, in signing the bill on July 6, 1979. "It will revise the rules of international trade to create a fairer and more equitable and more open environment for world trade."

But still the trade deficit rose, soaring 308 percent, from $27.6

billion in 1979 to $112.5 billion in 1984. Nevertheless, policy makers went back to work on yet another trade bill, the Trade and Tariff Act of 1984. It, too, promised to put teeth in the nation's trade policies and to expand exports.

By now it was clear that there were two policy problems: Congress had no intention of putting real teeth in any trade legislation, and the executive branch had no intention of using the teeth it had. Nonetheless, when he signed the bill on October 30, 1984, President Ronald Reagan spoke about the tough new provisions: "While promoting free trade, this new act insists on something just as important—fair trade. . . . The bill [will] help American producers and workers deal with unfair trade practices [and] should go far to strengthen American trade laws." Once more, it was Washington talking to voters, rather than acting.

Four years later, with the trade deficit still going up, from $112.5 billion in 1984 to $127 billion in 1988, Washington was back at work on yet another trade bill—the Omnibus Trade and Competitiveness Act of 1988. In urging the Senate to approve it, Lloyd Bentsen, then a Democratic senator from Texas, spoke of the bill's benefits on August 2, 1988: "This bill says 'No' to the status quo. It says America is going to insist on opening up those markets. It says America will no longer roll over and accept the situation. . . ."

Once again, it was a legislative charade from Capitol Hill, backed up by a White House that had no intention of actually doing what it promised voters it would do. In the six years following passage of the 1988 bill, the United States recorded a total of $693.1 billion in merchandise trade deficits—or more than all the deficits combined for the first 85 years of this century.

True to form, Washington was back at work in 1994 on yet another trade bill—legislation ratifying the General Agreement on Tariffs and Trade (GATT). In calling for congressional approval, President Clinton said the bill would open markets abroad and create jobs at home: "GATT will require all nations to do what we've already done—to cut tariffs and other barriers and open up trade to our products and our services. It will level the export playing field for American companies and American workers all around the world, and in so doing, will create hundreds of thousands of new high-paying jobs right here at home."

For the record, when Congress debated the 1973 trade bill, the United States posted a $900 million trade surplus. In 1995, the nation registered its 20th consecutive trade deficit—that's

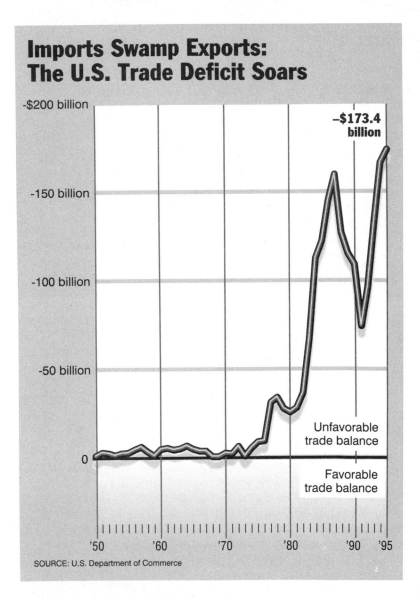

Imports Swamp Exports:
The U.S. Trade Deficit Soars

-$200 billion

–$173.4 billion

-150 billion

-100 billion

-50 billion

0

Unfavorable trade balance

Favorable trade balance

'50   '60   '70   '80   '90 '95

SOURCE: U.S. Department of Commerce

deficit, not surplus. After five major pieces of trade legislation to spur exports and improve the standard of living of American workers, the United States has run up trade deficits totaling $1.7 trillion. More significantly, it has eliminated the jobs of millions of American workers and helped drive down living standards.

If manufacturing jobs are being eliminated, then what kinds of jobs are being created? The theme sounded over and over by Washington and the business community is that the American workforce must become more high-tech. Labor-intensive industries, they say, will continue to move offshore and new, better-paying high-tech jobs requiring more education and training will take their place.

This view is widely held by economists, politicians, corporate executives and newspaper editorial pages. As theories go, it sounds nice.

But reality is quite different.

By the government's own projections, there isn't going to be an abundance of high-tech jobs in the future.

The Department of Labor publishes a thick catalog every two years on the job outlook for the coming decade. It is called *The Occupational Outlook Handbook*, and it covers some 250 occupations. They range from corporate executives, lawyers and engineers to locksmiths, dispatchers and detectives. For each career, the handbook estimates future demand for workers.

Based on data about jobs that have been created in recent years, the 1996-97 edition lists 20 occupations that are expected to have the greatest job growth over the next 10 years. And what might those jobs be? Heading the list are cashiers, followed by janitors, retail salespersons, waiters and waitresses. Other leading job-generating fields are home health aides, guards, nursing aides, truck drivers, secretaries, child-care workers and maintenance repairers. Among the 20 occupations expected to generate the greatest job growth, only one could be considered high-tech—systems analysts.

Conclusion, based on the Labor Department projections: High-paying jobs are becoming scarcer for the workforce as a whole and especially for one segment—women.

CHAPTER • FIVE

Keeping Women Down

Why Are These People Worried?

Alan Greenspan, the chairman of the Federal Reserve Board, whose income was upward of a half-million dollars in 1995—planting him firmly among the top 1 percenters—can't understand why people are worried about their jobs.

"Today, a truly puzzling phenomenon confronts the American economy," he told an economic conference in June 1996. "I refer to the pervasiveness of job insecurity in the context of an economic recovery that has been running for more than five years. . . . This sense of job insecurity is so deep that many workers fear their ability to make ends meet in the future. Many appear truly concerned about a prospective decline in their standard of living."

And jobs were plentiful. As Greenspan had put it in January 1995, "Cumulatively, payrolls have now increased roughly six million over the past couple of years, belying in dramatic fashion the notion that had developed earlier in this decade that our economy had lost its job-generating ability."

Betty Lizana knows a little bit about those jobs. She's held two of them. Both paid less than the job she lost.

For 16 years, Lizana was the payroll officer at an assembly plant in Biloxi, Miss., that made electrical wiring components for vehicles and household appliances. In May 1992, the plant's owner, Fleck Inc., closed the Biloxi facility, packed up the machinery and shipped it to a plant in Juarez, Mexico, where labor is cheaper. Lizana was dismissed, along with about 50 other office and production workers.

Betty Lizana's odyssey since then says much about how working Americans—especially women—are faring in today's job market. And it helps to explain the anxiety about jobs that Greenspan and other people in Washington can't grasp.

In July 1993, about a year after she was let go by Fleck—and long after her unemployment benefits had run out—Lizana found another job. She became a cashier aboard the *Biloxi Belle*, one of the glistening new floating casinos that line the Mississippi Gulf Coast. But shortly after she started work, the *Biloxi Belle* ran into trouble. Too many casinos were chasing the same dollars at a time when neighboring states were also establishing legalized gambling. The *Biloxi Belle*'s owners filed for bankruptcy court protection. Then, in January 1994, court officers were dispatched to close down the ship and secure its assets.

"They just came in one day and locked the place up," Lizana recalled. "I was at work when they came. Naturally, I had to close out the money and make the [bank] drop. There were managers who came in for the next shift and their places were locked. Padlocks on the door. I had never seen anything like it."

This time, it took a year and a half to find another job. The Lizana family got by on her unemployment compensation and on her husband's small disability pension Lizana's new job was with a contractor for an employer that has been trimming its payroll for five years, dismissing more than 260,000 workers: the U.S. government.

In September 1995, Lizana began managing the food-service inventory at Keesler Air Force Base, the Biloxi area's largest employer. But it's only part-time. "I don't get full-time," she said. "I go in and work two hours, then go back later and work two hours. I'm lucky if I get 20 or 25 hours a week."

In four years, Betty Lizana, 52, went from full-time payroll supervisor in an assembly plant at $9 an hour to full-time casino cashier at $5 an hour to part-time food-service worker at $7.97 an hour—whenever she can get work. Welcome to the jobs of the 21st century.

The working lives of millions of Americans have been upended by Washington policies. But of all those affected, the burden has fallen most heavily on women. At a time when unprecedented numbers of women are diving into the workforce—often because their households desperately need the income—the tide is going out. High-paying jobs, never common for women, are becoming even scarcer.

In the past 30 years, Washington trade policies have encouraged the movement of manufacturing jobs overseas, to low-wage countries. In one industry that was among America's largest—the making of apparel—it was primarily women who staffed the factories. Nearly half of those jobs are now gone.

Except for those in the professional class, most women must resort to the service sector: the clerking and cleaning and table-waiting and cashiering jobs that provide little money, few or no benefits, and part-time or irregular hours.

This is true for veteran, well-established workers like Betty Lizana who are forced to find new occupations, just as it is for women seeking their first paycheck.

And for women, the harm is all the greater because they were already at the bottom of the wage scale. It is generally understood that women earn less than men. In 1995, the median weekly earnings of women—meaning half earned more, half earned less—was 75 percent of men's wages. What is not understood so well is this: Barring a dramatic shift in government economic policies, women will always draw a smaller paycheck than men—sometimes substantially smaller.

This disparity persists across occupations. Of the 614,000 marketing, advertising and public relations managers employed in 1995, a total of 208,000—or 34 percent—were women. Their median annual income was $32,800, or just 59 percent of the $55,300 earned by men.

Of the 348,000 people employed as insurance adjusters, examiners and investigators, 258,000—or 74 percent—were women. Their median yearly income was $22,300. That worked out to 69 percent of the $32,200 earned by men.

Of the 799,000 people employed as computer analysts and scientists, 235,000—or 29 percent—were women. Their median annual income totaled $40,700. Or 86 percent of the $47,300 earned by men.

Even in occupations that women have historically dominated, men enjoy an edge.

A total of 426,000 people were employed as general office supervisors in 1995. Of that number, 279,000—or 65 percent—were women. Their median annual income was $24,500. Or 70 percent of the $35,200 earned by men.

A total of 1,039,000 people were employed as bookkeepers, accounting and auditing clerks. Of that number, 946,000—or 91 percent—were women. Their median annual income was $19,900. Or 86 percent of the $23,100 earned by men.

A total of 1,476,000 people employed as elementary schoolteachers. Of that number, 1,233,000—or 84 percent—were women. Their median annual income was $32,600. Or 88 percent of the $37,100 received by men.

Women's Wages Lag

Median annual income in selected occupations by gender, 1995.

SOURCE: U.S. Bureau of Labor Statistics

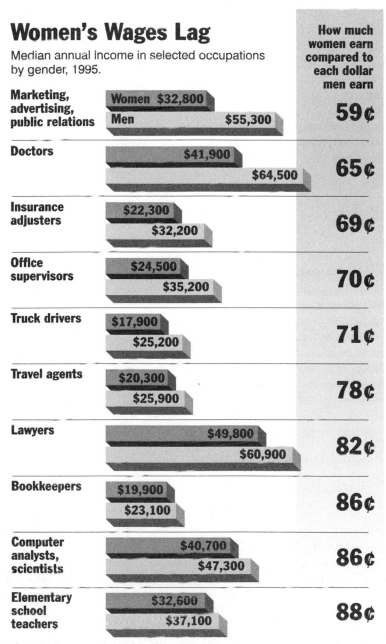

	How much women earn compared to each dollar men earn
Marketing, advertising, public relations — Women $32,800 / Men $55,300	**59¢**
Doctors — $41,900 / $64,500	**65¢**
Insurance adjusters — $22,300 / $32,200	**69¢**
Office supervisors — $24,500 / $35,200	**70¢**
Truck drivers — $17,900 / $25,200	**71¢**
Travel agents — $20,300 / $25,900	**78¢**
Lawyers — $49,800 / $60,900	**82¢**
Bookkeepers — $19,900 / $23,100	**86¢**
Computer analysts, scientists — $40,700 / $47,300	**86¢**
Elementary school teachers — $32,600 / $37,100	**88¢**

America: Who Stole the Dream?

There are, of course, some jobs in which men and women are paid the same: those that pay minimum wage or a little more. Not surprisingly, women hold more of these jobs. In 1995, a total of 6.4 million people aged 25 and older earned between $4.25—the minimum wage—and $5.99 an hour. Of that number, 4.3 million—or 67 percent—were women. This total can be expected to grow substantially since new welfare rules require recipients—most of whom are women—to work.

As for the increase in the minimum wage enacted by Congress in August 1996, it will have little effect. The minimum will reach $5.15 an hour, in two steps, in September 1997.

The $5.15 an hour, by the way, adds up to $10,712 a year, which means the minimum-wage earners of 1997 will be behind their counterparts of 30 years ago. They earned nearly $2,000 more in inflation-adjusted 1995 dollars.

While men have always earned more than women, this stubborn gap is taking on much more urgency now, because women are making up an increasingly greater share of the workforce. In fact, sometime in the early part of the next century, women—for the first time—will outnumber men in the American workplace.

Over the last 30 years, the number of working men has gone up 45 percent, from 46.3 million in 1965 to 67.4 million in 1995. During that same period, the number of working women jumped three times as fast, rising from 24.7 million to 57.5 million— an increase of 132 percent. In 1965, women held 35 percent of all jobs. By 1995, that swelled to 46 percent. And it's still going up. One reason: More and more women are solely responsible for a household.

Internal Revenue Service statistics show that the fastest growing group of tax-return filers is "heads of households." The category consists of single, unmarried or legally separated people supporting children or parents, but is made up mostly of single mothers. From 1970 to 1993, the latest year for which statistics are available, the number of head-of-household tax returns jumped from 3.6 million to 15.2 million—an increase of 322 percent. But a better measure of that growth is this: In 1970, heads of households accounted for 4.8 percent of all tax filers. By 1993, they represented 13.3 percent.

While single mothers and other heads of households are the fastest growing group, their *incomes* aren't growing at all. Their average adjusted gross income went from $6,100 in 1970 to $19,200 in 1993—an increase of 215 percent. That lagged far behind the inflation rate of 272 percent for the period. So single mothers today are worse off than the single mothers of 1970.

The inevitable result of all these factors: Nearly twice as many adult women as men are below the poverty level. For 1995, the poverty levels were: one person, $7,761; two persons, $9,935; three persons, $12,156, and four persons, $15,570. In all, 14.1 million women over the age of 18 were classified as living in poverty in 1994, compared with 8.6 million men. In addition, 15.3 million children lived below the poverty line. Perhaps more telling, the incomes of another 28.5 million women were only 25 percent above the poverty point.

What this means, of course, is that an ever-increasing number of American children are growing up in poverty. In 1994, more than 15 million children lived below the poverty line. That was up from 13 million the decade before, in 1984.

At the other end of the age spectrum, the outlook for retirement is no better. While there are more working women, the longtime promise of a secure pension has been canceled. The number of workers participating in a guaranteed monthly pension plan peaked in 1984 at 30.2 million. Their ranks have declined every year since, falling to 25.4 million in 1992, the latest year for which figures are available. These are plans that guarantee payment of a fixed sum each month at retirement and are backed by the federal Pension Benefit Guaranty Corp.

The picture, though, is far more bleak than those figures suggest. That's because the number of workers with a guaranteed pension, when measured as a percentage of all private wage and salary workers, fell from 39 percent in 1975 to 26 percent in 1992. If the 1975 percentage had remained unchanged, some 37 million workers today would be eligible for a guaranteed pension.

As for those women already collecting retirement benefits, their monthly checks, as you might expect, are well below those of men. The median pension benefit for 2.2 million women in 1994 was $3,000, or a little less than $60 a week. That was just 39 percent of the $7,800 pension benefit for 4.9 million men. And those figures represented the top-of-the-line pensions, the guaranteed, or defined benefit plans.

The Jobs of Tomorrow

Lest you think things are going to get better for women, take a careful look at the federal government's job projections for the period 1996 to 2005. These projections list the occupations that the Department of Labor says will show the greatest growth in numbers, and therefore offer the greatest opportunities for employment. Just what might these employment opportunities be in an era that Washington policy makers say, over and over, depends on our ability to create high-tech jobs?

The No. 1 occupation, with a projected increase of 562,000 jobs during these years: cashiers. In 1995, a total of 891,000 women were employed as cashiers in retail establishments. They filled 77 percent of those jobs. Their median weekly wage—meaning half earned more, half earned less—was $233. Or $12,116 a year. Men earned $13,312—or 10 percent more.

The No. 2 occupation, with an expected gain of 559,000 jobs: janitors and cleaners. In 1995, a total of 345,000 women were employed as janitors and cleaners. They filled 26 percent of those jobs. Their median weekly wage was $259. Or $13,468 a year. Men earned $15,964—or 19 percent more.

The No. 3 occupation, with a projected increase of 532,000 jobs: retail salespeople. In 1995, nearly 1.8 million women were employed as retail sales clerks. They filled 56 percent of those jobs. Their median weekly wage was $253. Or $13,156 a year. Men earned $18,980—or 44 percent more.

The No. 4 occupation, with an expected increase of 479,000 jobs: waiters and waitresses. In 1995, a total of 418,000 women were employed serving food. They filled 71 percent of those jobs. Their median weekly pay was $258. Or $13,416 a year. Men earned $16,328—or 22 percent more.

The No. 5 occupation, with a projected increase of 473,000 jobs: registered nurses. In 1995, a total of 1.3 million women worked as registered nurses. They filled 91 percent of those jobs. Their median weekly pay was $693. Or $36,036 a year. Men earned $37,180—or 3 percent more.

The No. 6 occupation, with a projected increase of 466,000 jobs, is general managers and top executives, and No. 7, expected to grow by 445,000, is systems analysts. While both are among the higher-paying occupations, both are dominated by men.

The No. 8 occupation, which is projected to generate 428,000 new jobs: home health aides. In 1995, a total of 238,000 people were employed as health aides. Of that number, 179,000—or 75 percent—were women. Their median weekly pay was $285. Or $14,820 a year. Men earned $17,940—or 21 percent more.

The No. 9 occupation, with a growth rate of 415,000 jobs: guards, a largely male, low-paying field.

Keeping Women Down

And finally, the No. 10 occupation, which is projected to produce 387,000 jobs: nursing aides, orderlies and attendants. A total of 1.202 million people worked in this field in 1995. Of that number, 1.069 million—or 89 percent—were women. Their median weekly pay was $275. Or $14,300 a year. Men earned $17,212—or 20 percent more.

Let us summarize: Six of the ten occupations that the U.S. government says will provide the largest number of jobs for America's high-tech future are in fields paying women annual wages that would qualify a family of four for the earned-income tax credit. Meaning they are working poor. Two of the occupations are in fields that pay good wages—general managers and top executives and systems analysts—but women hold comparatively few of those jobs. One is in a low-wage field—guards—where most workers are men. And the tenth—registered nurses—is the only one that pays middle-class wages to women. Under managed health care, it is destined to shrink.

It wasn't always this way. There was a time when the American economy offered reliable and permanent employment, with benefits, to women. Many of these jobs were in factories.

While manufacturing is traditionally thought of as a male bastion, women dominated the assembly lines in a wide range of industries where sewing, fastening, connecting, sorting, collating and processing were at the heart of the work. Because those were considered labor-intensive tasks, such industries were among the first to move offshore to cheaper labor markets.

Betty Lizana worked in such a business—the wire-harness industry. The name may mean little to you, but wire harnesses are one of the most common and indispensable items that are a part of everyday life. Found in products from automobiles to appliances, they range from the complex circuitry in the electrical system of your car to the power cord that connects your refrigerator to an electrical outlet.

Since 1990, wire-harness factories, in small towns and big cities, have closed as corporate executives moved production to low-wage countries or lost business to competitors who had made the move. National Industries eliminated the jobs of 370 workers who made automotive wire harnesses in Union Springs, Ala. In Wabash, Ind., 550 workers who made automotive wire harnesses for United Technologies Corp. were fired. About 300 people lost their jobs at General Dynamics Corp. in Fort Worth, Tex., where they were making aircraft wire harnesses. Circuit

Wise Corp. eliminated the jobs of 45 workers who made automotive wire harnesses in New Haven, Conn.

In many cases, corporations have relocated operations to Mexico, particularly along the U.S.-Mexico border, where the United States government, since 1965, has encouraged establishment of assembly plants to bolster the Mexican economy. U.S. companies sent materials across the border for assembly on the Mexican side, then brought assembled products back duty-free.

So many wire-assembly installations have sprung up that boosters of Mexico's industrialization program refer to the country as "harness heaven." Most of the jobs that have left the country were held by women.

"A man's hands just will not fit in the places they have to go to assemble a wire harness," says Patricia Wilbanks, who managed a wire-harness plant in Biloxi, Miss. Wilbanks worked at the same plant where Betty Lizana was the payroll officer. And like Lizana, she lost her job when the owner moved the plant to Mexico.

There was one other reason the wire-harness field attracted fewer men: low wages. "They are not going to get a man to do what is involved for the pay," Wilbanks said. The pay at the Biloxi plant, she said, averaged just over the minimum wage for female production workers—about $5 an hour. Even this was more than Fleck wanted to pay. In 1992, it sent the work to Mexico.

Plant closings are affecting both men and women, of course. But they are often harder, Wilbanks believes, on women. "Most of the time in the male positions the men can move their families to where the job is," she said. "A woman is not so willing, and a lot of times, if she is married, she is not going to be able to because her husband has a job. She can't just pack up and move her family unless she has a very understanding husband."

Wilbanks faced the relocation decision. Fleck offered her a job in a company plant in Mexico near El Paso, Tex. But she was reluctant to move. As a single mother raising a young son, she did not want to face the daily anxiety of being separated from her child by the U.S.-Mexico border. "If anything happened and the border closed, and I'm on the Mexican side, what do I do?" she said.

So she stayed in Mississippi. For months she looked for work, eventually finding what she described as a "pay-nothing" clerical job. Finally, she found her current job, as a secretary. At Fleck, she earned about $35,000 a year; today she earns $14,000.

Both Wilbanks and Lizana responded the same way when

asked their reaction to news accounts of a vibrant economy that is creating millions of good jobs. "People wonder where they are getting [that] information," Lizana said. "There just are no jobs. One of the construction companies building a casino advertised for 25 positions. . . . There was a huge traffic jam, people showing up to apply for those jobs. There must have been four or five times more people than there were jobs. . . . People want to work. There just aren't any jobs paying much. There is no manufacturing anymore. . . . It seems like the only people who advertise are K-Mart. But sometimes those are part-time jobs and they don't pay much, either."

As Wilbanks sees it, nothing is being done to treat the epidemic of plant closings and job loss. She also believes that most Americans do not realize fully what is happening. "I think if a lot of the American people realized what was going on, they would quit buying a lot of products," she said.

As for the ability of many middle-class Americans to earn a solid income in the years ahead, Wilbanks said she isn't hopeful. "I know I sound very pessimistic, but I just don't see it happening."

Rich People, Little People

Some 1,200 miles to the north of Patricia Wilbanks and Biloxi, Miss., are Tomasa Kershner and Williamsport, Pa. Like Wilbanks, Kershner lost her job in a manufacturing plant. And like Wilbanks, she frets about the future, especially for her son, who began his freshman year at Lock Haven State University in the fall of 1996.

"You want your kids to have something," she said. "I think of my son and what's going on and it's all very sad. They want to lower everyone's wages. They want just rich people and little people. There won't be a middle class."

In 1973 Kershner, a soft-spoken Texas native, went to work at a GTE plant in Williamsport, where the company manufactured electronic components for the military. She earned about $3 an hour, or nearly twice the minimum wage of $1.60 at the time. Twenty-one years later, in December 1994, she was making $11 an hour—but that was soon to come to an end.

Kershner's troubles began in early 1993, when GTE sold its North American lighting division, which included the Williamsport plant, to Osrams Sylvania. Sylvania was interested in GTE's lighting-products plants, not the defense-related facilities. So in September 1993, several former GTE executives acquired the

Williamsport plant and renamed the business Primus Technologies Corp.

At the time, the company's contract with the International Association of Machinists union, of which Kershner was a member, had a little more than a year to go. Kershner recalled what happened next: With the contract due to expire in December 1994, the union sought to continue to work under the old agreement. But the new owners presented a take-it-or-leave-it package that called for a 30 percent wage cut (to eight dollars an hour for Kershner), a 25 percent increase in health insurance payments, and the loss of some vacation time.

Out of 53 employees, 13 went back to work under the new contract terms and 40 struck the plant. Primus hired replacement workers, and the striking workers picketed from Christmas 1994 until March 1996. At one point, the Primus owners offered to put the striking workers on a preferential hiring list for new jobs that would pay six dollars an hour.

"At six dollars," Kershner said, "you can't make it. They want the wages down, but your utilities keep going up. Taxes are going up. Property taxes are going up. None of the prices are coming down. There's got to be a reason for this." Then she answered her own question: "I think it's a lot of greed."

Except for a brief stint as a temporary postal worker over Christmas 1995, Kershner's income the past 16 months came largely from walking a picket line—$100 a week. That ended in March 1996, when the union ceased to exist at Primus.

Kershner herself spent months looking for a job that paid more than the minimum wage. "It really takes two people, with the bills we have," she said. Finally, in April 1996, she found work that matched what she earned at Primus—for one day a week. As a substitute rural postal carrier, she delivers mail on Saturdays and whenever the regular carrier is ill or on vacation. In the meantime, she continues the search for yet another job.

"I'm trying to find part-time [work]," she said, "where they would be flexible to my schedule [with the Postal Service]. Sometimes, they call you the day before [to deliver mail]."

As in so many small towns and medium-sized cities across the country, the options of out-of-work people here are severely limited. In that respect, Williamsport, a city that became famous as the home of Little League baseball, is typical.

There used to be plenty of jobs. Back in the 1950s, Williamsport, located in Lycoming County in central Pennsylvania, billed itself as "the Main Street of industry and distribution in the United States." The area boasted 111 manufacturing plants employing upward of 15,000 people.

That was then. This is now. Widespread plant closings and layoffs have blighted the town. Between 1960 and 1990, according to U.S. Census data, nearly half of Williamsport's manufacturing jobs disappeared, and its population dropped from 42,000 to 31,900. Factory employment fell from 6,171 to 3,340. Men were hardest hit, losing 2,190 jobs. Women accounted for 641 of the layoffs. More significant, the overall number of jobs in town held by men plunged 31 percent, from 9,874 to 6,850. In all, 3,024 jobs held by men vanished.

At the same time, jobs held by women edged up 1 percent, from 6,097 to 6,168. As a result, by 1990 women made up 47 percent of the workforce in Williamsport. That was up from 38 percent in 1960, which was up from 34 percent in 1950. Like so many other places where manufacturing died, women became the breadwinners. Invariably, the jobs were at lower pay than the men had made.

Since the 1990 census, jobs, especially good-paying jobs, have continued to disappear in the Williamsport area, many as the result of cheap imports that have flooded into the country under Washington's "free trade" policies. C.A. Reed Inc., a manufacturer of paper and party products—crepe paper, napkins, paper hats and plates—closed, throwing 325 people out of work. Those workers had earned $10 to $15 an hour. Sylvania closed two plants that made flashbulbs and electrical components. About 500 jobs were eliminated. Stroehmann Bakeries closed its main plant, putting 120 people out of work.

The list continues. Erman Ryveld's Son Corp., 160 workers. High Steel Structures Inc., 136 workers. Footwear Temps Inc., 130 workers. Wundies, 210 workers. Woolrich, 340 workers. Philips ECG, 48 workers. Tampella Power Corp., 120 workers. Muncy Building Enterprise, 79 workers. With few exceptions, the surviving companies are not hiring or do not pay wages that match those that closed.

Tomasa Kershner says that other former Primus workers have found jobs, but "not good-paying jobs—minimum-wage jobs." And what about those still working at Primus for six dollars an hour? "I talked to one of our ex-union members that still works there," she said, "and he told me that a lot of these people also have a second job. . . . That's the only way you can really make ends meet. . . . [People] are working more hours and they're not getting as much pay. And they're at work all the time. It's really sad that people don't realize, yeah, you can create jobs that pay six dollars, but you can't live on that. You can't."

Richard Hritzko has watched, on a much broader scale, what Tomasa Kershner has experienced. He's the director of the Job Training Partnership Act in Williamsport, which provides training for displaced workers in Lycoming and Clinton Counties.

"The majority of the jobs we have lost have been the well-paid jobs," Hritzko said. "What's available for people are jobs starting out at minimum wage. We lost a lot of good, skilled jobs. These were secure jobs. The people were hired right after high school. It's hard to tell them, when they were making $15 an hour, not to turn their noses up at $7. And that's sad. Many of the jobs are service-oriented, computer and lower-paying. And they are competing with graduates right out of high school."

There are, to be sure, some exceptions. Kellogg Co. and Shop-Vac Corp. have come to Williamsport in recent years, offering some manufacturing jobs. And there is one booming service-sector business: rehabilitation centers for drug and alcohol addicts, largely from Philadelphia. Over the last 15 years or so, about 3,000 substance abusers and their families have moved to Williamsport to undergo government-funded treatment for their addictions and to live in halfway houses or recovery homes, forever changing the character of the bucolic community.

While manufacturing jobs have dried up in Williamsport, employment in one other occupation has soared, shooting up 737 percent, from 142 workers in 1960 to 879 in 1990. It's the food-service industry—waiters and waitresses, cooks, busboys. The pay is usually minimum wage or slightly above. And most of the workers are women.

The Collapse of Apparel

On the list of Williamsport-area shuttered plants were two operated by Woolrich Inc., the sportswear manufacturer. Jobs eliminated: 340. Nothing remarkable there—except it's a story that has been repeated hundreds upon hundreds of times over the last two decades, as one apparel manufacturer after another shut down or laid off workers when production was moved offshore, to the Caribbean, Latin America and Asia.

In that, the apparel industry is just one more entry in a catalog of American businesses that have disappeared, or are in the process of disappearing. Recall shoes, microwave ovens, television sets, telephones, carnations, machine tools, flatware, roses and cellular telephones?

What sets it apart from all the others is that the large number of casualties are mostly women. From 1973—the year of peak employment in the apparel industry—to 1995, the number of jobs held by women plunged 39 percent, from 1,158,900 to 702,700. The 456,200 jobs that vanished was the equivalent of wiping out every woman's job in the cities of Miami, Charlotte, Cincinnati, Pittsburgh, Milwaukee and Portland, Ore.

As has been the case with most all other industries, the people in Washington said it couldn't happen, that domestic manufacturers would survive the waves of imported clothing. That was the view that prevailed back in 1987, when some textile and apparel makers sought, unsuccessfully, to curb the rising volume of imports. During a congressional hearing, Philip M. Crane, the Republican representative from Illinois, summed up the opposition this way: "There was a loss [in] 1986 over 1985 in the apparel industry of approximately 10,000 jobs. But that is certainly not an indication of a severe dislocation, and I would suggest that the industry . . . has already come out of its worse plight and is making remarkable progress."

If that sounds eerily like those other Washington pronouncements on shoes, roses, flatware and microwave ovens—all industries that were portrayed as doing nicely in the years before they collapsed—that's because it is. Since Rep. Crane dismissed concerns over a 10,000-job loss, 12 times that number of jobs (126,000) have disappeared. And more are going with each passing year.

In interviews across the country, the authors talked to women who once worked in apparel factories in cities and small towns from Pennsylvania to Mississippi, from Virginia to California. With few exceptions, they related similar stories. They talked about the work, which was always hard. They talked about production schedules, which were difficult to meet. But they were a community inside those plants. And the pay, while not good, was steady. The benefits, while modest at best, at least assured them that their families had health coverage.

One by one, with startling regularity, these plants are closing, putting out of work women who had long depended on them for a paycheck. The roll call reads like a Norman Rockwell review of small-town America.

In Linden, Ala., Linden Sportswear eliminated the jobs of 250 workers who made women's sportswear. In Wynne, Ark., Reltoc Manufacturing Co. fired 250 workers who made men's slacks. In Conyers, Ga., USA Enterprises laid off 450 workers who made men's pants. In Lancaster, Ky., Cowden Manufacturing Co. let go 1,370 workers who made denim pants.

In Federalsburg, Md., Fed Sportswear eliminated the jobs of 90 workers who made ladies sportswear. In Ruleville, Miss., Noel Industries eliminated the jobs of 500 workers who made jeans. In Albemarle, N.C., J.E. Morgan Apparel eliminated the jobs of 225 workers who made underwear. In Temple, Okla., Haggar Apparel Co. eliminated the jobs of 200 workers who made men's suits and slacks.

Many communities have been confronted with multiple apparel-plant closings or layoffs. In Pittston, Pa., Lori Sports eliminated the jobs of 50 workers; Andy Fashions fired 117; an additional 32 lost their jobs at Sallies Fashions; and Pittston Fashion fired 116. All these workers made women's dresses.

The closings are affecting everyone in the industry, from those who have spent a lifetime sewing to those who have worked their way up to management.

Until 1992, Linda Crane was the manager of a 150-person apparel plant in the small Mississippi town of Fulton, population 3,500. Today, she is a nurse at a 130-bed nursing home.

Crane, born and raised in Mississippi, spent 11 years working her way up the management ladder at the Denton Mills plant in Fulton. Maker of Dr. Denton sleepwear, a familiar name to generations of parents, the Fulton plant was one of a half-dozen facilities that the New York–based manufacturer operated in the South.

Crane, who started in production, moved up to personnel manager and was named plant manager in 1989. Along the way, she and her husband, Roger, a junior high school social studies teacher, raised a son and a daughter.

For many years, the plant provided dependable employment for women in the Fulton area. Its most appealing benefit was a health plan, which Linda and Roger Crane considered superior to the school district's plan that covered Roger. "We just felt good about the place," Linda Crane later recalled. But over time, Denton Mills, like other domestic manufacturers, found itself fighting a losing battle as low-cost imports—coming in under Washington's open-door trade policies—began overwhelming the American market.

Keeping Women Down

Even wages in Mississippi, the nation's poorest state, were no match for cheap foreign labor. To cut costs, the company opened two plants in Mexico in the 1980s and shifted work there from Mississippi. By 1990, Linda Crane sensed that her plant's days were numbered. More and more work was being transferred to Mexico. Production orders were erratic. The parent company was in turmoil.

The company didn't tell employees its plans. "But it didn't take anybody with a high I.Q. to figure out that something was fixin' to happen," Linda Crane said. "And I said, 'We better get our ducks in a row because I've got a feeling they're [going] to close this place down.'"

The Cranes reviewed their financial situation and decided they'd better do a little belt-tightening to prepare for that day. They stepped up payments on their house and retired the mortgage within two years. They stopped making major purchases. It was a big change in their lives.

"When I started work there, we were not afraid to go out and buy something on a payment plan," Crane recalled. "We felt secure enough that that job would always be there. But the last few years, we got to where we were afraid to go out and buy anything on long-term."

Crane began to explore her options. She always had been interested in nursing, and that was a field the federal government was touting as a future source of jobs. To see if she had any aptitude, she took a night-school class in anatomy and physiology at a nearby community college. She said her husband kidded her about tackling such a difficult academic course for starters. "He told me, 'Boy. You don't wade off into the river. You just jump in head first,'" Crane said.

When she talked about resigning to go back to school full-time, a company manager prevailed on her to stay. "'Linda, please don't quit right now,'" Crane said the woman manager told her. "'We need you here.' I couldn't understand why she was so persistent that I stay on." It soon became clear. The company would close the Fulton plant soon and, as Linda Crane later saw it, "did not want to have to worry about replacing me with another plant manager."

When the shutdown came in early 1991, it was too late for Crane to be admitted to nursing classes. "They had 500 applicants that spring," she recalled. "They take in only 125. It was too late to get my papers approved. I talked to everyone and I couldn't get in. Here I am. I've lost my job to foreign imports. I've got a federally funded program that will send me to school, and I can't even get in a program in my county."

She was so determined that she enrolled in the next closest community college, which was in Hamilton, Ala., 35 miles from of her home in Golden, Miss. For 15 months, Crane commuted 70 miles daily to and from Hamilton. It was a difficult time for the Cranes. Linda Crane received unemployment pay, but it barely covered her expenses. "The hardest time was while she was in school," Roger Crane recalled. "All that expense and on that little income. It was tough."

But she stuck with her plan, and in November 1992, she graduated from nursing school. The following January, she took a temporary job at an Alabama hospital. It was 70 miles a day round-trip by car. But at least she was back in the workforce.

Two months later, a nursing home nearby called and hired her to work the third shift, 11 P.M. to 7 A.M. Roger Crane remembers this period well: "I never saw her."

Linda Crane has made the transition to a new career that many Americans are having to make these days. Eventually, she went on the afternoon shift, and then days. She likes the new job, the people she works with and the sense of helping others. But the family has lost ground financially.

As a mid-level manager, she earned more than $30,000 a year. Her first job as a nurse paid $6 an hour—about $13,000 a year. Gradually, her pay rate has gone up to $12 an hour—still less than what she earned five years ago.

Though she and her husband have adapted, they worry about the future for working Americans. The transfer of jobs out of the United States, they fear, is undercutting middle-class Americans' ability to earn a good living.

"I don't begrudge anyone in Mexico getting work," says Linda Crane. "But what is it doing to us? We have got to make a good wage to pay our own bills. I feel for the Mexican people, but we have to think of ourselves, too."

"It's not our fault the cost of living is as much as it is," says Roger Crane. "I know that we have probably talked ourselves right out of a job, demanding higher wages. But I don't know how we can make ends meet and pay our bills if we can't demand a higher wage. I can't help but wonder: What are people going to do?"

At the Top, a Winner

Not all women are losing ground in the apparel industry. Some, in fact, are making quite a nice living. Like Linda J. Wachner. She's the 50-year-old chairman of the board, president and chief executive officer of Warnaco Group Inc., and chairman of the board and chief executive officer of Authentic Fitness Corp., two apparel makers.

The New York-based Warnaco Group designs, manufactures and markets women's intimate apparel, including such brand-names as Warner's, Olga, Valentino Intimo, Calvin Klein. By its own reckoning, the company accounts for 30 percent of all women's bra sales in the United States. It also sells a range of menswear, including shirts by Hathaway and Chaps by Ralph Lauren.

Authentic Fitness, headquartered in Commerce, Calif., designs, manufactures and sells swimwear and activewear under Speedo, Catalina, Anne Cole, Sporting Life and Sandcastle brand names, among others.

Many products sold by Warnaco and Authentic Fitness are manufactured abroad. Warnaco operates its own plants in Mexico, Honduras, Costa Rica, the Dominican Republic and Ireland. Both subcontract production to other companies overseas.

A look at U.S. Customs records reporting foreign shipments to the two companies reads like a global Geography 101 course. Consider a sampling from two months, May and June 1996. These are shipments of clothing to be sold in the United States under the various Warnaco and Authentic Fitness labels.

Men's cotton shirts from Dubai, the United Arab Emirates, and shirts from Alexandria, Egypt, arrived in New York. Head straps from China and ladies' silk woven panties and cotton knit panties from Hong Kong arrived in Seattle.

Men's jackets from Colombo, Sri Lanka; silicone swim caps, garments and Olympic thongs from China; Speedo sunglasses from Kaohsiung, Taiwan; garments from Jakarta, Indonesia; garments from Singapore; woven jackets from Hong Kong; and ready-made garments from Taipei, Taiwan, all arrived in Oakland.

Wearing apparel from Puerto Cortes, Honduras, arrived in Miami. Cotton fabric from Santos, Brazil, arrived in Philadelphia. Sleepwear from Manila, the Philippines, and cotton garments from Karachi, Pakistan, arrived in Long Beach. Ladies wearing apparel from China, jackets and ladies wearing apparel from Hong Kong, and fabric from Kobe, Japan, all arrived in Los Angeles.

So how goes the apparel business? Let's look at the larger of the two companies—Warnaco. For the three years 1993–95, Warnaco reported revenue of $2.4 billion and profits of $134 million. Its U.S. income tax payments, according to reports filed with the U.S. Securities and Exchange Commission, came to about $10 million, giving Warnaco an effective tax rate of 7 percent. Which means that a company with annual sales approaching $1 billion paid federal income taxes at a rate below that paid by individuals and families with incomes between $25,000 and $30,000.

You might want to view Warnaco's low tax bill from another vantage point—the pay of its chief executive. Linda Wachner's salary and bonuses for the years 1993–95 added up to $11.4 million. Or more money than Warnaco paid in U.S. income tax.

The salary and bonuses, naturally, do not include stock options and other stock deals. In 1995 alone, for example, she received a salary and bonus of $4.8 million, plus $6 million in stock, for a total compensation package of nearly $11 million. In addition, her overall stockholdings in Warnaco and Authentic Fitness in 1996 were worth upward of $200 million.

All of which helps explain why Wachner fascinates Graef S. Crystal, an adjunct professor at the University of California at Berkeley Business School and an authority on executive compensation who compiles lists of underpaid and overpaid executives. In 1992, Crystal reported that "in these days of equal pay for equal work, it gives me great pleasure to announce that Linda J. Wachner, the 45-year-old CEO [chief executive officer] of the Warnaco Group Inc., passed all but two men to end up as the second runnerup for the most overpaid CEO of the year. Indeed, if you make the appropriate adjustments for her company's size and performance, she would even beat out the two men." In 1996, Wachner again headed Crystal's list of most overpaid chief executives.

Oh, by the way, just in case you missed it, at the same time Wachner's take-home pay soared into the millions, her company reduced the take-home pay of the workers at one of its plants.

In May 1996, Warnaco announced that it intended to close the plant in Waterville, Maine, where Hathaway shirts have been manufactured for more than 150 years.

The closing stunned workers. Michael Cavanaugh, assistant

manager for the northeast region of the Union of Needletrades, Industrial and Textile Employees, the union that represents Hathaway employees, explained why: "The amount of production went up from an average of 2,000 dozen a week to 3,000 dozen a week, and the cost of that production went down almost in half [through all of 1995 and until May 1996]. So there was some rather remarkable productivity improvements. . . and that was one of the major reasons why people were so shocked when this announcement came in May, that, you know, 'thanks very much, but good-bye.'"

After the announcement and a demonstration by union members, Maine politicians and investors explored the possibility of a private group acquiring the Hathaway brand name so the plant could be kept open. Wachner promised to keep the facility running until the fall of 1996.

Of the 450 people who work at the Waterville plant, about 90 percent are women—many single mothers. Their average pay is $8.00 an hour. That's $16,640 a year—a sum that qualifies families for the earned-income tax credit. Remember the credit, designed for the working poor?

The $16,640, naturally, is based on a 40-hour week. After Wachner said she would keep the plant open until an investment group could be formed to buy it, she cut the work week to 30 hours. That's $12,480 a year, which not only qualifies families for the earned-income tax credit, but places some of them in the official category of people the U.S. government designates as living in poverty.

Whatever number you pick, $12,480 or $16,640, think of it this way: Linda Wachner's $10 million compensation package for 1995—salary, bonus and stock—exceeds the total wages of the 400 women workers at her Waterville plant.

CHAPTER SIX

The Lobbyists

The China Lobby Moves In

Doral Cooper and Ronald Holley are from different worlds. She lives in Washington, D.C., and is a former trade official in the Reagan administration who used the experience gained in her government job to become a high-powered, high-paid and highly successful lobbyist. He lives in Batesville, Miss., a community of 6,400 in the northwest corner of the nation's poorest state, where he grew up, graduated from high school and went to work cutting cloth for the area's largest employer. In 1994, the worlds of Cooper and Holley collided.

At the time, she represented an alliance of big-name retailers who wanted to block efforts by a few members of Congress seeking to limit certain kinds of cheap imports. He wasn't represented by anybody. Except Congress.

She won a little, lost a little. He lost everything.

When the dust settled on Capitol Hill, Congress did what Doral Cooper, her fellow lobbyists and the big businesses they represented wanted—at least temporarily. It kept intact—for two more years—a trade-law provision that allowed ever more imports of clothing from low-wage countries.

That was just enough time for Holley to lose his job, when his employer of 20 years, Fruit of the Loom, closed its Batesville plant, laid off all 850 workers and moved production offshore. At the time, Holley earned $10.25 an hour, a little more than $21,000 a year. The bottom end of middle-class America. On this point, Holley poses a question that's on the minds of many working Americans: "How can someone who makes $10.25 an hour compete with somebody making 30 cents an hour? We can't live on that. How can you call that equal?"

How Indeed? After corporate executives and Washington policy makers, no group has played so large a role in eliminating jobs in America as trade lobbyists. These are the people who in many cases help to shape the government's policies on international trade. They represent U.S. multinational corporations, foreign-owned companies, foreign governments and other special interests.

Lobbying, to be sure, is hardly new to Washington. Attempts to influence American policy are as old as the republic. What is different today is the extent of those efforts, the huge increase in the number of lobbyists and the impact they are having on American workers.

As the number of trade lobbyists has gone up, the U.S. trade deficit has ballooned and the economic well-being of middle-class America has gone down. Take the 10 biggest foreign exporters to the United States in 1995: Canada, China, France, Germany, Japan, Mexico, Singapore, South Korea, Taiwan and the United Kingdom.

Twenty-six years ago, in 1970, the United States had a trade *surplus* with five of them. There was no trade with China, the deficit with Taiwan was small ($22 million), and the only serious deficits were with Canada ($2 billion), Japan ($1.2 billion) and Germany ($386 million). That year, 157 foreign agents were registered to lobby the U.S. government on behalf of those 10 countries.

By 1995, the number had jumped to 554— an increase of 253 percent. And the U.S. merchandise trade deficit with the 10 countries had shot up 7,950 percent—from $2 billion in 1970 to $161 billion in 1995. To put that growth in perspective: If the minimum wage had gone up at the same rate, a beginning hamburger flipper at McDonald's would earn $129 an hour. That's a quarter-million dollars a year.

But let's return to the real world, where there is a correlation between the successes of lobbyists for foreign producers and the falling standard of living of American workers. As the trade deficit soared during those years, the average annual wage of workers in American manufacturing, calculated in 1995 dollars, fell from $27,230 in 1970 to $26,650 in 1995. Even worse than the drop in wages was the job loss, as imported products replaced American-made goods in the marketplace. Several million jobs were wiped out due to the trade deficit with just those 10 countries.

What has been bad for American workers has been very good for foreign producers and U.S. multinational companies, which have helped frame the government's free-trade policies. They have profited handsomely by convincing Washington policy makers to trim or eliminate tariffs and ease or remove other trade barriers on imported goods. To gain access to the people who write the trade regulations, foreign interests buy the services of insiders who once did those jobs themselves: former government officials turned lobbyists.

The Japanese, of course, wrote the book on lobbying in Washington a generation ago. When Japan began exporting to the United States in large quantities, Japanese corporations, trade associations and government agencies retained powerful Washington law firms and consultants to represent them before Congress and the regulatory agencies.

Even today, Japan dominates the Justice Department's list of registered foreign agents. They range from large trade groups, such as the Japan Automobile Manufacturers Association, the Japan Auto Parts Industries Association and the Japan Iron and Steel Exporters Association, to huge corporations, such as Mitsubishi, Fujitsu and Hitachi. In 1991, the most recent year for which figures are available, the Japanese spent $83.9 million in consulting, public relations and legal fees for lobbying and related activities. That was up 577 percent from 1980, when Japan spent $12.4 million. In 1950, before making the run at the American market, Japan spent a mere $150.

Today, what the Japanese perfected is being replicated by others, from the smallest country in Latin America (El Salvador) to the largest in Asia (China). Officially, the Department of Justice says a total of 1,111 foreign principals—these are foreign governments, corporations, trade associations and others with foreign ties—have registered agents in the United States. No one knows precisely how many lobbyists actually work for them. The number ranges from as few as one to upward of 50 lobbyists per foreign principal. Which means that more than 10,000 lobbyists are working the nation's capital on behalf of foreign-owned corporations, foreign governments and U.S. multinational corporations with a stake in foreign countries.

To better understand the extent of the lobbying influence—and the consequences for people like Ronald Holley and you—consider the achievements of the newest player in town: the People's Republic of China. The Chinese may be having difficulty moving to a market economy, letting political prisoners out of jail, embracing Western-style ideas of democracy and tol-

Growing Foreign Influence

Registered agents
representing the
top 10 U.S. trading
partners (Canada,
China, France,
Germany, Japan,
Mexico, Singapore,
South Korea,
Taiwan and the
United Kingdom).

In **1970**

there were
157
foreign
agents.

In **1995**

there were
554
foreign
agents.

More Foreign Lobbyists Means More Dollars Flow Overseas

With the rise in lobbyists came an
increase in the U.S. trade deficit with
these 10 countries, from $2 billion in
1970 to $161 billion in 1995.

erating free expression. But in one important area, China has made the transition from the old Communist state to a sophisticated modern power in record time: influence-peddling in Washington.

Look no further than China's handling of its most important bread-and-butter trade issue—preservation of its preferential trading status with the United States. Every year, China's status comes up for renewal, and every year the Chinese have been bad boys. They have locked up and tortured political opponents. They have sold the ingredients for making poison gas to the Iranians and missiles to Pakistan. They have used prison labor to manufacture goods sold in stores across this country.

The United States vows punitive action unless China cleans up its act. The Chinese stiffen and warn the United States about interfering in their internal affairs. When relations worsen, the United States says it will impose sanctions against China and releases a list of products on which high tariffs will be levied. Retailers and importers howl. The media churn out stories about how the high duties will jack up prices of consumer goods, from toys to silk shirts. And then, when a rupture with China seems possible, its trading status, miraculously, is renewed.

"I have decided to extend unconditional most-favored-nation trade status to China," President Clinton said on May 20, 1996. "Revoking MFN, and, in effect, severing our economic ties to China, would drive us back into a period of mutual isolation and recrimination that would harm America's interests, not advance them."

The truth is, for all the sound and fury coming out of Washington every year, China's MFN status, which allows it to export its products to the United States at the lowest possible tariffs, was never at risk. Not in 1996. Not in 1995. Not in any year before that. That's because China and a host of American multinational corporations with their own self-interest at stake have created an extraordinarily powerful lobby, whose views on trade prevail year in and year out in Washington.

How did the Chinese achieve such a favorable trade position in so short a time? They began the same way Japan did—hiring lobbyists and channeling American decision making along lines beneficial to China. But there was one big difference. When the Japanese began exporting in volume, they had few allies here. The Chinese already have powerful corporate advocates in Washington.

The Lobbyists

General Motors and Ford, which fought Japanese imports of autos and auto parts for years, are among China's most ardent supporters. Like many American multinationals, they see China as both an expanding market for U.S. goods and as a potential manufacturing site—one where U.S. labor costs could be replaced by low-cost Chinese labor. So it's in their interest that Chinese-made goods be allowed entry to the United States with low tariffs. Indeed, because of low duties, imports from China have soared in the last decade, rising from $3.8 billion in 1985 to $15.2 billion in 1990 to $45.5 billion in 1995.

Proponents of trade with China are fond of saying that China, with its 1.2 billion people, will need many goods as the nation develops, meaning an expanding market for American companies. "China is becoming the largest market in the world for almost any product you can name: airplanes, construction equipment, consumer products, and virtually everything else that's produced and marketed," says Robert E. Allen, chairman of AT&T.

So far, though, the U.S.-China trade has been decidedly one-sided. The Chinese are selling to us, but buying much less in return, with increasingly adverse consequences for Americans. While cheaper Chinese-made products may give consumers a price break, the ongoing erosion of better-paying manufacturing jobs, aggravated by imports, is having a ripple effect, driving down wages and the standard of living of middle-class Americans.

But what is economically unhealthy for the nation as a whole is very good for the multinationals. Unlike small and medium-size companies that manufacture here, multinationals have operations around the world and export goods from those overseas facilities back to the United States. Which is why, when China's favorable trade status is up for annual review, the Chinese can count on American multinationals to be their strongest supporters for low tariffs.

Although MFN comes up annually, to understand just how powerful the China lobby has become, let's go back to the 1994 campaign. That year, by all accounts, China seemed destined to lose its favorable trading position.

In running for president in 1992, Bill Clinton had criticized George Bush for extending MFN status for China, saying Bush had "coddled" the Chinese dictators. After he was elected, Clinton extended MFN in June 1993, but, he insisted, only on one condition. Said Clinton: "I am signing an executive order . . . extending most-favored-nation status for China for 12 months. Whether I extend MFN next year, however, will depend upon whether China makes significant progress in improving its human-rights record. . . . I intend to put the full weight of the executive behind this order."

Clinton said the Chinese would have to stop using prison labor in their factories, allow freedom of expression by religious minorities, and provide an accounting of political opponents imprisoned by the Communist regime. In the year that followed, China made little progress on these points. If Clinton was to follow the spirit of his directive, it seemed he would have little choice but to revoke MFN status.

That's when the China lobby swung into action. The coalition of *Fortune* 500 companies that teamed up with agents of the People's Republic of China was as influential a lobby as Washington ever sees. In addition to the efforts of individual multinationals, such as AT&T, Motorola, General Electric, TRW Inc., Honeywell, Chrysler, Digital Equipment, Kodak and Boeing, powerful business consortiums raised large sums of money to underwrite the lobbying assault.

Typical of the amount raised: The United States–China Business Council, made up largely of some of America's biggest multinational corporations, took in $1.4 million in 1994 alone. The purpose, as set forth in an official filing with the House of Representatives: "Oppose legislation which would harm U.S. business's competitive position in China and/or harm bilateral trading relations." The contributors included Caterpillar Inc., TRW, Philip Morris Companies Inc., Wal-Mart Inc., Coca-Cola International, Xerox Corp., Deere & Co., Johnson & Johnson, Eastman Kodak Co., Air Products & Chemicals Inc., Bristol-Myers Squibb Co., Anheuser-Busch International Inc., DuPont China, Procter & Gamble Co., Whirlpool, Alcoa, Hewlett-Packard Co. and The Limited.

Another pro-China business lobby, the Emergency Committee for American Trade, built a war chest from cash contributions by some of America's most highly compensated executives. Tapping corporate chieftains for personal donations of $11,000 on average, the Emergency Committee raised $612,500 in 1994 from givers who included:

- John J. Murphy, chairman and CEO, Dresser Industries,

whose 1994 salary and bonus totaled $1.7 million—or 45 times median family income that year.

- Duane L. Burnham, chairman and CEO, Abbott Laboratories, 1994 salary and bonus, $1.6 million—or 61 times the average wage of a manufacturing worker.
- Leslie H. Wexner, chairman of the board and CEO, The Limited, 1994 salary and bonus of $2 million—or 131 times the income of a family of four at the poverty level.
- David W. Johnson, president and CEO, Campbell Soup Co., 1994 salary and bonus, $1.8 million—or 160 times the average wage of a retail sales clerk.
- Edwin L. Artzt, chairman of the board and CEO of Procter & Gamble, 1994 salary and bonus, $3.2 million—or 366 times the annual earnings of a minimum-wage worker.

The lobbying blitz that followed was described by one lawmaker, Rep. Frank Wolf (R., Va.), as bordering on a "feeding frenzy of lawyers." Beginning in the winter of 1994, lobbyists swarmed over Washington. They conducted briefing sessions at the capitol. They brought corporate executives to Capitol Hill to personally lobby lawmakers about the stakes. They mobilized letter-writing campaigns. And they distributed studies that purported to show the high cost to the American economy of revoking most-favored-nation status for China.

The type of pressure brought to bear was illustrated at a House Ways and Means subcommittee hearing on February 24, 1994, when one corporate speaker after another warned of the "devastating" consequences if MFN were revoked. Typical of the alarms sounded was one issued by Fermin Cuza, a vice president of Mattel Inc., the toy maker, who said higher import duties would have a "severe impact" on American importers, some of whom "would be quickly forced out of business." Higher tariffs, he added, would "raise retail prices by approximately 25 percent, at a minimum, [and] also put at risk many of the 32,000 U.S. jobs in the U.S. toy industry."

In addition to help from the U.S. multinationals, the People's Republic fielded its own impressive team. The Washington office of Cleveland's Jones, Day, Reavis & Pogue, the nation's third-largest law firm, represented the embassy of the People's Republic. The Washington office of Mudge Rose Guthrie Alexander &

Ferdon, the New York law firm of former president Richard M. Nixon, represented the China National Import/Export Corporation. Rollins International Inc., the consulting company of Edward Rollins, the former aide to Ronald Reagan and GOP political consultant, was the registered foreign agent for the China Chamber of International Commerce and the municipality of Nanjing, China.

One set of numbers shows how far China has come in the lobbying game. In 1970, China did not have a single lobbyist in Washington. Today, no fewer than 19 law firms and consultants, many of them representing multiple Chinese clients, have registered as foreign agents for the People's Republic. And, of course, that doesn't include the U.S. multinationals who can be called on when needed.

Confronted by this powerful lobby, Clinton backed away from his demand that China reform. Although China continued to jail political opponents, repress religious minorities and use prison labor to make products for sale in the United States, on May 26, 1994, the president announced: "I have decided that the United States should renew most-favored-nation trading status toward China."

While acknowledging there were "continuing human rights abuses," the president said that continuing trade benefits represented the "best opportunity" both to solve the human-rights questions and advance the U.S.'s "other interests with China."

Bejing not only had triumphed; it got more than it bargained for. In extending MFN, Clinton said that in the future, renewing China's trade status would not be contingent on progress on human rights. With that major stumbling block off the table, it has been renewed ever since.

Why does it matter that the China lobby won?

- Between 1986 and 1995, the U.S. trade deficit with China exploded from $1.6 billion to $33.9 billion—a 2,019 percent increase. If your credit-card bills had gone up at the same rate, a family that owed $3,500 in 1986 would now owe $74,000—plus about $13,000 a year in interest.
- The imports that caused those deficits eliminated an estimated 680,000 American jobs. Picture two states, Vermont and North Dakota; now picture every working man and woman in those states—630,000—suddenly

162

U.S. Trade With China in 1995

Which Is the Third-World Country?

Top 20 in each category in millions of dollars.

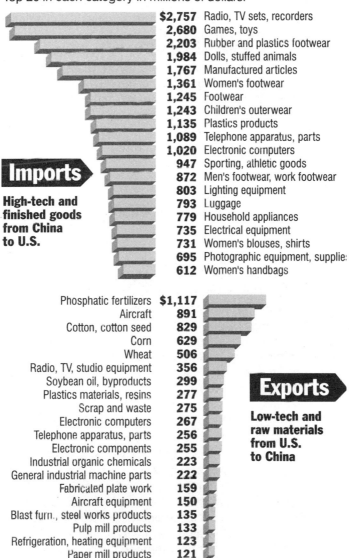

Imports

High-tech and finished goods from China to U.S.

$2,757	Radio, TV sets, recorders
2,680	Games, toys
2,203	Rubber and plastics footwear
1,984	Dolls, stuffed animals
1,767	Manufactured articles
1,361	Women's footwear
1,245	Footwear
1,243	Children's outerwear
1,135	Plastics products
1,089	Telephone apparatus, parts
1,020	Electronic computers
947	Sporting, athletic goods
872	Men's footwear, work footwear
803	Lighting equipment
793	Luggage
779	Household appliances
735	Electrical equipment
731	Women's blouses, shirts
695	Photographic equipment, supplies
612	Women's handbags

Phosphatic fertilizers	**$1,117**
Aircraft	**891**
Cotton, cotton seed	**829**
Corn	**629**
Wheat	**506**
Radio, TV, studio equipment	**356**
Soybean oil, byproducts	**299**
Plastics materials, resins	**277**
Scrap and waste	**275**
Electronic computers	**267**
Telephone apparatus, parts	**256**
Electronic components	**255**
Industrial organic chemicals	**223**
General industrial machine parts	**222**
Fabricated plate work	**159**
Aircraft equipment	**150**
Blast furn., steel works products	**135**
Pulp mill products	**133**
Refrigeration, heating equipment	**123**
Paper mill products	**121**

Exports

Low-tech and raw materials from U.S. to China

SOURCE: U.S. Department of Commerce

unemployed. Cancel all their wages, more than $11 billion a year, and taxes paid on that income. Forever.

- Chinese shipments to the United States are not raw materials, but finished goods. At the top of the list of products sold to the United States in 1995: radios, television sets, records and related items, $2.8 billion; games, toys and children's vehicles, $2.7 billion; rubber and plastic shoes, boots and sandals, $2.2 billion. These products used to be made in America by American workers.

China exports an even greater volume of certain high-tech products to us than we sell to them. In 1995, $1 billion worth of computers were exported to the U.S. from China. U.S. companies exported a mere $267 million in computers to China—one-fourth of what that country sold to us.

- America, the export powerhouse? While Washington talks about high-paying jobs created by high-tech goods, our exports to China resemble those of a third-world country. Of the top 20 products exported in 1995, ranked by their value, four were agricultural: cotton, ranked No. 3, at $829 million; corn, No. 4, at $629 million; wheat, No. 5, at $506 million; and soybean oil, No. 7, at $299 million. They accounted for 30 percent of the top 20. Or one-fifth of all exports to China. The only sizable export of a manufactured product: aircraft worth $891 million.

The United States' ninth-largest export to China was decidedly low-tech: scrap and waste, worth $275 million. That includes everything from scrapped cars to wastepaper and used clothing.

- The United States exported only one commodity to China with a value exceeding $1 billion: phosphatic fertilizers. Among the few U.S. businesses benefiting from this trade is a Tampa, Fla.–based company called U.S. Chem Resources. Formerly known as U.S. Agri-Chemicals Corp., the company has, since 1989, been a subsidiary of a global corporation called Sinochem International Petroleum Co. With annual sales of more than $122 billion, Sinochem is in the same league as Exxon Corp.

And where is Sinochem headquartered? Beijing, China. In short, one of the largest U.S. exporters to China is a Chinese-owned company.

Buying Know-How and Access

For most foreign interests, the way to succeed in Washington is to look to the revolving door—to people who have rotated out of the executive branch or Congress into the lobbying or consulting game.

Someone like William H. Houston 3d. Houston was the chief textile negotiator for the U.S. Trade Representative's Office in 1987. He negotiated agreements with foreign nations that set limits on the volume of apparel they could ship to the United States. The next year, Houston became a private consultant, and afterward helped offshore clients negotiate agreements with the U.S. government on the volume of apparel they could export to the United States.

The company he works for, Sandler & Travis Trade Advisory Services, secured a $25,000-a-month contract from an exporters group in the Dominican Republic to represent them in 1993 negotiations with the United States on a new textile agreement, stressing the "extensive experience" of the firm's members, including Houston, in international textile negotiations. The agreement was renegotiated, and the Dominican Republic's quota of apparel imports to the United States was increased.

There are thousands of people like William Houston 3d in Washington, using their government-gained know-how for private clients.

Brenda Jacobs was a lawyer for the International Trade Commission in the 1980s, then moved to the Commerce Department's Committee for the Implementation of Textile Agreements. In 1989, she entered private practice. In 1990, she registered to lobby Congress for the Toy Manufacturers of America on behalf of retaining China's most-favored-nation trade status. The lobbying campaign succeeded, and since then toy makers have closed plants in the United States and shifted more production to China.

According to the Toy Manufacturers of America, at least 75 percent of the toys sold in the United States are made wholly, or in part, overseas. To better understand the extent of the job loss in this industry—and the cause for it—look no further than American ports and ship arrivals on just three days, and one toy company, Mattel Inc., the nation's largest.

On Friday, June 28, 1996, at least 22 shipments of Mattel toys arrived from China, Indonesia and Malaysia. More than 300,000 pounds of toys were unloaded at ports in Los Angeles and Long Beach, Calif., Seattle and Tacoma, Wash.

One week earlier, on Friday, June 21, 1996, Mattel brought in at least 20 shipments of toys weighing more than 400,000 pounds from China, Hong Kong and Malaysia. This time, all were unloaded at Los Angeles and Long Beach.

And on Friday, May 31, 1996, Fisher-Price, a Mattel subsidiary, brought in 10 shipments of toys weighing more than 250,000 pounds from Hong Kong and Malaysia. Again, all were unloaded at Los Angeles and Long Beach.

As you might expect, Mattel—which sold $3.6 billion worth of Barbie Dolls, Cabbage Patch Kids dolls, Disney movie action dolls, Hot Wheels, preschool and other toys—has closed U.S. toy-making plants and dismissed hundreds of workers.

And if you would like more evidence as to why Americans are working for less, take a look at Mattel's chief competitor, Hasbro Inc., from another vantage point—a toy store. Wander the aisles and look at the boxes that helped to generate $2.9 billion in sales in 1995. The GI Joe action figures were made in China. The Sesame Street stuffed toy set figures, Big Bird and Ernie, were made in China. The *Batman Forever, Superman, Star Wars* and *Jurassic Park* action figures were all made in China. The Nerf guns and the Playskool musical mirror—they, too, were made in China.

For much of this, you may credit Washington's highly skilled trade lobbyists. How and where, you might ask, did they acquire the experience that has made them so successful? From you—the taxpayer.

Check their résumés and you likely will find that they served an apprenticeship with one or more government agencies—the Office of the United States Trade Representative, the International Trade Administration, the Export-Import Bank, the Antitrust Division of the Justice Department, the National Security Council, State Department, White House or Congress, to name only a few. Foreign interests recruit these government alumni not only for their experience in Washington, but for their contacts in Congress or the bureaucracy. And they pay handsomely for that access.

Early in 1994, the Embassy of India, eager to improve relations on Capitol Hill, retained the Washington law firm of Raffaelli, Spees, Springer & Smith to arrange a series of meetings for the Indian ambassador, Siddartha Shankar Ray, with members of Congress. The purpose, according to an embassy spokesman, was to discuss matters of mutual interest including "trade and foreign policy."

The lead partner, John Raffaelli, had been an aide to Sen. Lloyd M. Bentsen from 1980 to 1984, when the Texas senator was a power on the Senate Finance Committee, which oversees tax and trade legislation.

For the Indian embassy, Raffaelli, Spees arranged 141 meetings with lawmakers or their staffs, including face-to-face meetings with 69 members of Congress and senators during a six-month period.

During that time, the law firm received $322,000 in fees from the government of India. The firm is on a retainer from the Indian government, according to reports on file with the Clerk of the House. The fee: $57,500 a month, or $690,000 a year.

When asked why a lobbyist had been hired, the embassy spokesman said: "This is the way things are done in Washington. . . . The feeling was, everybody is doing it, there is a case to be made for it, and let's use some professional help to gain a better knowledge of legislative procedures."

The best lobby shops are always on the alert for fresh recruits to keep current their connections to government and assure them of continuing entrée, regardless of the party in power.

Just look at Global USA. The company, which represents Japanese clients, such as Komatsu, the heavy-equipment maker, got its start in 1983 during the Reagan administration. Its founders, William H. Morris Jr., William Timmons and Stanton D. Anderson, all had ties to the administration or other power brokers in the Republican Party. Morris had been an assistant secretary of commerce for trade development in 1981–83. Timmons was a power in Tennessee Republican Party politics and was close to Howard A. Baker Jr., the state's Republican senator who would become chief of staff for President Reagan. Anderson had worked at the White House in 1971–73 while Richard Nixon was president and served briefly as a deputy assistant secretary of state for congressional relations from 1973 to 1975.

As Global USA grew and took on more Japanese clients, the company brought in more associates with government connections. Bohdan Denysyk had been a trade official in the Department of Commerce under Jimmy Carter and Ronald Reagan. George S. Kopp, a Democrat from Arkansas, had been chief counsel of the House subcommittee on natural resources until 1988.

Rosamond S. Brown had been a tax aide for Arkansas Democratic representative Beryl Anthony Jr. on the House Ways and Means Committee until 1993.

Then there is that informal group called the Friends of Bill. After Clinton was elected, Global further cemented its ties to the incoming administration by hiring Lottie H. Shackelford, former Little Rock mayor and vice chairwoman of the Democratic National Committee; Paul C. Berry, an Arkansas banker who was Bill Clinton's roommate at Georgetown University and a golfing buddy; and Michael A. Brown, son of Ron Brown, the late Democratic leader who was Clinton's secretary of commerce.

"We're very, very fortunate," John M. Nugent Jr., Global USA vice president, told an interviewer in 1994. "There are a lot of people in this firm with deep Little Rock or Arkansas connections."

The files of the Justice Department's Foreign Agents Registration Office bulge with details about how foreign agents earn their retainers. It's not a bad life. They lunch at stylish Washington restaurants, attend meetings with members of Congress and senators and travel to foreign countries.

Take Ruth M. Kurtz, who represents a consortium of Mexican businesses. As with most Washington lobbyists, Kurtz received her early training courtesy of U.S. taxpayers. She worked at the Department of Commerce from 1970 to 1980 as an economist and trade negotiator. Then she was a trade adviser at the International Trade Commission, put in five years on Capitol Hill as a trade specialist for Sen. William V. Roth, Republican from Delaware, and helped draft the Omnibus Trade and Competitiveness Act of 1988, one of the most comprehensive trade bills in recent years.

In 1989, she left government and became a private consultant. She works for COECE, an organization of influential Mexican business groups that was formed to lobby for congressional approval of the North American Free Trade Agreement (NAFTA).

Since the early 1990s, when Kurtz began representing COECE, the association has pumped thousands of dollars into lobbying Congress and the bureaucracy—most of it on behalf of NAFTA, which lowered tariffs among the United States, Mexico and Canada.

Kurtz's reports filed with the Department of Justice provide a window on the Washington world of power lunching and how lobbyists seek to influence U.S. policy:

The Lobbyists

May 24–27, 1992:	Organized and participated in fact-finding trip to Mexico for congressional staff.
June 15–16, 1992:	Supported fact-finding trip to Mexico for a governor.
August 13, 1992:	Alice Block, USTR [Trade Representative's Office], Discussion re NAFTA.
August 14, 1992:	Rebecca Bannister, U.S. Department of Commerce meeting re NAFTA.
August 24, 1992:	Charles Hansen, International Trade Commission discussion re NAFTA.
May 10, 1993:	La Colline. Lunch meeting with Thelma Askey [House Ways and Means Committee] re NAFTA.
May 25, 1993:	Le Mistral. Lunch mtng. with Diane Sullivan [tax and trade counsel for Robert Matsui, a Democratic congressman from California] re NAFTA.
June 2, 1993:	The Monade Capitol Hill. Lunch mtng. with Eric Biel [trade counsel, Senate Finance Committee staff] re NAFTA.
June 8, 1993:	Cafe Berlin. Lunch mtng. with Mary Foley [legislative assistant, Max Baucus, a Democratic senator from Montana] re NAFTA.
August 9, 1993:	La Brasserie. Lunch mtng. with Meredith Broadbent [minority professional assistant, House Ways and Means Committee].
September 15, 1993:	Dominiques. Lunch mtng. with Eric Fredell [economic officer, Office of Mexican Affairs, Department of State] re NAFTA.
October 29, 1993:	Capitol View Club. Lunch mtng. with Al Raider [House export task force] re NAFTA.

November 18, 1993:	La Belle Florist. Gift to Tana Rosenblatt. Legislative assistant, Office of Cong. [Jim] Kolbe [R., Ariz].
November 20, 1993:	Everlasting Harvest Herb and Dried Flower Farm. Five Gifts. Four for Sen. Roth staff. One for Cong. Matsui staff.
Dec. 9, 1993:	Old Ebbitt Grill. Lunch with Karen Chopra, director of Commercial Programs, Division U.S. Department of Commerce.
June 7, 1994:	Le Mistral. Lunch with Brian Bieron, legislative assistant, Office of Cong. [David] Dreier. [R., Calif.]
September 27, 1994:	Les Halles. Luncheon with Jonathan Doh, director, Trade Policy Division, Office of North American Free Trade Agreement, U.S. Department of Commerce.

The COECE campaign, of course, was but one of many lobbying offensives by Mexican commercial interests and U.S. multinational corporations to swing votes in Congress for NAFTA and to work for implementation of the agreement afterward. The trade agreement with Mexico and Canada was ultimately adopted by Congress in November 1993. Kurtz continues to represent COECE in Washington at a salary of $120,000 a year.

Oh, yes. Congressmen Kolbe and Matsui and Senators Baucus and Roth all voted in favor of NAFTA.

The Fruit of the Loom Amendment

What difference does it make if former government officials go to work for private interests?

A lot.

Remember Ronald Holley and his coworkers, who lost their jobs when Fruit of the Loom closed an apparel plant in Batesville, Miss., in 1995? The Batesville shutdown was part of a larger Fruit of the Loom cutback in domestic manfacturing, following a little-known battle fought on Capitol Hill in 1994 over an obscure trade provision.

The Lobbyists

For years, American retailers have imported apparel labeled "Made in Hong Kong" but which actually is sewn in mainland China. The practice grew out of U.S. customs regulations that placed a cap on the volume of apparel that could be imported into the United States from any one nation. When mainland China reached the maximum, American importers and Hong Kong businessmen found a way to circumvent the limit.

By having the fabric cut in Hong Kong, then shipped to mainland China for sewing and assembly—the bulk of the work—and sent back to Hong Kong for export to the United States, a garment could have a Hong Kong label and come in under Hong Kong's unused quotas, even though it was largely made in China. It was all perfectly legal under U.S. customs regulations.

This worked fine for retailers such as The Gap, The Limited, J.C. Penney and Wal-Mart, which were always pressuring suppliers for the lowest prices on apparel. But it wasn't good for domestic producers such as Fruit of the Loom, whose factories were primarily in the United States. The importation of more low-cost goods from China put yet more cost pressures on the company, where Fruit of the Loom production workers earning $7 to $10 an hour were competing with 30-cent-an-hour Chinese seamstresses.

In the summer of 1994, Fruit of the Loom and other U.S. producers asked Congress to end the practice that allowed goods made in one country to come in under the quota limits of another. As Ronald Sorini, Fruit of the Loom's senior vice president, put it: "When China is doing 90 percent of the work, the label should read 'Made in China.'"

What followed was a high-stakes battle on Capitol Hill that pitted retailers, importers and foreign producers opposing the label change against Fruit of the Loom and domestic producers who favored it. Described as "total war" by one of the combatants, the fight over the "Fruit of the Loom Amendment," as it became known, swirled around the Senate Finance Committee, which had to okay the provision before it could go to the full Senate for a vote.

Among those lobbying the committee that summer, Doral Cooper, a former high official of the Office of the United States Trade Representative, was to play a pivotal role. An assistant trade representative for Asia, Africa and the Pacific during President Reagan's first term, Cooper had left the office in 1985 to become a trade consultant. She went to work for Michael K. Deaver, the onetime Reagan deputy chief of staff, who founded a consulting firm after he left the White House that year.

171

Deaver & Associates was a hot property in 1985 Washington. A close personal and professional friend of the president and first lady, Deaver quickly signed up a number of large corporations and foreign governments on six-figure retainers. But his activities soon sparked controversy and led to allegations that he had improperly used his White House connections on behalf of some of his new clients, which included the government of South Korea.

Deaver later was indicted by a federal grand jury for lying under oath to Congress and to a grand jury about his lobbying activities for South Korea. He was found guilty by a federal court jury in 1987 of three counts of perjury. He was given a suspended three-year sentence, fined $100,000 and ordered to perform 1,500 hours of community service. He has since returned to public-relations work in Washington and was one of the architects of the 1996 Republican National Convention.

Cooper, after leaving Deaver & Associates, joined C&M International, a consulting company affiliated with the Washington law firm of Crowell & Moring, and built up a successful trade practice. Her foreign clients included the Korea Foreign Trade Association, the Singapore Trade Development Board, the Board of Foreign Trade on Taiwan and the Indonesian Ministry of Trade.

As a lobbyist for The Limited, a major importer of men's and women's wear under such well-known brand names as Victoria's Secret, Structure and Abercrombie & Fitch, Cooper took part in the 1994 campaign to shoot down the Fruit of the Loom amendment. The strategy was simple: Swamp the Senate Finance Committee members with calls, letters and personal visits from corporate leaders warning that clothing prices would shoot up, hurting American consumers and the retail industry, if the committee members approved the Fruit of the Loom amendment.

Corporate chiefs telephoned committee members, urging them to vote no. Letters flooded Senate offices. And Cooper, along with others, lobbied Finance Committee members, focusing in particular on then-senator Bob Dole (R., Kan.), who was seen as holding the deciding vote. Of the full-scale campaign, Cooper later told the *Legal Times*: "This was a must-win for us."

The upshot: On August 2, 1994, the Finance Committee deadlocked, thus killing the Fruit of the Loom measure.

Afterward, Fruit of the Loom officials went back to lawmakers again, and that time the company prevailed and late in 1994 secured language in trade law similar to what had been rejected earlier.

The Lobbyists

But once again lobbying by retailers and foreign interests succeeded in getting a provision into the new law that would cushion the impact. Rather than taking effect on January 1, 1995, as the original Fruit of the Loom proposal had called for, the new provision did not take effect until eighteen months later.

That was too late for Ronald Holley and his fellow Fruit of the Loom employees. In May 1995, Chairman William Farley said the company was committed to a "gradual migration" of its sewing facilities to the Caribbean and Central America. The company was moving production offshore aggressively. From producing 30 million dozen garments offshore in 1995, the company said it would produce 50 million dozen in 1996, and 70 million dozen offshore by 1998.

Six months later, on October 30, 1995, the company announced it was eliminating the jobs of 3,200 of its U.S. employees because of the "difficult retail environment for apparel and increasingly competitive nature of the business." Fruit of the Loom closed six U.S. plants—in Florence, Ala.; Franklin, Ky.; Acadia Parish, La.; Batesville, Miss.; and Albemarle and Kings Mountain, N.C.—and scaled back employment at two others, in Bowling Green, Ky., and Rockingham, N.C. All told, the company cut back its domestic workforce by 12 percent.

In Batesville, Ronald Holley, who had cut cloth that seamstresses sewed into men's briefs and undershirts with the familiar Fruit of the Loom label, was out of a job for five weeks. He found work as a shipping clerk for a local furniture maker, at 30 percent less pay. Even so, he considers himself lucky. "Every time I go to the grocery store with my wife, I run into somebody I worked with for years," he said in the summer of 1996. "The ones I've been running into lately have not found work."

As it turned out, the impact of the Fruit of the Loom shutdown in Batesville went far beyond the 850 people who lost their jobs. Batesville learned what cities and towns all over America have been finding out: When a large employer, especially a manufacturing plant, closes, it has a ripple effect, spreading outward to those who supplied goods and services to the company and its employees.

When the mill closed, a local vending company that furnished snacks, soft drinks and sandwiches to the plant lost its largest account. The company had to lay off several longtime employees. One of them was Holley's wife, Vickie, who had prepared sandwiches and snacks. She still has not found work.

For many Fruit of the Loom employees, Holley said, jobs have been scarce, and many, by late summer 1996, were about to exhaust their unemployment benefits. "I don't think this town has seen the full effect of this yet," he said.

Like others interviewed by the authors, Holley is puzzled about Washington and can't understand why policy makers, through free-trade agreements, are sacrificing the nation's manufacturing base. "What are the young people going to do? When I was 19 I got a job at this plant," he said. "Later on, I used to coach Little League baseball, and some of the kids I coached, well, they went on to get jobs there, too, and were working there when it closed.

"Where are the new jobs going to be? We can't all be lawyers or computer experts. And some choose not to go that way anyway. So what will people do? What it looks like to me is that our government or our Congress—whoever it is—is taking some of the jobs away that they seem to think are not important."

Americans employed in manufacturing now represent 15.8 percent of all jobs. That's down 39 percent from 1960, when manufacturing jobs made up 26.1 percent of the workforce. None of the United States' leading trading partners has experienced anything approaching this loss in manufacturing jobs. Indeed, some have actually increased the percentage of those jobs.

Germany had 34.4 percent of its workforce employed in manufacturing in 1960; 33 years later, in 1993, the number had declined slightly, to 29.1 percent. In Italy, the percentage has remained virtually unchanged—24 percent in 1960 versus 23.2 percent in 1993. In Japan, the share of the workforce employed in manufacturing went up during the period that such jobs plummeted in the United States. It has grown from 21.7 in 1960 to 23.9 percent in 1993.

Educating Lobbyists—At Your Expense

Doral Cooper came out of what has become Washington's premier graduate school for trade lobbyists—the Office of the United States Trade Representative. Former trade representative officials are in top demand because they are out of the nation's most important agency dealing with trade. It coordinates and directs trade policy and is supposed to be a watchdog for U.S. business, negotiating with other governments when a U.S. industry is jeopardized by international trade practices or when American exports are blocked by foreign trade barriers.

The Lobbyists

Anyone in that office for even a short time learns how Washington operates and gains insights into the workings of many domestic industries and their foreign competitors—invaluable information for a later career as a lobbyist or consultant.

Steven R. Saunders was an assistant U.S. trade representative for congressional and public affairs for less than two years, 1981–82. But that was long enough for him to gain the experience necessary to become a registered foreign agent. After leaving the Trade Representative's Office, he founded Saunders & Co., a public-relations firm, and signed up a number of Japanese clients, including the Embassy of Japan, Mitsubishi Electric and the Seiko Epson Corp. In one six-month period in 1992–93, for example, Saunders billed his Japanese clients $145,000 for advising them on U.S. trade policy and economic relations with the United States, and for arranging luncheon meetings with congressional staffers.

For years, the Trade Representative's Office was a bureaucratic backwater, until surging imports in the 1970s led a succession of presidents and Congresses to beef up its powers. One major overhaul came in 1979 under President Jimmy Carter, who brought the office under the direct control of the White House. For the first time, proponents of the change claimed, the nation would have a "central authority capable of planning a coherent trade strategy." As Carter informed Congress: "This reorganization. . . will sharpen and unify trade policy direction, improve the efficiency of trade law enforcement, and enable us to negotiate from a position of strength."

The office has had no success in reducing the merchandise trade deficit, but the reorganization wasn't a total bust. It has provided a wondrous career path for future trade lobbyists. The files of registered foreign agents kept by the U.S. government are full of alumni from the Trade Representative's Office.

Alexander Platt was associate general counsel of the office from 1983 to 1985. He then became a partner with the Washington law firm of Akin, Gump, Strauss, Hauer & Feld, whose clients included the Japanese External Trade Organization, Colombia Flower Council, Fujitsu America Inc., Matsushita Electric Industrial Co. Ltd., Mazda Motor Corp. and COECE, the Mexican business consortium.

Jeanne S. Archibald was associate general counsel of the Trade Representative's Office from 1980 to 1986 and worked at the Treasury Department from 1986 to 1993, rising to the position of general counsel. Then she became a partner with Hogan & Hartson, a Washington law firm whose foreign clients included the Embassy of Japan, the China External Trade Development Council, Nippon Telegraph & Telephone Corp. and the Korean Foreign Trade Association.

Julia Christine Bliss was an assistant general counsel at the Trade Representative's Office from 1982 to 1986. She became a partner with the Washington office of Mudge, Rose, Guthrie, Alexander & Ferdon, whose clients included Toshiba Corp., Asociacion Nacional de Industriales (Colombian textiles), China National Textile Import and Export Corp., Japan Lumber Importers' Association, Footwear Open Trading Coalition (Hong Kong), Hong Kong Trade Development Council and the Salvadoran Apparel Manufacturers Association.

Former trade representatives often do best of all. William Brock, for instance. Brock was U.S. trade representative from 1981 to 1985 under Ronald Reagan. After leaving office, he established the Brock Group, a Washington consulting company specializing in international trade.

Clients flocked to his company, including Airbus Industries North America, the Panama Trade and Development Committee, the Federal Republic of Germany, the government of Mexico and the Board of Foreign Trade of the Republic of China on Taiwan. Taiwan turned to Brock for help in drumming up support on Capitol Hill for its admission to the General Agreement on Tariffs and Trade [GATT], the international body that administers the global trading system.

Brock peppered Congress with letters urging lawmakers to endorse Taiwan's request, including this one dated January 19, 1990, to Sen. George J. Mitchell, the Maine Democrat who then was majority leader of the Senate: "Despite my disinclination to represent foreign governments, the admission of Taiwan into the GATT is so clearly in the interest of the United States and its workers that I have agreed to help." For agreeing to help, Taiwan paid the Brock Group $480,000 a year.

Lest you think the revolving door only turns *out* from the Trade Representative's Office, then consider the case of the nation's top trade negotiator—Charlene Barshefsky. As acting trade representative, Barshefsky is the most powerful person in government on trade matters next to the president. She negotiates with foreign governments about opening their markets to American products and protests unfair trading practices that harm

U.S. industries. In sum, her job is to represent America's interests in global trade.

But for most of her career, Barshefsky has been on the other side—representing foreign interests. Before she entered government in 1993, Barshefsky was a partner at the Washington law firm of Steptoe & Johnson, where she specialized in international trade law and cochaired the firm's 35-lawyer International Practice Group. Steptoe & Johnson represented a substantial number of foreign clients from Japan, Mexico, Hong Kong, Canada and Britain.

As a Steptoe partner, Barshefsky filed a registration form with the Department of Justice on January 8, 1992—required of lobbyists under the Foreign Agents Registration Act— in which she described her work as providing "legal advice and representation and trade counseling to clients in the firm." The Steptoe foreign principals listed on Barshefsky's form were "COECE [the consortium of Mexican business groups], Hercules General Cement Co., Embassy of Canada, Turkish Republic of North Cyprus, Canadian Sugar Institute, Nippon Steel Corp., Canadian Forest Industries Council, Canadian Wheat Board."

Nippon Steel had retained Steptoe & Johnson to handle legal work for them with U.S. trade agencies. For years, U.S. steel producers have charged that Nippon Steel and other Japanese steelmakers have harmed the U.S. industry by "dumping" steel for sale in the American market—that is, pricing their products artificially low to gain an advantage. Earning fees of $2.4 million from Nippon Steel in one six-month period, Steptoe & Johnson drafted briefs and filed responses "in defense of antidumping cases" and monitored other trade issues for the Japanese steel giant.

At Senate hearings on her nomination as deputy trade representative on May 19, 1993, Barshefsky was questioned by senators about her work for foreign clients. While acknowledging that she had registered as a foreign agent, she said none of her activities involved "lobbying of any kind." In the case of COECE, the Mexican business consortium, she said: "The scope of the representation with COECE was rather limited and narrowly focused. That was to review various drafts of the NAFTA text for legal consistency." As for Nippon Steel, Barshefsky told the senators: "I do not represent Nippon Steel, although they have been a client of my firm."

She said her work on behalf of foreign clients had been of such a limited nature that, in retrospect, it was "questionable" whether she needed to register. But she had done so anyway.

"There are many gray areas under the act," she told the senators, "and I tend to look at these things extremely conservatively and carefully." She pledged that, if confirmed as deputy trade representative, she would "not participate" in any activities involving clients she had previously represented.

On May 28, 1993, the Senate confirmed Barshefsky as deputy trade representative in a voice vote. By the time she was sworn in, the path between the government's trade office and her old law firm was becoming a little worn. One of Barshefsky's predecessors as deputy trade representative, Michael B. Smith, had taken the reverse route. When he resigned the post in 1988, he went to Steptoe & Johnson to establish a trade consulting firm.

Whatever Barshefsky did or did not do for the foreign interests that her firm represented, the fact that she filed a registration statement on January 8, 1992, under the Foreign Agents Registration Act made her a registered agent for a foreign government. That posed a dilemma for the Clinton administration. It wanted to nominate Barshefsky for the job of U.S. trade representative. Federal law, it would seem, prohibits it.

In December 1995, Congress enacted, and President Clinton signed, the Lobbying Disclosure Act of 1995. Widely hailed as an attempt to plug loopholes in the law by compelling more lobbyists to register, the act also contained, in Section 21, this provision:

> A person who has directly represented, aided, or advised a foreign entity (as defined by Section 207 (f) (3) of title 18, United States Code) in any trade negotiation, or trade dispute, with the United States may not be appointed as United States Trade Representative or as a Deputy United States Trade Representative.

Section 21 was fathered by Bob Dole, who was then Senate majority leader. It not only prohibited anyone who had represented a foreign interest from serving as the trade representative or the deputy; it also barred anyone who had served in those jobs from ever representing a foreign interest in the future.

As Dole told his Senate colleagues on July 25, 1995: This "provision says that no one shall be appointed to the important posts of U.S. trade representative or deputy U.S. trade representative if that person had, in the past, directly represented a foreign government in a trade dispute or negotiation with the United States."

Dole's amendment might have remained tucked away in lobbying law had Commerce Secretary Ron Brown's plane not gone down in Croatia on April 3, 1996, killing Brown and 34 others.

To succeed him at Commerce, President Clinton nominated Mickey Kantor, the U.S. trade representative. And to succeed Kantor, the president named Charlene Barshefsky, who had been Kantor's deputy for three years, as acting trade representative. This was considered the first step toward formally nominating Barshefsky to be trade representative.

But there's no way the Senate could confirm her, given the language that lawmakers adopted in 1995—right? Perhaps. By the late summer of 1996, the president had not yet formally nominated Barshefsky, but there is every indication he planned to.

Speaking for the White House and the Trade Representative's Office, a spokesman said White House lawyers were studying the matter to determine if Barshefsky's activities "having to do with working for foreign countries" posed any problem under the new law. The spokesman seemed optimistic that there would be no obstacle to the nomination. Once they've gone through the record, the spokesman said, "then they will presumably nominate her because I am sure she will be fine."

Manipulating the Media

American policies and attitudes on free trade and the global economy are shaped by more subtle forces than simply arm-twisting in Washington. Public opinion can be influenced by the quote of an expert in the press, a column on the op-ed page of a newspaper, or a statement by a spokesman who purports to represent the public. But sometimes those who claim to speak on behalf of the public interest also have other interests—and some have foreign connections, although that is rarely, if ever, revealed to the public.

Note, for example, some of the opinions expressed by columnist George Will, who is syndicated in more than 450 newspapers and who appears regularly on television on the ABC program *This Week With David Brinkley*. Will has frequently criticized certain legislation or regulatory actions as violations of free-trade principles. In the spring of 1995, when the Clinton administration was considering high tariffs on luxury autos from Japan to force Japanese automakers to buy more American-made auto parts, Will lashed out at the administration over the proposed import duties. In a column that appeared in newspapers on May 19, 1995, Will wrote:

The administration may be a 98-pound weakling when dealing with Russia, Iran, Cuba, North Korea, NATO allies regarding Bosnia, and many others, but it knows how to punish Lexus, Acura, Infiniti, Mazda and Mitsubishi dealers. The 617 such dealers, who have invested an average of $2 million in their businesses and employ an average of 50 people, will be injured or destroyed if the tariffs become final in June.

What readers of Will's columns would have no way of knowing, however, was that his wife was a public-relations consultant for the Japanese automobile industry. Mari Maseng Will has her own Washington public-relations company, Maseng Communications, which operates out of the office building of the historic Willard Hotel, two blocks from the White House. In 1994, Maseng Communications was retained by another Washington public-relations company, Porter/Novelli, to perform "professional services" for the Japan Automobile Manufacturers Association.

Maseng spelled out her company's work on behalf of the Japanese trade group in documents filed with the Justice Department:

> [Maseng Communications] provided strategic communications counsel, drafting and editing services, as well as media contact activities for the foreign principal [Japan Automobile Manufacturers Association], in conjunction with Porter/Novelli. The registrant participated in drafting and editing of the following: op-eds—"High Stakes Trade Policy Jeopardizes Currency Market" and "Trade Brinkmanship"; press releases—"Major Step for U.S. car sales in Japan," "U.S. Auto Parts Sales to Japan's Auto Makers Increase More than 14 Percent in FY 1993 to $15.5 Billion," "Super 301 Action Against Japan's Automotive Industry Would Violate GATT . . ." "JAMA Warns Administration Against Buckling to Big Three and U.S. Auto Parts Company Pressure . . ." "Big Three Auto Sales Jump in Japan; Automakers Strengthen Efforts to Buy U.S.-Made Parts." . . . Letter to the editor of the *New York Times* and letter to the editor of the *Detroit Free Press* . . ."

For "professional services" on the Japanese account in 1995, Maseng Communications received $81,774.

Washington abounds with trade associations, think tanks and

organizations such as the Japan Automobile Manufacturers Association that are instrumental, thanks to people like Mari Maseng Will, in helping shape public perceptions of free-trade issues through their input to policy makers and the media.

Of the many groups in Washington that have played a role in molding opinion, one of the longest-running and most successful is Consumers for World Trade, which bills itself as the "only national consumer organization" dealing exclusively with trade. It is regularly quoted in the press. Its president frequently testifies on trade before congressional committees. It sponsors an annual dinner where awards are handed out to those the group annoints as champions of free trade. It publishes a newsletter that is widely circulated among the media and policy makers. It serves as a type of research arm for congressional and media sources on trade-related issues. Mainly, it acts as a self-appointed spokesman for American consumers, extolling the benefits of free trade and opposing any domestic legislation that it considers protectionist.

It was started in 1978 by Doreen L. Brown, the Bryn Mawr College—educated widow of a Washington construction-industry executive, who says she launched it because no one else "was taking care of the public interest in trade." Whenever a trade issue arose—whether the United States should endorse the North American Free Trade Agreement or whether a domestic industry was entitled to import relief—reporters invariably turn to Doreen Brown or one of her associates for a comment.

The *Washington Post*, November 22, 1981: "Free traders, such as Consumers for World Trade, a Washington-based international-trade watchdog organization, oppose government protection of domestic industries through tariffs, quotas or 'Buy American' legislation, and favor forcing American industries to compete or die."

Newsday, May 18, 1992, in a story on the impact of higher import duties: "'Consumers are paying the price,' said Doreen Brown, president of Consumers for World Trade, a consumer advocacy group in Washington."

The *Journal of Commerce*, March 31, 1993: "Consumers for World Trade is the country's only consumer group exclusively dedicated to freer trade."

The impression conveyed by these stories is that it's a broad-based organization working on behalf of the American consumer, much like Consumers Union, which evaluates products for reliability and cost. But where Consumers Union has 4.8 million

members, Consumers for World Trade has fewer than 1,000—
only a fraction of 1 percent of the nation's consumers. And they
are a very elite group of consumers, it turns out. The organization's board and national advisory council comprises registered
foreign agents, lobbyists, former government trade officials,
economists, academics, officials of multinational corporations
and an heir to a multimillion-dollar shipping fortune.

"We are not a mass-membership organization," Doreen Brown
told the authors. "Our members are around the country, but they
are in small numbers. We have trade associations and corporations who contribute money but are not participatory or voting
members of the organization. We carefully delineated that, because we don't want anybody to think we are working for corporations."

Consumers for World Trade may not want the public to think
it works for corporations, but that's who benefits from its efforts.
As a tireless spokesman for unrestricted free trade, the organization is aligned most of the time with multinational and foreign
interests that benefit from such free-trade policies. Records on
file with the House of Representatives show that contributors to
the organization include Nissan North America, Toyota, Honda,
Hyundai, Matsushita, Automobile Importers of America, American Association of Exporters and Importers, Procter & Gamble,
3M Corp., the Yamashita-Shinnihon Steamship Co., Warnaco,
The Limited, Sea-Land Service, Rockwell International, Cater-
pillar, the International Mass Retailers Association, and COECE,
the Mexican business consortium.

Not surprisingly, given the source of its support, Consumers
for World Trade's position on global trade issues has been pre-
dictable over the years. It has opposed any duties, tariffs or
quotas on imports and has called for the elimination of all trade
barriers. No domestic industry should be shielded in any way
from imports. Anything less harms the consumer. "Our philosophy," Doreen Brown has said, "is that the consumers are the ultimate victims of protectionist policies and the ultimate benefac-
tors of an open-trade policy."

Asked what the United States should do when a major trading
partner such as Japan, which has benefited enormously from
America's open-door trade stance, fails to reciprocate and bars
American products, Brown says the answer is simply to keep
talking. "I think continuous negotiations are the only way to do

it," she says. "Making a big enemy out of Japan isn't going to end up being to the benefit of the United States."

For all the rhetoric about trade during political campaigns, there are few substantive differences from one administration to another. Doreen Brown has advocated free trade during the administrations of four presidents—two Democratic, two Republican. In her view, they have pursued remarkably similar policies.

"I would say pretty much every one of the administrations has been reflecting what the private sector in the United States has been saying," Brown said. "I don't think there has been a tremendous amount of difference in administrations on free trade."

The Revolving Door Turns On and On

Because there is little real difference between the political parties on trade, there has been little real difference in dealing with an issue at the heart of the formulation of national trade policy—the revolving door. Occasionally, a president or Congress purports to strike a blow at influence-peddling by onetime government officials. But these efforts invariably fall short.

In 1978, Congress enacted the Ethics in Government Act, which, among other things, banned high officials in the executive branch from lobbying their former agencies for a year after leaving office.

In 1989, Congress enacted new restrictions on lobbying by former executive branch officials and, for the first time, placed limits on lobbying by former congressmen and key staff members.

After President Clinton took office in 1993, he signed an executive order prohibiting top executive branch officials from lobbying their former agencies for five years and from ever representing foreign governments or foreign political parties. In December 1995, Congress passed the Lobbying Disclosure Act of 1995 and codified Clinton's lifetime ban on lobbying by top trade negotiators on behalf of foreign interests. The new law went a step further by prohibiting anyone who had ever represented a foreign government from holding either of the top two trade positions—the provision that entangled Charlene Barshefsky.

But these measures, as ambitious as they might sound, have not gone very far. None bars legislative aides from lobbying the executive branch. Senior staff members of the House Ways and Means Committee and Senate Finance Committee, which oversee trade legislation, are free to start lobbying the Commerce Department or the Trade Representative's Office the day they leave the government payroll.

Nor do the lobbying restrictions affect the vast bulk of the federal trade bureaucracy, such as assistant trade representatives. They, too, are free to lobby on trade-related matters after they leave government.

When Clinton campaigned for the presidency in 1992, he singled out Washington lobbyists and influence-peddlers for special scorn and vowed that his administration would be different. And after his executive order prohibiting lobbying by top executive branch officials, Mickey Kantor, then Clinton's trade representative, told reporters: "I think we've locked the revolving door."

But not much really has changed. Look no further than the Trade Representative's Office under Clinton. In addition to Barshefky, there are other appointments worth noting.

The office's senior counselor and negotiator, Ira S. Shapiro, was a partner specializing in international trade for the Washington office of Winthrop, Stimson, Putnam & Roberts before he joined the Trade Representative's Office in 1993. Jeffrey M. Lang, the new deputy trade representative, came out of the same law firm, where he, too, specialized in international trade. Both previously worked on Capitol Hill, Shapiro as a staff member of the Senate Governmental Affairs Committee and Lang as chief international trade counsel for the Senate Finance Committee. Today, after stints representing the private sector, they are back in government.

But Winthrop, Stimson, Putnam & Roberts doesn't have to worry about losing too many of its lawyers to government service. The revolving door continues to turn. After Shapiro and Lang left to join the trade representative's staff, an assistant trade representative, C. Christopher Parlin, resigned late in 1995 and headed to—you guessed it—Winthrop, Stimson, Putnam & Roberts.

On February 14, 1996, Winthrop, Stimson filed lobby registration papers with the clerk of the House of Representatives reporting the name and title of each employee "who has acted or is expected to act as a lobbyist" for the firm's clients. Parlin was listed as a lobbyist for two influential foreign groups: the Korea Semiconductor Industry Association and Korea Automobile Manufacturers Association.

Which means that nothing much really has changed since

The Lobbyists

June 21, 1992, when candidate Bill Clinton had this to say in a position paper on the revolving door:

"It's long past time to clean up Washington. The last twelve years were nothing less than an extended hunting season for high-priced lobbyists and Washington influence peddlers. On streets where statesmen once strolled, a never-ending stream of money now changes hands—tying the hands of those elected to lead. . . . This betrayal of democracy must stop."

CHAPTER SEVEN

Retraining for Nonexistent Jobs

Learning to Earn Less

You may have missed the commercial on television, or the advertisement in your newspaper. The one aimed at you folks who were making between, say, $10 and $20 an hour. The one that urges you to return to college or a technical school or a trade school to acquire skills for a new profession or occupation in a global economy. The one that says that after you have completed your advanced education, you will be able to earn between $5 and $10 an hour. Five dollars to $10 when you were making $10 to $20?

You bet.

There is no such commercial, of course. If there were, no one would sign up for the retraining courses. Nevertheless, that's what the people in Washington are encouraging jobless workers to do. In fact, they are spending tens of billions of taxpayer dollars to retrain and reeducate American workers so they can make less money. Except they aren't telling workers that once their education is completed they will receive smaller paychecks. And their benefits—most notably health care and pensions—won't be as good as they had at their last job. It's another one of Washington's little secrets.

But before the litany of statistics that show how things are, it may be useful to understand what the people in Washington believe is an appropriate income for you.

In conducting studies of workers who have lost their jobs when companies cut back or closed because they were unable to compete against cheap imported goods, the government considered one of its retraining programs a success if workers moved into a new job "that paid or had the potential to pay suitable wages."

Retraining for Nonexistent Jobs

And what was the U.S. government's definition of "suitable wage"? It's 80 percent or more of the displaced worker's former wages.

Thus, if you earned $35,000 at a company that shut down and moved to Mexico, and you completed a retraining course and found a new job that paid—or might one day pay—$28,000, the people in Washington chalked you up as one of their success stories.

Now the findings from an audit report prepared by the Office of Inspector General of the U.S. Department of Labor. Its investigators tracked a group of displaced workers who qualified for retraining under the Trade Adjustment Assistance program, enacted in 1974 to aid workers who lost their jobs as a result of imports.

- Just five of every 10 displaced workers who were eligible to attend retraining courses did so.
- Of those five workers who completed retraining, only two found work in their new field.
- And only one of the five retrained workers found a job in the new field "that paid or had the potential to pay suitable wages." Remember, suitable wages means the potential to make 80 percent or more of what they earned in their old job.
- The median weekly wage of workers in their new jobs was $320. That was down 25 percent from the $425 median wage in the jobs they lost. The median wage means half earned more, half earned less.
- The more money workers made in the jobs they lost, the less likely they were to earn as much or more in their new jobs.
- Of those workers who earned $300 to $399 a week, 54 percent found new jobs "that paid or had the potential to pay suitable wages."
- But of those workers who earned $800 a week or more, only 32 percent found new jobs that paid or might one day pay 80 percent of their former earnings.
- Of those workers who completed retraining and responded to the government survey, 54 percent said the program did not assist them in getting another job.

The Inspector General's Office findings from 1993 buttress those of the authors, gleaned from interviews of displaced workers conducted from 1994 to 1996 across the country.

Item. With few exceptions, retrained workers are earning less in their new jobs than they did in the ones they lost when their old employers trimmed workforces or closed plants—in some cases, up to 50 percent less money.

Item. They are unable to find employment in the new fields in which they received specialized training and have been forced, in many cases, to take jobs that require few or no special skills.

Item. They are either going without health insurance or are paying a portion of the premiums for coverage that is inferior to what they had in their old jobs.

Item. They are working two or more part-time jobs that add up to more hours but less money than their former job paid, traveling greater distances to work and spending more time away from their families.

Item. And finally, many workers enrolled in the Trade Adjustment Assistance program not to get the retraining but so they could collect income-support payments for an extra year. Workers who lose their jobs receive unemployment compensation for 26 weeks. Those who qualify for TAA training can receive support payments equal to their unemployment benefits for an additional year.

The situation is no better in other government training programs, such as the one designed for men and women who never worked or have held only marginal jobs. The General Accounting Office (GAO), the investigative arm of Congress, reported in March 1996 that a study of such workers showed that five years after they completed training, there was no "statistically significant" difference between their wages and the wages paid to workers who did not receive training. In addition, the GAO concluded that "individuals assigned to participate in the program did not have . . . employment rates significantly higher than individuals not assigned to participate."

None of this discourages members of Congress, government officials and American presidents from talking about the wonders of the training and retraining legislation they have proposed or enacted and signed into law, and all the high-tech jobs waiting to be filled by formerly unemployed workers who have successfully completed retraining courses.

President Clinton in April 1994: "We want instead of an unemployment system, a reemployment system, so the minute people lose their jobs, they're immediately eligible for retraining and for job help to find new jobs and different jobs. . . ."

Retraining for Nonexistent Jobs

Secretary of Labor Robert Reich in January 1996: "As this country continues to adjust to a changing national and international economy, it is critical that we retain the talents and skills of individuals whose work lives are affected but whose contributions to society are as vital as ever. This is why training and retraining services are so critical to our nation's workforce development."

Truth to tell, the single largest group of beneficiaries of retraining is not the workers themselves, but the people employed in the cottage industry that it supports. In fact, far and away the best-paying jobs available are not for the graduates of retraining but rather for those associated with the programs. They range from teachers, educators and administrators in trade schools, technical schools, colleges and universities, to workers in federal, state and local governments who administer a bewildering array of courses.

So far in the 1990s, under dozens of programs designed for everyone from workers who lose their jobs because of imports to illiterate teenagers, the U.S. government has spent more than $100 billion. That's enough to pay tuition bills to send upward of one million students through Harvard. But retrained workers aren't looking for a Harvard degree. All they want is a job that pays what they earned in their last one. On that score—perhaps the most important to working people—retraining has been a dismal failure.

Daniel M. Heitsenrether, who manages the Williamsport Regional Office of the Pennsylvania Dislocated Worker Unit in the Pennsylvania Department of Labor and Industry, offers this assessment based on his two decades of experience in dealing with the jobless: "About 5 percent obtain jobs paying comparable or higher wages. The other 95 percent move into lower-paying jobs, even after retraining."

A Symbol of Distress: The Transformer Plant

To better understand the failure of just one of the government's many retraining programs—the Trade Adjustment Assistance program—as well as the circumstances that force displaced workers into retraining, let's look at what happened at one facility and the employees who once worked there.

The place is Canonsburg, Pa., about 30 miles south and west of Pittsburgh. It's a town of 9,200 people, the home of pop singers Perry Como and Bobby Vinton, the birthplace (1791) of the Whiskey Rebellion, perhaps the nation's first tax revolt.

The factory was known for decades simply as "the transformer plant." Owned by Cooper Power Systems, the plant, which in the early 1990s employed as many as 1,000 people, manufactured custom-designed transformers for electric utilities and other large users of electricity.

In the spring of 1994, Cooper Power, a subsidiary of a Houston-based conglomerate, Cooper Industries Inc., decided to close the transformer plant—the last American-owned facility of its kind. Layoffs began that fall and the shutdown was completed by Thanksgiving.

This is a walk through the lives of some of the people who worked there. What you will see, what you will hear, in these conversations is everything that has gone wrong in America—from failed retraining programs to government policies that treat one jobless worker quite different from another, to the elimination of entire occupations so that jobs skills and expertise built up over decades are lost forever. And you will hear about the frustrations of people who have worked 10, 20 and 30 years at one place and suddenly find themselves on the street. In all of this, the employees of "the transformer plant" are representative of workers at other shuttered plants, in other industries, across America.

Like John Bizub. After 25 years, Bizub, a 48-year-old widower with two grown children, lost his job as an electrical draftsman in September 1994.

Because Cooper workers qualified for assistance under the Trade Adjustment Assistance (TAA) program, he signed up for a heating and air conditioning course at Penn Commercial, a business and technical school in his hometown of Washington, Pa., about 12 miles south of Canonsburg. Bizub was one of 10 people who began classes in January 1995. "All 10 were from Cooper," he recalled. "So it was like everybody knew each other." In December 1995, he received his associate degree in heating and air conditioning and began to search out the job market.

"I put in applications everywhere," he said. But there were no offers. "I had an interview with one guy about three days after I graduated. He said, 'Okay, we'll give you a call for your second interview.' And I never heard nothing from him."

Unable to find work in the field he had been retrained for, Bizub lowered his expectations. He saw an ad in the paper for a cleaning supervisor at Futtrel Inc., a company that trains mentally and physically challenged people. In February 1996, he was

190

hired to supervise a Futtrel work crew that cleaned the Army Aviation Center in Washington. It was a part-time job without benefits. The hours were from 3:30 to 8:30 P.M. The pay: $5.25 an hour. That represented a 60 percent cut in hourly wages from the $13.27 that Bizub earned at the transformer plant.

You may want to look at those dollar amounts on a yearly basis. The $13.27 an hour at Cooper gave Bizub an annual salary of $27,600, placing him in the middle class. The $5.25 hourly pay for a part-time job gave him an annual salary of $6,800, placing him among the more than 16 million individuals and families the federal government classifies as living in poverty.

Recognizing that he could not make it on the income from one part-time job, and with his unemployment benefits gone, Bizub sought out another part-time job. He found it—not in heating and air conditioning, for which he had been retrained, but, once more, in cleaning.

Bizub went to work for Hennson Maintenance, a company with cleaning contracts in a half-dozen counties in southwestern Pennsylvania. His workdays are full.

"I work for Hennson Maintenance in the mornings. I start there at 7:00 in the morning and normally we quit around 12:00 [noon]. So I get five hours in the morning and then I come home, get cleaned up, and at 3:30 I have to be down at Futtrel to go pick up my clients."

Bizub's pay at Hennson Maintenance: $5.50 an hour. Now John Bizub's employment and pay profile looks like this: He works 10 hours a day for a total daily pay of $53.75. That amounts to one-half the daily pay of $106 that he made at the transformer plant. Of course, the $106 was earned over eight hours.

Bizub is philosophical about his situation: "I'm at half of what I was making there at Cooper, plus no benefits. So the only thing I'm doing is working to pay bills. Put a little food on the table. Maybe go out once a month.

"I'm making enough money to pay the bills. But God forbid if something should happen. You know, like the car breaks down, or the water tank goes, or this or that. And then I might have to forgo paying the bills for one month to try to get something fixed. . . . Luckily, I don't have a mortgage [he owns his own home], don't have a car payment. . . .

"I consider myself fortunate because of the fact I do have two part-time jobs. And I know some guys that don't have any jobs. . . .

One guy, a real good friend of mine I went to school with for heating and air conditioning, the bank's knocking on his door.

"He does own his car. But the bank's knocking on his door for the mortgage. He's had to go through consumer credit and all that kind of stuff. I'm hoping and praying that things work out for him. . . . He's 55 years old."

As for the government's retraining program, Bizub echos the view of other displaced workers interviewed by the authors. Many, if not most, sign up for retraining just to continue collecting unemployment checks.

"They should have just gave us two years unemployment and forgot about the retraining program. Because of the fact a lot of the guys that went to school are now finding jobs that aren't related, and if they are, they're starting at the bottom rate, which is normal.

"Personally, I think they should have just gave us two years unemployment and you're on your own. Because that way guys two years ago could have got jobs making $5 an hour or $6 an hour and possibly they might have been up to maybe $7 an hour, $8 an hour now. Well, now they're two years older, and they're starting out at $5 and $6 an hour. I mean, some guys they get lucky. They got jobs in the field of studies that they went to. But they're few and far between."

Bizub said that of the 10 Cooper workers in his heating and air conditioning course, only two found work in that field. As for pay, Bizub said, "one guy's making $6, the other guy's making $7. Now these guys were making $16 an hour [at Cooper]. They were like $16-plus an hour when they left Cooper. And they're taking $6- and $7-an-hour jobs."

Sometimes, though, in other locales under other circumstances, the jobs do pay more—at least when they're offered to foreign workers. In 1995, the Department of Labor certified that no American workers were available to take heating and air conditioning service and installation jobs in Annandale, Manassas and Vienna, Va. The department authorized a company in that area to bring in foreign workers at a pay rate of $17.26 an hour— or $35,900 a year, assuming a 40-hour week.

The foreign workers were recruited under the Permanent Labor Certification Program, which grants them permanent residency status and allows them to become U.S. citizens. The only requirement, you may recall, is that the government must attest that "there are not sufficient U.S. workers who are able, willing, qualified and available at the place where the alien is to perform the skilled or unskilled labor."

When the Layoffs Came

Built as a wartime facility by Alcoa, the transformer plant was a fixture of Canonsburg from the close of World War II on. The facility was so massive that workers used bicycles to move about. Like so many other factories and plants in so many other towns and cities across America, it provided lifetime employment for residents of the area. Entire families worked there—fathers and sons, brothers and uncles, husbands and wives. At its peak in the 1970s, it employed 3,000 people. It was good pay. The benefits, especially health care insurance, were generous.

Over the years, the plant built transformers for factories, coal mines and many of the nation's largest electric utilities. The custom-designed transformers ranged in size from small units attached to utility poles to ones as large as a two-story house that had to be transported by specially built railcars to electric utility power plants.

But the transformer business, like so many businesses, is cyclical. Periods of high demand for the product are followed by slack periods. None of this mattered until the takeover craze of the 1980s when ever-larger profit demands led the plant through an ownership change, a bitter strike, concessions by employees, and ultimately, in 1994, to a decision to close the plant.

In the spring of that year, Cooper advised the United Steelworkers Union, which represented office and production workers, that it planned to shut down the facility. By Thanksgiving, only a skeleton crew remained, largely to fulfill repair requests.

When the layoffs began, the union hall just outside the plant was converted into a displaced-workers office, which later was moved across town to the American Legion post. It was staffed by several former employees and funded by the state and $200,000 from Cooper Industries.

Each day, workers congregated in the office to learn about forthcoming retraining courses; the types of health care coverage available, which ranged from little to none; the area employers with job openings, and lists of agencies where they could secure assistance—food pantries, credit counseling, homeowners' emergency mortgage assistance. Perhaps equally important, in addition to all those real services, the office offered a place for workers to vent their anger over losing their jobs and their frustration in dealing with the unemployment office for the first time in their lives.

They worried about selecting the right kind of retraining course—one that hopefully would lead to a permanent job—and what they would do about health care. Said one office counselor: "There's people who come in here. They sit in that chair. They sound like they're okay, Then they get hot. You try to explain they're not the only one in this position. They don't want to talk at home. This is where they come to talk about their problems . . . .

"These people come in here, they could go to a psychiatrist and he couldn't help them any better than I can. They don't have a job—and that's what they need. This is not the fault of the average guy, what happened here. But tell your kid that. Tell your wife that. See how far it goes."

In the end, all that mattered was a job. And that was hard to find. At least a decent-paying one. The center's staff routinely posted employment openings available across the Pittsburgh area. With an occasional exception, the list read like a catalogue of low-wage, low-tech jobs:

Armed guard, $6.50 an hour. Maintenance repairmen ("two years experience preferred"), $6.50 an hour. Customer service representative ("Must be able to stand for eight-hour shifts. Bend, stretch and lift 25 pounds"), $4.50 an hour. Sales clerk ("need to work two hours per day"), $4.50 an hour. Telephone solicitor ("temporary position"), $5 an hour. Exterminator ("treat lawns with pesticides"), $8 an hour.

Receptionist ("high-profile front desk"), $5.50 an hour. Dishwasher ("employer will train"), $5 an hour. Cook ("spin pizza dough, make sauces, fry food, make sandwiches"), $5 an hour.

Day-care worker ("two years experience"), $4.25 an hour. Manager of retail store ("open, close, make schedules"), $6 an hour. Driver—sales ("refill perfume dispensers in restrooms"), $6 an hour. Housekeeper ("train to clean hotel rooms"), $5.50 an hour. Laundry clerk ("check in clothing"), $4.25 an hour. Waiter-waitress, $2.34 an hour ("plus tips").

In some cases, the jobs required travel time of one hour or more. All this for work that paid no more than double the minimum wage at the time—$8.50 an hour. Once more, put that income in yearly numbers: $17,680. Before Social Security and Medicare taxes are withheld. Before federal and state income taxes are withheld. For a family of four, it's slightly above the poverty line of $15,570.

In the year that followed the transformer plant closing, Cooper workers would submit thousands of employment applications. Listen to what they found.

Ed Lemley, who worked at the plant 32 years, looked at one job that was a combination stock clerk and prescription delivery person: "It paid $5 [an hour] with no benefits. Fifty hours one week. Forty to forty-five hours the next week. Five days one week. Six days the next. They just flatly tell you, 'These are the hours.'"

Vince O'Shea graduated from Carnegie High School in 1963, cut crystals for shortwave radios, served a tour of duty with the army in Korea, then went to work at the transformer plant for the next 26 years: "I looked really hard for a job for about six months. One guy looked at my application and said, 'Boy, you have a lot of experience.' That meant I was too old."

Ed Banko went to work at the plant in 1963 and over the next three decades worked as a cost accountant, inventory control, purchasing and production scheduling: "With 30 years of clerical experience, I didn't get one offering. . . . The few good interviews told me they were just building up their dossiers." Eventually, he found work at Thrift Drug. "I'm starting off at $4.50. At Cooper, I made $13.90."

Some former Cooper employees turned to temporary agencies for jobs, but those experiences, too, have been demoralizing. When temp workers take jobs, O'Shea said, they often are told that it's going to be a permanent position. "But right before they get that probation period in, they're let go. And it's like a big revolving door."

He said that "there's been guys who have had three or four jobs at this point. . . . The companies are in the driver's seat. They can get anybody they want. . . . And they know they can do it. They're not going to pay any benefits. They just let them go before it comes time to get into any kind of benefits."

O'Shea said that his wife has had six or seven different jobs through temporary agencies. "She's told they're temp to perm, but they never end up being permanent. The shame of it is that some people can't handle this—their first thing is, 'What did I do wrong?' These [companies] want a turnover. And they don't want anybody to get comfortable in there . . . . It really is sad. I don't know where it's going to . . . ."

Joseph M. Amorose, one of the managers of the displaced workers office, echos this view. A Vietnam War veteran who is married with two teenage sons, Amorose had 25 years in at the transformer plant. His father had retired after 27 years. Two uncles also worked there.

Amorose said that representatives from a temporary agency had visited the displaced workers office and told him they were contacting area employers. "What they do is, they go in and talk to these employers," he said. "They say: 'If you want to keep your workforce at a certain level, you don't have to worry about the comp issue [workers compensation], the hospitalization issue; that if you've got a project coming up, why don't you come through us. We'll turn around and staff your project and when it's done, you release all these people and you're not stuck with them.'"

Health Insurance Crisis

Severely depressed wages and a constant turnover in temporary employment are not the end of the grim news for the one-time Cooper employees. Workers who accepted low-paying jobs to put food on the table also had to forgo health insurance. Most of the companies hiring, even for full-time positions, provided no health care or required a substantial copayment.

Of course, they had the option of continuing their health care package they had at Cooper by paying the premiums under COBRA, yet another government program designed more for the affluent than for the jobless. That's because the premiums are so high that few people who lose their jobs can afford to pay for the insurance. "There's no way people can afford this," said Vince O'Shea, the longtime Cooper veteran who helped man the displaced-workers office. "I would have to say many, if not most, are going without insurance. When we sent out the price lists [explaining the insurance costs]," he said, "the calls started coming in. A woman called me the other day and she said we can't afford this [health care premium]. What are we going to do? I feel bad because there's nothing they can do. This lady that called, she even went to welfare. They said, 'You own a home. You have money in the bank.' And she said, 'Not for long.' There's something wrong with this. The average person wants a livable wage and dignity. That's all."

John Bizub is one of them. "I just hope and pray nothing happens to me," he says. "And if it does, it's quick. You know what I mean. Don't make me sick. Just kill me. . . . ."

Retraining for Nonexistent Jobs

Bizub recalls that shortly after the plant closed there was a health insurance seminar to lay out the options for workers. "We went and this guy's giving us this song and dance about health insurance and to see what it was going to cost. And a real good friend of mine stood up. . . and he says, 'Now what about these people that have to make a decision between health insurance and food on the table? What do they do?' And he says, 'Well, it's a decision they have to make.' My friend says, 'Well, I'm putting food on the table.'"

Kenneth R. Dombrowski is a quiet, soft-spoken, 57-year-old man who worked at the Cooper plant for more than 31 years. A 1957 graduate of Canonsburg High School, he spent three years in the U.S. Navy and several more years working with his father as a painter before starting at the transformer plant on April 29, 1963.

Through the years, he held a variety of jobs, from general laborer to mechanical assembler to core fabricator.

"I enjoyed working down there," he says. "We did our work and at the same time we had fun doing it. If you did your job, they left you alone. . . . I thought I was going to work until I retired. And I think everybody else did."

When he was first interviewed by one of the authors in March 1995, Dombrowski had been out of work five months. He was still searching for a job that paid a decent wage, while at the same time mulling over the possibility of attending a retraining school.

Most of all, he was concerned about medical insurance. With a wife who had one cancer operation in 1990, and two children still at home—a daughter in nursing school and a son in high school—health care coverage was an absolute necessity. His wife's costly treatment was covered almost entirely by the Blue Cross–Blue Shield plan at the transformer plant.

Under the severance agreement negotiated with Cooper, workers received fully paid health insurance for nine months.When Dombrowski's was due to run out in July 1995, he then faced three choices—two of them unacceptable.

He could continue the existing coverage under COBRA, the government program that allows workers to retain their existing coverage if they pay for it. That would cost him more than $500 a month, or roughly 50 percent of his after-tax income.

He could sign up for a special-care alternative package that would cost him less money, $156 a month, but did not provide major medical or "cover that much."

He could find a job—hopefully—that paid a comparatively small wage but provided health insurance. There were no good-paying jobs available, especially for someone then 56 years old.

Indeed, Dombroski's job search mirrored that of most Cooper workers. "I had about 25 résumés and applications out there," he said. "Every time there was something in the paper, I ran out. But the places aren't hiring. Some places, all they want are your name and address and they say they will call you."

What did the jobs pay? "Most start at $4.50," he said, "and they go to maybe $6.50. You're lucky if you can start at $6.50. You go to the unemployment office and look at the bulletin board and it's $4.50 to $5.50." At the transformer plant, he was making $16.48 an hour when he was terminated. The $16.48 translates into a solid middle-class income of $34,000 a year. The $6.50 an hour adds up to $13,500 a year—a poverty-level income for a household of four.

"When I put my unemployment application in," Dombrowski recalled, "the man looked at the salary and said you're never going to get that. If I can get $7 or $8 an hour with benefits, I'm going to work. I know I'm not going to get $16. But where do you draw the line? If I have the medical insurance, that's the most important thing to me. I hate this. I still got kids. How do I get my youngest boy an education?

"The people want you to work for nothing. A neighbor went to one place and he [would have] started at $4.50, would go to $5. But he would have been held at that rate for four years. But they did provide insurance."

Dombrowski eventually found work at a company that assembles literature into packets for corporate training seminars. It pays about $7 an hour, which means a 58 percent reduction from his Cooper wage.

The work actually opened up when he was in his second week at a training school but he quit to take the job, he said, because "it provides health insurance." As for his coworkers who completed retraining, Dombrowski said, most are still "out looking for work. There ain't nothing out there."

Sometimes workers were obliged to give up even before starting—through no fault of their own. Ed Banko enrolled in a computer course at a trade school. "They gave me a schedule. When I started the first day, the first class was computer programming. The second class was beginning computers. The third class was advanced computers. I went to the programming class and I said,

Retraining for Nonexistent Jobs

'What am I doing here?' The second class was okay. The third class—I couldn't do that. I said this isn't right."

What happened to Banko was the equivalent of placing a junior high school student in calculus for his first class of the day, and beginning math the second class. Banko said that he asked the instructor and "she said that was it. . . . I told [the admissions office] it would be foolish to continue and dropped out."

In some instances, former Cooper workers enrolled in courses in such large numbers that there was little likelihood they would ever find employment when they graduated. At just one of the technical schools, 106 workers from the transformer plant signed up for 12 different retraining classes. But 42—or 40 percent of them—enrolled in building maintenance. Another 16 workers—15 percent of the total—took quality food classes. And 14 workers—or 13 percent of the total—took business data processing.

That means 68 percent of the displaced workers were receiving training for jobs that would pay, at best, only a few dollars above the minimum wage—and substantially below what they earned at Cooper. The other courses, and the number enrolled, were: carpentry (8); machinist (7); electrician (6); heating and air conditioning (5); auto body (3); health assistants (2); and drafting, masonry and welding (1 each).

For many older workers who lose their jobs but are too young to consider retirement, returning to a classroom for retraining is the most difficult hurdle to overcome. Some are skilled craftsmen who never finished high school and are fearful they will be unable to master the academic material. Some are reluctant to start over at 45 or 55.

Many are simply embarrassed because they have lost their jobs. They believe it reflects on them personally, that they are a failure. Ray Shook, who has witnessed the feeling close up many times, explains: "If your wife is working and you are sitting at home, you feel very badly. Money's not everything. It's pride. Someone says, 'Hey, where do you work?' 'I worked at The Transformer 30 years building transformers.' A mill worker has the same feelings as the bank president who loses his job."

Label all these people as retraining's casualties. And keep in mind that no one in government counts them, knows or cares about them.

Vince O'Shea talked about the stress on workers who have been out of school for years who suddenly have been forced back into a classroom. "These people knew how to build transformers.

199

Some might not have been able to write their names, but they could build a transformer. What is happening to them," he said, "isn't right."

On Monday, March 13, 1995, Donald L. Mosier, a 56-year-old U.S. Navy veteran who had built transformers at Cooper for three decades, attended his first retraining classes with other Cooper employees at Western Vo-Tech.

The classes ran from 3 P.M. until 9 P.M. Shook recalls talking with some of Mosier's colleagues: "They said he felt it was hard to cope. 'Here I've been working 30 years and now I have to start all over again.' Most guys feel the same way. Why should I go to school, what can I learn? But they need the extra weeks [of unemployment compensation].

"This is like walking across the creek, from one rock to the next. I can't swim and that last rock is the final unemployment compensation check. They are getting $1,200 a month. They can get by month to month. But it's running out."

In any event, Shook said, one of Mosier's buddies noticed that he was depressed. "He told his wife when he got home that he didn't know if Mosier could cope with school and that he would call him the next day to offer him a ride."

The friend called the next day, Shook said, but was unable to reach him.

Mosier, the father of three grown children, was found in his garage, car running, dead of carbon-monoxide poisoning.

CHAPTER • EIGHT

What Can Be Done?

Restoring Fairness

The times are trying.

Corporations merge to form megacorporations with far-reaching power and influence. Workers put in ever-longer hours to make ends meet. Families feel under siege. The gap between the country's richest citizens and average workers widens daily. The government imposes its most onerous tax burden on working individuals and families. And it taxes most lightly the nation's wealthiest citizens.

Political attacks have become so personal that good people are discouraged from running for office. Local governments are competing against each other to lure new businesses by giving economic incentives to their owners. Stories of government corruption appear with startling regularity on the front pages of newspapers.

America in the 1990s, right?

Wrong.

America in the 1890s.

To understand where you are today—and why—you might just turn back the clock a century. To understand where you can be tomorrow, you might just recall how citizens in that earlier era dealt with the same forces you confront.

There are, to be sure, differences between the America of the 1990s and a century ago. One stands out above all the others. Back then, a powerful reform movement took shape and a third party, the Progressive Party, brought about wholesale changes in the way government operated.

The Progressive Party's reforms were gradually co-opted, one by one, by the two major parties, the Democrats and the Republicans. By the time the Progressive Party passed out of existence, many of the changes it had proposed were in place:

- Because government needed more revenue and the rich were not paying their fair share, the income tax was enacted.
- Because businesses were peddling tainted meat, food and medicines, pure food and drugs laws were enacted.
- Because companies were forming trusts that wielded unprecedented powers, the antitrust and monopoly laws were enacted.
- Because half the nation's population was denied the right to vote, the women's suffrage law was enacted.
- In other instances, the reformers set a tone that produced yet more legislation in the decades that followed—from child labor laws to unemployment compensation, from minimum wage to Social Security.

All these changes resulted in a legislative framework to protect the average citizen and small businesses from the excesses of big business, special interests and individuals who exploited others and used government to their own personal advantage. More important, over time that framework gave rise to the largest middle class in history.

Now that framework is being dismantled. The evolving economy is balkanizing America—pitting social groups against one another, widening the gap between the have-mores and the have-lesses. What is at stake is nothing less than the cohesiveness of American society.

This is not to say that Washington policy makers deliberately set out to enact laws and programs to set citizen against citizen, or to reduce American living standards. Indeed, many have acted out of the best of intentions. But whether well-intentioned, or influenced unduly by corporate or other special interests, government policy makers too often have based their decisions on faulty assumptions or erroneous beliefs that have had unforeseen consequences. Nowhere is that more true than in policies that affect the U.S. economy.

How can we begin to restore a measure of fairness in American society, ease the gap between the have-mores and the have-lesses, halt the loss of good manufacturing jobs and improve the condition of the beleaguered middle class? Some specific suggestions will follow in a moment. But first, it's important to recognize the mistakes that some of "the best and the brightest" in

Return to a Two-Class Society

The shift in wealth upward is moving America closer to the society of the 1890s, when most of the wealth was owned by a small elite.

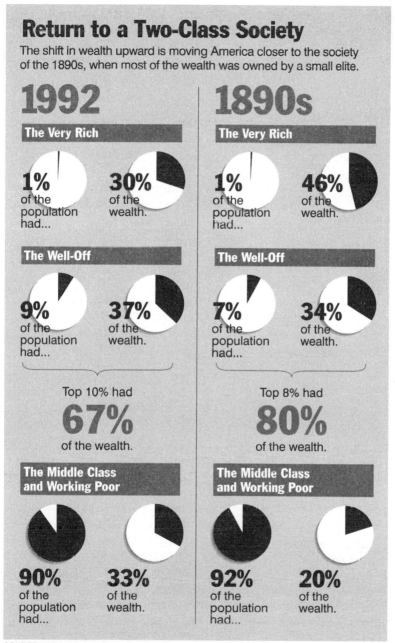

1992

The Very Rich

1% of the population had...

30% of the wealth.

The Well-Off

9% of the population had...

37% of the wealth.

Top 10% had

67%

of the wealth.

The Middle Class and Working Poor

90% of the population had...

33% of the wealth.

1890s

The Very Rich

1% of the population had...

46% of the wealth.

The Well-Off

7% of the population had...

34% of the wealth.

Top 8% had

80%

of the wealth.

The Middle Class and Working Poor

92% of the population had...

20% of the wealth.

SOURCE: 1890s data from Estate Records of Massachusetts, 1889-1891 government and finance have made in the past—and to learn from them.

For those who would put absolute faith in the infallibility of economic experts, there is this reminder:

On October 16, 1929, Charles E. Mitchell, president of National City Bank of New York and the nation's leading banker, sent a cable to financier Bernard Baruch, who was in Scotland at the time, with this advice on the stock market: "General situation looks exceptionally sound with very few bad spots. . . . I doubt if anything that will not affect business can affect the market, which is like a weather-vane pointing into a gale of prosperity." Thirteen days later, the weather vane was pointing into an unprecedented storm, as the stock market collapsed, leading to the Great Depression.

In the 1950s, as government officials and scientists sought to persuade Americans of the wisdom of building a nuclear-power industry, B. Lewis Strauss, chairman of the Atomic Energy Commission, and Edward Teller, father of the H-bomb, painted a bright picture of an atomic future. Strauss promised that "our children will enjoy . . . . electrical energy too cheap to meter," and Teller dismissed even the concept of nuclear waste, saying that "these radioactive byproducts will turn out to be useful and will not be considered as waste at all."

You may check your electric bill to determine the accuracy of Strauss's forecast. As for the valuable nuclear by-products, they've turned out to be so hazardous that they have cost taxpayers and electric utility customers billions of dollars to store. And the final bill hasn't been tabulated yet.

Perhaps the ultimate bad judgment in the last 30 years was made by a man who in 1966 topped a list of "greatest living businessmen in American history" in a poll conducted by the Graduate School of Business Administration at the University of Michigan: Robert S. McNamara. As U.S. secretary of defense in 1966, McNamara had this comment on the decision to pour American troops into South Vietnam to turn back the North Vietnamese: "To prevent that disaster, the United States put into South Vietnam over 100,000 men in about 120 days. The potential disaster was averted. . . . Whereas the North Vietnamese and the Viet Cong forces were approaching possible victory some 15 months ago, I think it is clear to all that today a military victory is beyond their grasp."

Thirty years later, in 1995, private citizen McNamara had this

What Can Be Done?

to say: "My associates in the Kennedy and Johnson administrations were an exceptional group: young, vigorous, intelligent, well-meaning, patriotic servants of the United States. How did this group—'the best and the brightest,' as we eventually came to be known in an ironically pejorative phrase—get it wrong on Vietnam? . . . I want to put Vietnam in context. . . . We were wrong, terribly wrong." The "errors of judgment" over Vietnam resulted in the deaths of 47,000 military personnel and the wounding of 300,000 others.

U. S. economic policy has been marked by the same kind of errors of judgment. For decades, policy makers have consistently miscalculated the impact of their decisions on the American workforce.

In 1962, as Congress debated President Kennedy's Trade Expansion Act that called for lower tariffs on imported products, Wilbur Mills, the Arkansas Democrat who chaired the House Ways and Means Committee, sought to allay concerns of some congressmen who worried the bill would cost American jobs. Citing a letter he had received from shoe workers in his state who feared that shoe imports would soar under the trade bill, Mills told lawmakers on June 28, 1962: "I do not believe this will happen to my shoe people. . . . In 1961 . . . imports of shoes as a percentage of U.S. production were still only 2.6 percent. This bill is not here, with my name on it, to bring about the sacrifice of any of these industries about which we are talking. This bill has safeguards in it."

Wilbur Mills was flat wrong.

His bill, others that followed and decisions by presidents and trade administrators from both parties brought about that very "sacrifice" that Mills denied could ever happen, not only for the shoe industry—where imports now account for 85 percent of the American market—but for other American industries, as well. Remember machine tools, telephones, microwave ovens and roses, to name only a few.

Many of the themes currently shaping economic policy are based on equally false assumptions. One of the most popular—and one that is bound to cause disillusion in the future—is the widely touted theory that America's future depends on the creation of high-tech jobs.

Over and over we are told that high-tech jobs will be the salvation of the American worker. "America's future is in high-tech work," Senator John Breaux, the Democratic senator from Louisiana, said in November 1993. "We're going to be making 747s and computers and the medical equipment for the rest of the world. Nobody can compete with American workers in those areas."

Actually, foreign workers already are "competing"—and at much lower wages. The Chinese, in a requirement insisted upon by their government in exchange for buying Boeing airplanes, are manufacturing sections of Boeing 747s as well as 737s in China. And, as you may recall, the United States now has a trade deficit in computers even with China. In 1995, China shipped $1 billion worth of computers here, while American companies exported a mere $255 million in computers to China.

The belief that the United States will enjoy a monopoly on high-tech jobs while developing nations concentrate on making labor-intensive products is one of the fictions of American economic policy. Developing countries already are targeting the high-technology field for job creation, much as they once targeted labor-intensive industries, such as apparel and electronic assembly.

Listen to this excerpt from a 1995 report of the Ministry of Finance of Malaysia, a country bordering the South China Sea, between Indonesia and Vietnam, with a population of about 20 million people. The report's language about the challenge facing Malaysia—the need to move away from labor-intensive work and toward high-tech development—sounds eerily similar to the statements U.S. politicians, corporate executives and economists make about the challenge facing the United States in the global economy:

> The need for Malaysia to move towards high technology industries is becoming increasingly necessary, given that the country now faces shortages of labor with the rapid growth in the economy since 1988. Furthermore, other surplus labor countries, like Vietnam and China, are opening up their economies to foreign investors and Malaysia will no longer be able to compete for labor-intensive industries against these countries. Malaysian industries must also restructure to go upscale in technology in order to remain efficient and competitive in a rapidly changing global environment.

Even under the best of conditions, there will never be an abundance of high-tech jobs—certainly not enough to replace the low- and medium-wage jobs that are being eliminated by imports.

If the people in Washington can't get it right on such basic economic issues as shoe making and high-tech jobs, what does it say about their handling of broader economic policies?

Not much.

An illustration of how the view of America from Washington gets distorted: Many of these policies are tied to the chief statistical yardstick that the government relies on to measure our progress as a society: GDP. That is, the gross domestic product, the sum total of all goods and services produced in the United States. Every month, newspapers, magazines, radio and televison print and air the latest government report on the GDP:

New York Times, January 29, 1994: "Stocks surged to record highs in a second day of heavy trading yesterday, after the Commerce Department reported that the economy grew at a 5.9 percent pace in the last three months of 1993—the best quarterly performance in six years. But even better was the news, included in the report on the gross domestic product, that inflation remained low. . . ."

Los Angeles Times, January 28, 1995: "The nation's economy grew at a supercharged rate of 4.5 percent during the final three months of 1994, the government said Friday. . . . The economy gained 4 percent for all of 1994—its strongest showing since the end of Ronald Reagan's first term as President when it soared 6.2 percent in 1984. . . . While the President and others in his administration portrayed the fourth quarter growth in gross domestic product—which measures the total value of the nation's goods and services—as healthy, some economists worried that the nation's economic engine was running too fast."

Philadelphia Inquirer, May 3, 1996: "Neither blizzards nor a government shutdown nor a strike at General Motors Corp. could keep the U.S. economy down. The nation's gross domestic product showed surprising strength in the first quarter of this year and grew at a faster-than-expected 2.8 percent rate."

This steadily rising GDP, the people in Washington and on Wall Street will tell you, is evidence that Americans are doing better than ever. But judge for yourself. During the three decades between 1965 and 1995, the U.S. population grew 37 percent, from 194 million to 265 million. In that period, the GDP shot up 901 percent, from $719 billion to $7.2 trillion. But between those years of a spiraling GDP:

- The number of persons unemployed went up 118 percent, from 3.4 million to 7.4 million.
- The number of those unemployed for 27 weeks or longer jumped 270 percent, from 351,000 to 1.3 million.
- The unemployment rate for blacks and other minorities went from 8.1 percent to 9.6 percent.
- The number of new housing units started annually fell from 1.473 million units to 1.350 million units.
- The number of business failures soared 427 percent, from 13,500 to 71,200. The business failure rate went up from 53 percent to 86 percent.
- The number of personal bankruptcies filed went up 365 percent, from 180,300 to 837,800.
- The number of persons receiving food stamps rocketed 6,386 percent, from 424,000 in the program's fourth year to 27.5 million in 1995.
- The number of households in poverty headed by females went up 121 percent, from 1.9 million to 4.2 million.

The statistics fail to show any connection between a rising GDP and the economic well-being of average Americans.

Perhaps an even more troubling question about the validity of the GDP statistic, and all those news reports that accompany its release, is this: Does the GDP—which counts only those transactions where money changes hands and assigns no value to the purpose of the expenditure—measure the kind of society you would like to live in?

Consider: If the cancer rate went up, more money would be spent on costly medical procedures, more people would be sent to hospitals for longer stays, all requiring the expenditure of ever-larger sums of money, thereby pushing up the GDP and creating good news. If the number of people convicted of crimes went up even faster, more money would be spent to build more prisons and hire more guards, thereby pushing up the GDP and creating more good news. And if more pollutants were spewed into the air, more money would be spent on cleanups and the medical bills of people requiring treatment, thereby pushing up the GDP and creating still more good news.

By now, you get the idea of what constitutes "good news" in the view of Washington, Wall Street and the economists of both.

But there's still more to think about. For you cannot use GDP to assess the health of a society any more than a doctor can use a thermometer to take your blood pressure.

Consider once more: If your mother-in-law watches your children so you can go to work, that's bad for the economy. No money changes hands and so it doesn't count in the GDP. But if you pay a day-care center to look after your children, that's good for the economy. If you serve as a volunteer counselor in the neighborhood drug and alcohol treatment facility, that's bad. But if the counselor is paid, that's good. If you care for your aged father, who suffers from Alzheimer's disease, at home, that's bad. But if you put him in a nursing home and pay someone to care for him, that's good. If you volunteer to tutor at your children's elementary school, that's bad. But if a learning center is paid to tutor, that's good.

In short, the government's most widely publicized economic indicator—the one newspapers routinely report on their front pages, the one that television and radio broadcasters lead off their nightly reports with—tells nothing about the health, well-being or stability of society.

Some Needed Reforms

So what specifically can be done? The list of possible reforms is a long one. The suggestions that follow are starting points, a place to begin the debate. Some of the recommendations could be easily implemented. Others would be difficult.

Trade. Global trade was promoted on the basis that it would benefit everyone, exporting and importing nations alike. But the concept is valid only if there is true reciprocity—if each nation provides equal access to its own market. That hasn't happened.

Instead, as America's competitors learned that Washington lacks the will to get tough on trade, they lowered their tariffs but raised other barriers to block entry of U.S. products into their markets. Washington's response—as it has been for decades—was to continue to negotiate agreements with individual countries that promise to open their markets, yet never do, at least not to the extent the United States does.

This has been the story of U.S.-Japanese trade relations. Now history is repeating itself with China.

When President Clinton went to Washington in 1993, developing the Chinese market was a high priority. At hearings on her nomination as the No. 2 trade official, Charlene Barshefsky

spelled out to senators the tough approach the Clinton administration intended to take: "China's large and growing trade deficit
with the United States, which in 1992 was $18.2 billion, is un-
acceptable. Multiple, overlapping barriers to U.S. imports exist,
as do high tariffs that make it very difficult for highly competitive
U.S. industries to penetrate China's markets. To address this
problem, the administration is vigorously pursuing access
through the October 1992 market access agreement, which will
sharply reduce or eliminate principal obstacles to U.S. trade."

When Barshefsky testified, the U.S. trade deficit with China
was $18.2 billion. In 1995, after three years of "vigorously pur-
suing" access to the Chinese market, the United States trade
deficit with China stood at $33.8 billion—up 86 percent over
1992.

Inadvertently, Barshefsky's testimony showed why U.S. trade
policy has failed so badly. Stated simply, the problem is this: For
years, U.S. policy makers have focused, single-mindedly, on exports. And they have dismissed imports as of no concern. That
attitude explains why the U.S. merchandise trade deficit went
from an annual average of $10 billion during the 1970s, to $94
billion in the 1980s, to $125 billion in the 1990s.

Now the government's emphasis needs to be changed from exports to imports, at least until trade is brought into balance. That
means controls need to be placed on imported goods. In other
words, access to the world's richest consumer market should be
granted on the basis of national interest, not because of a blind
adherence to an abstract economic theory like "free trade."

This is especially true when one considers that so-called "free
trade" has never existed in all of recorded history. Every nation
has imposed controls on the flow of goods across its borders, in
its own self-interest. The United States has come closer than any
other country to the free-trade concept—all at the expense of
working Americans.

Critics will complain that such a policy could set off a global
trade war, that it would force up wages and risk inflation. Perhaps. But the Japanese have been managing trade for years and
no war has erupted. As for the wage issue, you might ponder this
question:

Why do the people in Washington dismiss executive pay increases that go up 100 percent or 200 percent as of no consequence, yet call for restraints when the wages of working people
go up 5 or 6 percent?

What Can Be Done?

In any event, a new trade policy needs to look beyond simply balancing the books on imports and exports. That's because, dollar for dollar, imports cost more American jobs than exports create. The reason: Imported products, especially those from developing countries, most often are made in labor-intensive industries, such as apparel. Goods exported by the United States, on the other hand, tend to be produced by industries that require less labor, such as agriculture.

To curb imports would require raising tariffs and other trade barriers on products from countries that have consistently failed to open their markets. If other nations, for whatever reason, limit access to their markets, then the United States needs to respond in kind. It's called fair trade. Similar actions could be taken against countries whose governments support industries competing with American industries as well as against countries whose governments require that part of the manufacturing be done locally if U.S. companies want to sell products.

Such changes must happen if the United States is to eliminate the trade deficit and preserve its remaining manufacturing jobs. Only by restoring balance to the imports/exports ledger will this country keep vital those essential industries that it must have to remain a world power.

Immigration. Restore immigration to pre-1990 levels and scale back the skilled-worker and guest-worker visa programs that have led to widespread abuses in employment-based immigration. The practice of using immigration policy to create a labor surplus, thereby helping to hold down wages or limit wage increases, should be ended.

An army of illegal aliens adds to the foreign-worker glut. No one knows their exact numbers, but it is estimated they are in the millions. And that's after 2.7 million illegal aliens were granted amnesty in 1986 and allowed to become U.S. citizens.

The U.S. Commission on Immigration Reform, which was headed by the late Barbara Jordan, former congresswoman from Texas who died in 1996, described the need for action this way: "Curbing illegal movements into the country would. . .benefit the wage structure, working conditions, and employment opportunities of U.S. citizens, legal permanent residents and other authorized workers."

The commission took special aim at the group responsible for attracting illegal aliens: American businesses that hire them, especially those businesses that tend to violate other labor and

211

workplace laws. The most prominent nonagricultural industries that hire illegal aliens: "construction companies, manufacturers of food products, manufacturers of apparel and textiles, eating and drinking establishments and hotel and lodging services."

The commission reported that "a significant number of employers in these same industries are also involved in a variety of labor law violations, placing law-abiding employers at a serious competitive disadvantage. If employers were forced to comply with labor laws and reduce their reliance on unauthorized workers, it is likely that wages and working conditions would improve for the legal workforce."

To that end, the commission said it believed that stepped-up enforcement of all labor and workplace laws—from minimum wage to work safety—would be "an effective tool in reducing unauthorized work." The commission added: "Requiring employers to adhere to a set of labor standards for all workers can ensure that businesses have no economic incentive to hire illegal aliens rather than authorized workers."

Stepped-up enforcement will require more federal spending—not less.

Global Wages. Companies that produce goods in foreign countries to take advantage of cheap labor should not be permitted to dictate the wages paid to American workers.

A solution: Impose a tariff or tax on goods brought into this country equal to the wage differential between foreign workers and U.S. workers in the same industry. That way, competition would be confined to who makes the best product, not who works for the least amount of money.

Thus, if Calvin Klein wants to make sweatshirts in Pakistan, his company would be charged a tariff or tax equal to the difference between the earnings of a Pakistani worker and a U.S. apparel worker. Similarly, if Microsoft wants to have its computer programming done in India, the company would be charged a tariff or tax equal to the difference between the salaries of Indian and U.S. programmers.

If this, or some similar action is not taken, the future is clear. Wages of American workers will continue to slip, as well as their standard of living.

A 1992 World Bank study pinpointed what will happen if Washington stays the current course. Without mentioning the United States by name, economist Herman Daly of the University of Maryland and ecologist Robert Goodland of the World Bank had this to say about the consequences for a nation with a high standard of living when it embraces a global trading system in which most of the other nations are poor:

> If by wise policy or blind luck, a country has managed to control its population growth, provide social insurance, high wages, reasonable working hours and other benefits to its working class (i.e., most of its citizens), should it allow these benefits to be competed down to the world average by unregulated trade? . . .This leveling of wages will be overwhelmingly downward due to the vast number and rapid growth rate of underemployed populations in the third world. Northern laborers will get poorer, while Southern laborers will stay much the same.

Taxes. Reestablish the progressive income tax, which rests on the principle that tax rates should rise with income. This structure was in place from the beginning of World War II until the early 1960s, a period that coincided with the great expansion of the American middle class. In 1963, President Kennedy, a Democrat, began the process of dismantling the progressive income tax. Two decades later, President Reagan, a Republican, finished the job.

During the 1940s and 1950s, the top tax rate ranged between 81 percent and 91 percent. It should be emphasized that no taxpayers paid out 91 percent of their income in taxes. From 1954 to 1963, for example, the maximum rate of 91 percent was applied only to taxable income over $400,000.

In other words, after all deductions, and after income reached $400,000, the amount above that figure was taxed at 91 percent. That $400,000 would be worth about $2.3 million in 1996. The top tax rate today might apply to, say, taxable income over $5 million, with the top rate at, possibly, 70 percent, rather than 91 percent. To spread the tax burden more equitably, a dozen or so brackets should be added, down to 5 percent. The bottom rate in 1996 was 15 percent; the top rate was 39.6 percent.

To further simplify the system, all deductions should be eliminated. So, too, the preferential capital gains tax. All dollar bills would be treated alike. A middle-class working family whose income is derived solely from a paycheck would not be taxed at a higher effective rate than someone whose income is derived from speculating on Wall Street.

All this deals with the federal income tax. Truth to tell, state and local taxes are weighted even more heavily against middle-income and lower-income workers. To right this situation, the federal government could create a system of rewards and penalties when distributing revenue-sharing money to the states. The more progressive a state's tax structure, the more federal aid it would receive.

And finally, the corporate income tax. Thanks to sharply lower rates and a variety of tax concessions, corporations in the 1990s pay comparatively less income tax than corporations in the 1950s. During that earlier decade, corporations accounted for 39 percent of all income tax revenue; individuals supplied 61 percent. For the years 1990 to 1995, the corporate share dropped to 19 percent, while the individual share rose to 81 percent.

To restore some measure of balance, the top corporate tax rate should at least be raised above the highest personal rate of 39.6 percent. In the 1950s, it was 52 percent. By 1996, it was 35 percent. A variety of corporate deductions should be eliminated or scaled back. These include the essentially unlimited deduction for interest payments and the carryover deduction of losses, both of which fuel mergers and takeovers. Also, foreign tax provisions need to be amended so that multinational companies no longer would be able to move income around the world to escape payment of taxes.

Government Regulations. Like many things in life, some regulations are good, some are bad. The trick is to separate one from the other. Keep the good; throw out the bad. Instead, the government moves between two extremes, either overregulating business and society or, as is happening in the 1990s, seeking to end most, if not all, regulations.

We must preserve the rules that assure the quality of American life: the food you eat, the medicines you take, the air you breathe and the water you drink. They have evolved over a century. Third-world countries, indeed, even countries on the next tier up, have no such protective rules.

U.S. businesses must spend money to comply with these regulations, while their competitors in foreign countries are spared that expense. Sometimes the competitors are American-owned, sometimes foreign-owned. Whichever, the result is a most uneven playing field. One way to remedy the situation: Impose a tariff on imported products equal to the amount of money that American businesses must spend to comply with government regulations.

What Can Be Done?

Social Security and Medicare. It is generally understood that sometime shortly after the turn of the century, if not before, both the Social Security and Medicare systems will have to be drastically revised. They are running out of money. That means either a hefty tax increase on working Americans, a reduction in benefits for retirees, a delayed retirement age or some combination of all three.

One solution would be means-testing of benefits. The system should be changed from a retirement plan for everyone to a retirement plan for those who need it. Once again, the issue is one of balance.

In 1993, a total of 453,833 retired people with incomes over $100,000 collected Social Security benefits. In all, they received checks amounting to $6.6 billion. You might want to think of that money—and where it came from—this way: It's the equivalent of all the Social Security taxes paid by 1.3 million young working families with incomes of $40,000 a year. A direct transfer from them to retirees whose incomes range from two-and-one-half to more than 25 times their incomes.

Future Social Security payments should be ended to individuals and families whose incomes exceed, say, two to three times median family income. That would be between $80,000 and $120,000. Payments would be stopped only after retirees had collected what they had paid into Social Security, with interest.

As for Medicare, it, too, should be means tested. A story we have related before best describes the inequity of America's health care system. A Philadelphia physician summed up the issue this way: "I have patients who come to my office in chauffeur-driven limousines. They own three or four homes. And Medicare pays their bills. Does this make sense?" This in a society where 40 million or more people go without health care because they cannot afford it.

Retraining. Completely overhaul the existing retraining system, which now seems to benefit government and educational bureaucracies more than it helps displaced workers. Inequities abound.

If workers lose their jobs because their company moves to Mexico, where wages are lower, they qualify for 78 weeks of unemployment benefits. But if workers lose their jobs because their company closes its factory in, say, New York, and moves to Mississippi, where wages are lower, they receive only 26 weeks of unemployment benefits.

The benefits are tied directly to retraining. Thus, the workers at the plant that relocated to Mexico can afford to take extended courses for up to a year and a half in another field. Workers at the factory that went to Mississippi, on the other hand, are limited to those retraining classes that can be completed in six months, meaning many will have fewer employment opportunities.

The types of retraining classes offered to displaced workers also need to be rethought. Too many of the courses are in fields where there are few jobs, or where pay is comparatively low.

Executive Salaries. Corporations are free to pay their executives whatever they want. But that doesn't mean companies should be permitted to write off the full salary amount on their tax returns, thereby shifting the cost to taxpayers.

One possible solution: Tie tax deductibility to a multiple between the highest- and lowest-paid workers. For example, if the lowest-paid worker earns $20,000, then the company would be precluded from deducting more than, say, 15 times that amount, or $300,000. While the company could pay its top officer any amount, only $300,000 could be written off on the corporate tax return. The balance would come out of the shareholders' pockets, rather than the taxpayers' pockets.

Government Statistics. As a result of ongoing cutbacks in federal spending, the statistical branches of all federal agencies have been slashed, bringing into question the quality of information covering everything from employment numbers to taxes. This at a time when the government needs accurate data more than ever to make critical economic decisions.

The cutbacks are further tinged with irony in that they have occurred at the height of the computer age, just as the United States is about to enter the 21st century. In short, government statistics were more accurate and complete before the computer than since—yet the computer gives a seeming precision to the numbers that is not justified.

In addition, longtime standard statistical yardsticks, such as the gross domestic product, should be scrapped, and new formulas devised that more correctly reflect the health of both the American economy and society.

To that end, more than 400 economists have signed on to a proposed index called the GPI—the genuine progress indicator—which takes into account a variety of social and ecological factors that the GDP ignores. Just one of those differences, according to a public-policy think tank in San Francisco called Redefining

Progress: "GPI corrects for income and wealth distribution, so that economic gains going largely to the wealthiest Americans are not mistaken for benefits to the nation as a whole."

Campaign Finance and Lobby Reform. Absent sweeping reforms in campaign financing, all other reform efforts are likely to fail. That's because the money flowing into the coffers of political candidates and political parties is staggering. It comes from corporations, wealthy individuals, political action committees and other interest groups—all with agendas that often are at odds with what is good for average Americans.

In 1995, according to a study of the Center for Responsive Politics, the Democratic and Republican National Committees alone took in nearly $60 million from donors, in what was a nonelection year. And that did not include millions more given to individual candidates.

Campaign contributions not only elect candidates, but they give the donors access to the lawmakers after they are in office. That's another benefit beyond the reach of average Americans.

Over the years critics of the current system have generally agreed on a number of reforms, including these:

- Impose a limit on the amount of money that can be spent to run for office.
- Ban contributions by political action committees (PACs) to political candidates.
- Close the loophole in current campaign finance law that allows wealthy individuals and corporations to circumvent limits on contributions to political candidates by making contributions in any amount directly to political parties.
- Place restrictions on the amount of out-of-state money a congressional candidate can accept while running for office.

Only by limiting the money that pours into the political arena will the power of special interests be curbed. Their grip is so strong that even when relatively moderate reforms are proposed to help middle-class Americans, they are usually shot down. Look no further than the 1995–96 effort to revise the immigration law.

The Immigration Act of 1990, which opened America's doors to record numbers of immigrants, also greatly changed the categories of immigrants granted admission. It paved the way for an influx of skilled foreigners as well as so-called guest workers with visas to work in the United States for extended periods of time.

As evidence mounted that the program had been abused and exploited by corporations—both to secure more low-cost help and to hold down the pay of their American employees—the House and Senate took up separate bills. Each would have scaled back, but by no means eliminated, employment-based immigration.

Legislation proposed by Alan K. Simpson, a Republican senator from Wyoming and a principal author of the 1990 immigration act, would have reduced the number of annual visas, instituted more rigid controls for issuing visas, put a cap on the number of immigrant workers companies could employ and required companies that import workers to contribute to a fund to train their own employees in the future. "For too many U.S. workers, the impact of immigration includes adverse effects on their own wages and individual job opportunities," Simpson noted on introducing his bill in the Senate on November 3, 1995. "The bill's proposed changes in the employment-related classifications are intended to protect . . . U.S. workers, especially those who are first entering upon their careers. . . ."

Simpson's proposals never had a chance.

Corporate lobbyists and groups such as the American Immigration Lawyers Association, whose members represent corporations and potential immigrants, linked arms to scuttle the reforms.

Describing the proposals as "draconian," they lobbied lawmakers and especially members of the Senate Immigration Subcommittee, of which Simpson is chairman, to persuade other members to reject Simpson's proposed changes. They also mounted a public relations campaign to project the image that America's high-technology companies would suffer if Congress curtailed the hiring of foreign workers. "Our ability to get the best talent in the world is critical to us," Kenneth M. Alvares, a vice president of Sun Microsystems, a Silicon Valley computer chip company, told the *Washington Post*. Restricting that ability "is going to kill us," he said. "We will not be able to compete."

By March 1996, Simpson found he had been outmaneuvered by corporate lobbyists and, lacking support on his own committee, withdrew his proposal to trim back employment-based immigration—but not without a parting shot at the corporate lobbyists who had sabotaged his efforts. "I was working with the business community. . . to address their concerns," he said at a Senate hearing on March 7, 1996, "[but] each time we resolved one, they became more creative, more novel. . . . The business community so distorted everything we were up to, everything. . . ."

Overcoming the View from Washington

As Simpson's immigration experience suggests, overcoming the influence of Washington's lobbyists will not be easy. Further complicating any reform efforts is the fact that the view of America from Washington is decidedly different than it is from other parts of the country. It's important that you understand just how different. For the people in Washington who write and implement the economic rules that govern your daily life do not live in the same world that you do. Nor do they think like you do.

Take Alan Greenspan, who as chairman of the Federal Reserve Board exercises influence over everything from the interest rate you pay on your home mortgage to the amount of your annual wage increase. In a speech in June 1996 at the 40th economic conference of the Federal Reserve Bank of Boston, Greenspan puzzled over why so many American workers felt insecure about their jobs when "the overall state of the economy" is so good.

What's more, he said, another indicator that all is well is the growing equality in the ownership of consumer goods. The data show, he said, "that for motor vehicles and a number of appliances—for example, dishwashers, clothes dryers, microwave ovens, and even garbage disposals—the distribution of ownership rates by income [group] moved toward greater equality between 1980 and 1994. . . . Nearly all poor families have access to a refrigerator, stove and color TV. In addition, three-fourths of poor households have telephones, and nearly two-thirds have microwave ovens and VCRs."

In any event, the concern that people have over jobs will pass, Greenspan said. Or, as he put it: "With the inexorable turnover of the population, people will adjust."

Translation: In the long run, everyone's dead.

But Greenspan's view of life beyond the nation's capital is hardly unique in Washington. Consider, for a moment, the question of taxes, and the personal perspective brought to that subject by two men—Robert J. Dole, the Republican candidate for president in 1996, and Democratic incumbent president Bill Clinton.

Dole says that taxes are too high and must be cut. Clinton boasts of having raised taxes on the very rich. You may judge

Families with radically different incomes...

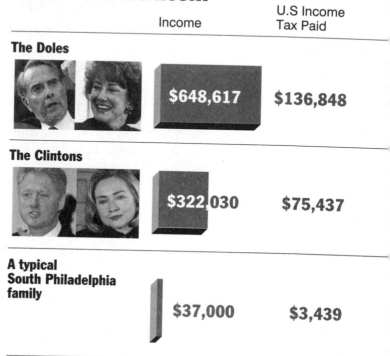

	Income	U.S Income Tax Paid
The Doles	$648,617	$136,848
The Clintons	$322,030	$75,437
A typical South Philadelphia family	$37,000	$3,439

SOURCE: Federal income tax returns

their statements for yourself, by looking at the tax bills of Dole, Clinton and a South Philadelphia family.

For 1995, the Doles reported total income of $648,617. That figure includes $64,748 in tax-exempt income. Their total taxes—federal income tax, Social Security and Medicare, and all state and local levies—added up to $191,692. That meant the Doles paid taxes at an overall effective rate of 29.6 percent.

The Clintons reported total income of $322,030. That figure, too, included tax-exempt income, of $5,956. Their total taxes—all federal, state and local levies—added up to $101,578. That meant the Clintons paid taxes at an overall effective rate of 31.5 percent.

Now consider the South Philadelphia middle-class family with

...have almost the same effective tax rate.

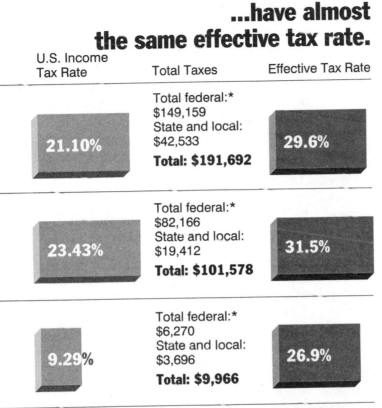

U.S. Income Tax Rate	Total Taxes	Effective Tax Rate
21.10%	Total federal:* $149,159 State and local: $42,533 **Total: $191,692**	29.6%
23.43%	Total federal:* $82,166 State and local: $19,412 **Total: $101,578**	31.5%
9.29%	Total federal:* $6,270 State and local: $3,696 **Total: $9,966**	26.9%

*Includes Social Security and Medicare taxes

one child that lives in a rowhouse. The husband works full-time at a salary of $25,000. His wife works part-time to supplement family income by bringing in another $12,000. Total income: $37,000. The middle-class family's taxes—federal, state and local—total $9,966. That meant they paid taxes at an overall effective rate of 26.9 percent.

Let us summarize: The Doles, with nearly 18 times as much income as the South Philadelphia middle-class family, paid taxes at a rate just 2.7 percentage points higher than that family.

The Clintons, with nearly nine times as much income as the South Philadelphia family, paid taxes at a rate just 4.6 percentage points higher than that family. Or, looked at from another perspective, the Doles, after paying their taxes, had $456,925 to live on. The Clintons, after paying their taxes, had $220,452. And the South Philadelphia family, after paying its taxes, had $27,034 to live on.

The moral: Whenever anyone in Washington talks about what they are going to do for your taxes, make sure you take into consideration your total tax burden. That's because the people in Washington over the last three decades engineered three critical revisions in the nation's tax structure:

- They slashed by more than half the top federal income tax rate paid by the wealthiest citizens.
- They raised Social Security and Medicare tax rates so that a surplus would be created and the money could be spent to pay for other government programs. Those two taxes hit middle- and lower-income people hardest.
- They transferred onetime federal responsibilities to state and local governments, which also tax those at the top lightly, reserving their heaviest tax bites for people in the middle and at the bottom.

Forty years ago, the tax rates of an earlier generation of Doles and Clintons would have been several times higher than that of a South Philadelphia family.

While official Washington has enacted a succession of economic policies that have proven harmful to the middle class, not everyone in the capital subscribed to them. Over the years, a handful of lawmakers has forecast—with uncanny accuracy—the consequences of legislation enacted by their colleagues. This has been true whether the issue was taxes, immigration or trade. The only problem is that few people paid any attention to them.

When Congress debated the Trade Expansion Act of 1962, to lower tariffs and promote global trade, some opposing congressmen foresaw exactly what would happen. As Glenn C. Cunningham, a Republican congressman from Nebraska, told lawmakers more than 30 years ago, on June 28, 1962: "I am convinced that we can never compete favorably with foreign countries, even when all trade and tariff barriers are removed. The cheap labor used in foreign plants mean that their products can be shipped here and sold at less cost than comparable American-made products. Whenever this happens, thousands and perhaps millions of workers will be laid off and become unemployed. Furthermore, it will downgrade and undermine our entire economy. . . ."

Other lawmakers said "free trade" would work only if American products were allowed equal access to foreign markets. As Victor A. Knox, a Republican congressman from Michigan, put it on that same day in June 1962: "Under the bill our domestic markets would be exposed to a rising tide of imports without sufficient safeguards against injury to domestic producers and without sufficient assurance of expanding oversea markets for American produced goods. The bill promises more of the same in one-way reciprocity with America giving and our so-called trading allies taking."

When Bad News Is Good News

As it turned out, over the years not everyone viewed the loss of jobs as bad news. In fact, some people came to consider the elimination of jobs as decidedly good news. Newspaper headlines tell the story:

Providence (R.I.) *Journal-Bulletin,* March 12, 1994: "Fleet's job cutback plans play well on Wall Street," read the headline over a story reporting on Fleet Financial Group's decision to eliminate 5,500 jobs.

USA Today, October 7, 1994: "Investors fear strong job growth," read the headline over a story reporting the federal government was expected to announce a sharp increase in the number of new jobs created in the past month.

New York Times, August 29, 1995: "As more banks vanish, Wall Street cheers," read the headline over a story on bank mergers.

Bridgewater (N. J.) *Courier-News,* January 3, 1996: "Wall Street applauds layoff announcement," read the headline over a story reporting on AT&T's decision to lop off 40,000 employees.

Montgomery (Ala.) *Advertiser,* January 10, 1996: "Layoffs please Wall Street; investors rack up the profits," read the headline over a story summing up decisions by several corporations, including Boeing and BellSouth, to lay off workers.

Detroit News, March 17, 1996: "Wall Street cheers as GM plays hardball," read the headline over a story reporting on a 12-day strike at GM plants over a decision to buy parts from outside vendors.

Whatever the corporate decision, if it reduces costs and improves profits in the short term, thereby contributing to the growth of the bottom-line society, Wall Street loves it. It matters not whether it's laying off employees, cutting health care benefits, restructuring pensions, hiring part-time workers, contracting out work or dumping the aged and infirm out of their nursing home beds.

Dumping the elderly?

Listen to Joyce Albers, a health care stock analyst with CS First Boston, who was quoted in March 1995 on nursing home decisions to move out patients on Medicaid—the state-funded plan that pays the medical bills of the indigent—and replace them with more ill patients from hospitals, whose bills would be paid more generously by Medicare: "What's important for these nursing homes is they're converting a $100-a-day patient into a $300-a-day patient. It's a significant uptake in revenue and the margins are higher."

Another stock analyst, Rose Ann Tortora of Donaldson Lufkin & Jenrette, was quoted in September 1994 on a plan announced by American Airlines to contract out jobs at smaller airports it serves, describing Wall Street's ideal workplace: "What airlines are doing is remolding themselves into what an airline would be today if it started all over again. If you started today with a clean piece of paper you wouldn't own anything. You'd rent the pilots if you could."

So it is that the future for tens of millions of workers as envisioned by Wall Street and Washington will be quite different from what you may have expected or hoped for.

James T. Hill knows all about that future. It's his present. For 20 years, Hill was a tool and die maker at AT&T's huge Shreveport, La., works, which manufactured residential and business telephones. Then in the 1980s, AT&T began the process of laying off thousands of workers and shifted much of the production abroad. Hill and his wife, who also worked at the plant, lost their jobs in 1988.

For the next two and half years, Hill worked part of the time making plastic injection molds for a Louisiana company, though at much less pay than he had earned at AT&T. In 1991, he heard that AT&T had openings for experienced tool and die makers. When he inquired, an AT&T supervisor told him, "You can go to work in Kansas City." Hill said he asked, "'Can't you find anything closer than that?' He said, 'Reading, Pennsylvania.' I said, 'I'll take Kansas City.'"

What Can Be Done?

So in 1991, the Hills relocated to Lee's Summit, Mo., a suburb of Kansas City and home to what was once one of the largest manufacturing plants in the Bell system. Built in 1963, the sprawling 43-acre Western Electric plant had once employed 7,500 persons making electronic circuits and switches. When Hill arrived, it employed fewer than 1,000, a victim, like Shreveport, of AT&T cutbacks. Though he was glad to be back in the Bell system, Hill soon found out that his new job was not secure either.

"When I got here they said they were going to move this stuff to Richmond, Va.," he recalled. "All these pins, the connector business. So don't worry about buying a house and settling down. So I didn't buy a house. Then all of a sudden about a year and a half ago [1994] they said, 'We're going to stay here.' So my wife and I started earnestly looking to buy a house. And we had found one that we were going to buy. Then about that time they made the announcement that they were going to sell the business."

Faced with this new uncertainty, the Hills held off on buying the house to see what developed. Rumors swirled around the plant. In the end, the business was sold in 1994 to Berg Electronics of St. Louis, which was vague about its long-term plans.

"They've had people [messed] up for four years now," says Hill. "The mess that people have had to go through is awesome—the never knowing what is going to happen next. It's like every week or every month they thought they might come out with an announcement 'we're going.' That kind of [thing] works on people."

Eventually, Hill secured a transfer early in 1996 to an AT&T operation in Dallas, that later was spun off as a division of Lucent Technologies. In the meantime, Berg announced it would phase out the remaining jobs at Lee's Summit and transfer some of the work performed there to other plants in the States, leaving the plant which once provided jobs for 7,500 manufacturing employees without one production worker.

Hill blames Washington policy makers for applying the pressure that is driving down the earnings of manufacturing workers. "They want all the manufacturing people to go back to $4.50 an hour," he says. "They are saying people shouldn't be making $11 an hour. They are killing us. People who make $15 an hour are able to buy cars and houses and things that keep the economy going. They want everybody to take a cut in pay but they don't want anybody who's making big money to take a cut in pay."

Hill, though, thinks there is a potential light at the end of this dark tunnel. Says he: "If the government keeps allowing these

225

companies to send [goods] overseas, we're not going to make enough money to pay the politicians. That's probably when they're going to stop it."

It will stop, of course, only when people send a message that they want it to stop. For it is up to the people, needless to say, to determine the kind of society in which they want to live.

Whether it is a caring, interdependent society in which citizens assume certain responsibilities for one another. Or an indifferent one in which it is every individual for himself or herself.

Whether it is a society that believes every working American should be entitled to a living wage, sufficient to allow one working spouse to support a family. Or one in which income is ever more concentrated at the top and two spouses are compelled to work to raise a family.

Whether it is a society where working people—blue-collar, white-collar and professional—are treated with a measure of dignity, and encouraged to contribute to the growth of a business, industry or profession. Or one where working people are looked upon as rental equipment, hired for a few days, a few weeks or a couple of years, and then traded off to another employer.

Whether it is a society that believes government has a role in protecting its most vulnerable citizens and assuring opportunities for everyone. Or one that favors those who have access to the people who write the laws.

A century ago, Americans were confronted with similar choices, and they made their feelings clearly heard. Across the land, societies and leagues and committees sprung up to bring about sweeping changes in society, government and business, both at the national and state levels.

Through these individual efforts, the reform groups—many of them headed by women—halted the employment of one million children under the age of 14 in factories. They succeeded in their efforts to limit the workday to 10 hours; first for women, and later for men. To provide relief for the aged poor. To secure the right to vote for women. To guarantee that meat and food products were safe for human consumption.

One of the driving forces behind the reform movement was the growing concentration of wealth. A study of the estates of men who died in Massachusetts from 1889 to 1891 showed just how concentrated:

• One percent of the population owned 46 percent of the wealth.

What Can Be Done?

- The next 7 percent owned 34 percent of the wealth.
- And the other 92 percent of the population divided up the remaining 20 percent of the wealth.

During the 1890s and early 1900s, magazines and newspapers published story after story detailing how a few people were controlling ever-larger fortunes. As the *North America Review* put it in November 1893: "Rapid accumulation of wealth by a few citizens, as we have seen it in the United States during the last 30 years, is evidence of morbidly abnormal conditions. It is inconsistent with free institutions. It is breeding anarchy and trouble."

Will history repeat itself?

As before, the people will decide.

A Note on Sources

This book is based on interviews and public records and data from a wide variety of federal, state and local agencies.

With a few exceptions, the statistics used in this book were drawn from government and corporate sources. They include the U.S. Internal Revenue Service, the Bureau of Labor Statistics, the Federal Reserve Board, the Annual Budget of the U.S. Government, the Economic Report of the President, corporate filings with the U.S. Securities and Exchange Commission, the Organization for Economic Cooperation and Development, the United Nations, the International Monetary Fund, the Export-Import Bank of the United States, the Immigration and Naturalization Service, the State Department, the International Trade Administration, the Social Security Bulletin, and the Census Bureau.

Other sources of information at the federal level included the U.S. International Trade Commission, the Employment and Training Administration of the Department of Labor, the Bureau of Economic Analysis, the United States Trade Representative, the Foreign Agents Registration Office of the Department of Justice, the Senate Records Office, the House Clerk's Office, the Department of Agriculture, public papers of the presidents, the *Congressional Record*, and congressional hearings related to trade, taxes and other economic issues spanning more than half a century.

We also collected information from a range of other sources, including the Embassy of the Netherlands, the Association for Manufacturing Technology, the Brazilian Association of Footwear Manufacturers (Abicalcados), the Rand Corporation, the Japan Economic Institute, the Floral Trade Council, the Colombian Flower Council, the Footwear Industries of America, the Aerospace Industries Association, the Florida Tomato Exchange, and the National Association of Computer Software and Services Companies (NASSCOM) in New Delhi, India.

State and federal courts as well as state employment security offices turned out to be a valuable source of information about the status of working America, and we drew on filings in many jurisdictions, from Virginia to California.

Lastly, the most valuable sources were the people we interviewed. Many had lost their jobs. Others were still employed, but expressed alarm at the economic trends they saw all around them. We spent more than two years talking with these people, who live in small towns and big cities. Their observations are at the core of this book.

Index

Index

Index

Index

Maryland Department of Housing and
Community Development, 78
Mascon, 105–6
Maseng Communications, 180
Mastech, 93
Mata, Hilda, 111
Matsui, Robert, 169–70
Matsushita, 126, 175, 182
Mattel Inc., 161, 165
offshore manufacturing by, 165–66
Mazda Motor Corp., 175
McNamara, Robert S., 204–05
media, 122, 124–25, 179, 180, 181,
223–24
Medicaid, 224
Medicare, 11, 194, 215, 222, 224
Mergerstat Review, 18
Merrifield Garden Center, 85
Metropolitan Life Insurance Co., 92
Mexico, 20, 23–26, 45, 54, 106–8, 134,
142, 149, 155, 168–69, 177
tomato imports from, 64–66
Meyer, Jody, 15
Meza, Gil, 65
Miami International Airport, 62
Mickey Mouse, xi
Microsoft Corp., 21, 92, 98, 212
microwave ovens, 125–27
middle class, 15–16, 113
decline in, 13,
definition of, xi, xii
government policies and, 31–32,
202
job insecurity of, 224–26
tax burden of, 220–22
Miles & Stockbridge, 88
Miles, Mark T., 107
Mills, Wilbur, 205
Ministry of International Trade and
Industry of Japan (MITI), 117
Ministry of Trade of Indonesia, 172
Mitchell, Charles E., 204
Mitchell, George J., 108, 176
Mitsubishi, 156, 175
Moisier, Donald L., 200
Monocle Restaurant, 76
Montgomery (Ala.) *Advertiser*, 223
Montview, 111
Morris, William H. Jr., 167

Motorola, 92, 98, 160
Mudge, Rose, Guthrie, Alexander &
Ferdon, 161–62, 176
Muncy Building Enterprise, 145
Murphy, John J., 160

N

NAFTA *see* North American Free
Trade Agreement
National Association of Home
Builders, 109
National Association of Manufactur-
ers, 102
National City Bank of New York, 204
National Council on Crime and
Delinquency, 79
National Foreign Trade Council, 24
National Industries, 141
National Organization for Victim
Assistance, 79
National Science Foundation, 100,
103
National Security Council, 166
Nelson, Gerald G., 128–29
Netherlands, 46
New York Life Insurance Co., 47–48
New York Times, 24, 66, 112, 118,
124, 180, 207, 223
Newsday, 181
Newsweek, 124–25
Nicaragua, 33–34, 37
Nippon Steel, 177
Nippon Telegraph & Telephone Corp.,
176
Nissan North America, 182
Nixon, Richard M., 55, 73, 107, 162,
167
Noel Industries, 148
North American Free Trade Agree-
ment (NAFTA), 24–26, 54, 108, 168,
169, 177, 181
North American Review, 227
Novell, 98
Nugent, John M. Jr., 168

Index

Index

Wrangler, 36
Wundies, 145
Wyatt, Michael R., 109–10

X
Xerox Corp., 160
Xian Aircraft Co., 49–50
Xuiwen Wang, 89–90

Y
Yamashita-Shinnihon Steamship Co.,
    182
Yancey, Patricia, 93–97, 100

Z
Zenith, 98